T0303232

Jane Austen & the Price of Happiness

Jane Austen & the Price of Happiness

INGER SIGRUN
BREDKJÆR BRODEY

JOHNS HOPKINS UNIVERSITY PRESS • BALTIMORE

© 2024 Johns Hopkins University Press
All rights reserved. Published 2024
Printed in the United States of America on acid-free paper
2 4 6 8 9 7 5 3 1

Johns Hopkins University Press
2715 North Charles Street
Baltimore, Maryland 21218
www.press.jhu.edu

Library of Congress Cataloging-in-Publication Data

Names: Brodey, Inger Sigrun, author.

Title: Jane Austen and the price of happiness /
Inger Sigrun Bredkjær Brodey.

Description: Baltimore : Johns Hopkins University Press, 2024. |
Includes bibliographical references and index. |

Identifiers: LCCN 2023024692 | ISBN 9781421448206 (hardcover) |
ISBN 9781421448213 (ebook)

Subjects: LCSH: Austen, Jane, 1775–1817—Criticism and interpretation. |
Austen, Jane, 1775–1817—Authorship. | Closure (Rhetoric) | Happiness in
literature. | Narration (Rhetoric)—Psychological aspects. | Reader
response criticism. | LCGFT: Literary criticism.

Classification: LCC PR4038.A9 B76 2024 | DDC 823/.7—dc23/eng/20230601
LC record available at https://lccn.loc.gov/2023024692

A catalog record for this book is available from the British Library.

Special discounts are available for bulk purchases of this book.
For more information, please contact Special Sales at
specialsales@jh.edu.

Contents

Figures

Jane Austen & the Price of Happiness

INTRODUCTION

"Perfect Felicity"

The good ended happily, and the bad unhappily.
That is what Fiction means.

OSCAR WILDE, *The Importance of Being Earnest*

My characters shall have, after a little
trouble, all that they desire.

BECOMING JANE, screenplay by Sarah Williams and Kevin Hood

Jane Austen is the quintessential author of romantic happy endings. Her novels provide love, appreciation, and marriage for all her heroines. Her happy couples model love and mutual respect; they restore hope to readers in a cynical world that domestic happiness is attainable without sacrificing personal standards. Austen's pervasive effect on storytelling and expectations of romance on both sides of the North Atlantic is hard to exaggerate. The ghosts of Elizabeth and Darcy haunt contemporary courtship and dating, providing an alternative model to the star-crossed fate of equally influential lovers like Juliet and Romeo. Contemporary readers and moviegoers who are familiar with Austen can feel her presence not only in every rom-com that ends in marriage, but also in those where marriage is explicitly rejected—whether it's *Four Weddings and a Funeral*,

Frozen, or *Fire Island*. Austen's name has become synonymous with the "marriage plot."

Or so people say. But Austen's endings are not quite as simple—nor as simply *happy*—as they might at first appear through the lens of her adaptations. While her endings may superficially resemble the happy endings of fairy tales, scholars who study word usage have found just the opposite. Contrary to expectations, Austen's word counts prove how different her endings are from the happy endings of fairy tales. The words simply aren't happy enough.[1]

Austen weaves a resistance to marriage into the fabric of her novels that seldom appears in film adaptations. Not only can readers cheer at Elizabeth Bennet's refusals of the wrong man—the odious Mr. Collins—but Austen also encourages some admiration for her refusal of the right man—Mr. Darcy—when he proposes in the wrong way. Headstrong, obstinate, and idealistic heroines like Elizabeth have a complex relationship to the choice of a husband. Austen goes further: she imbeds an anti-romantic strain in her novels, one that gets louder and more strident toward the conclusion of each novel, distracting readers from the buildup to the self-indulgent harmonies of a romantic conclusion. When analyzed, her endings consistently undermine the *inevitability* of the marriage plot's happy ending.[2] In fact, Austen actively encourages readers to uncouple happiness and marriage. She subtly encourages her reader to focus on forms of happiness that are more within our control, such as learning to be a better person or reconciling with friends or family. And in most of her novels, she works to give readers "resources for solitude" in the likely case that they do not find the right partner at the right time. Even in her happiest endings, Austen reminds us of the cost of romantic happiness—whether to realism, effort, self-knowledge, or good fortune. With all of these caveats, how romantic are her trademark happy endings?

As a teen reader of Austen, I relished the flush of pleasure at the union of star-crossed lovers at the end of her novels. Yet I was also annoyed and puzzled by the way Austen distances herself from her happy endings, laughs her readers out of romance, and speeds us through the final longed-for events in a blur of narration. Sometimes, like in *Northanger Abbey*, she uses metafictional flourishes, breaking the fourth wall, doffing the narratorial robes, and revealing herself, fingers still wet with ink, as the author behind the fiction.[3] And while the narrator's revelation that we are "hastening together towards perfect felicity" is delightful and humorous, it also takes the wind out of our collective narrative sails. I wanted, as I think most readers do, to suspend disbelief and immerse myself in the glorious resolutions, attributing all the choices to the characters themselves. I did not want to be reminded that I was reading falsehoods—the product of someone's imagination, that I was subject to the whims of its author. The features of Austen's endings that bothered me as a teenager are only a few of the anti-romantic arrows in Austen's quiver. Many others escaped my observation.

Austen's choices give rise to what Deanna Kreisel calls "that famous problem of let-down" in reading Austen novels.[4] Some readers think that the anti-romantic aspects of her novels are not choices at all, but rather character flaws: novelist Anna Quindlen, for example, says that Austen is "temperamentally unsuited to happily-ever-afters."[5] Regardless of her motivation, these techniques all contribute to the "let-down" that I felt, and many other readers have said they experience reading Austen's novels, particularly if they are reading them primarily for the romantic plotline and its resolution in marriage. Generally speaking, the less she punctures the romance of her happy ending, the more popular her novels are: her anti-romantic darts are much harder to spot in *Pride and Prejudice* and *Persuasion* than they are in *Sense and Sensibility*; they are perhaps most pronounced in her least loved novel, *Mansfield Park*. Her contemporary popularity might be selective: Do people love Austen *for* her happy endings? Or do people love the Austen where we can most easily *ignore* her limitations on the happy endings? The mystery persists in how Austen can enjoy the reputation of seminal romance novelist in the face of her elaborate anti-romantic maneuvers. This book hopes to explain that dynamic.

Cozy Consequences

The single strongest reinforcer of Austen's reputation as seminal romance author may well be Hollywood, or the rom-com in general. The past 25–35 years have seen the release of dozens of Austen film adaptations and hundreds of fictional adaptations. Judging by the composition of my classrooms over a similar period, Austen's reputation has been increasingly gendered and romanticized as well: where my classes used to be nearly half male, they've become 95% female. Increasingly, movies and fan fiction—not her books—draw students to Austen classes. Students respond with glee, for example, when they discover that *Clueless* is really an adaptation of *Emma*, spawning a newfound, deepening interest in Austen. In my most recent Austen class, about 40% of students had seen *Clueless* (many repeatedly) before reading *Emma*.

This gendering of Austen reception contributes to her reputation as a novelist of domestic happiness. Enter the warm and comfy Austen: the Austen of teapots and tea cozies, of crochet and knit shawls, of incense, perfume, and aromatic teas (figure 1). Coziness is associated with the life she portrays in her novels and by extension the world in which she lived. As much as I love Austen, as a Dane, I struggle to see Austen as the queen of "hygge." Coziness nonetheless becomes associated with her happy endings most of

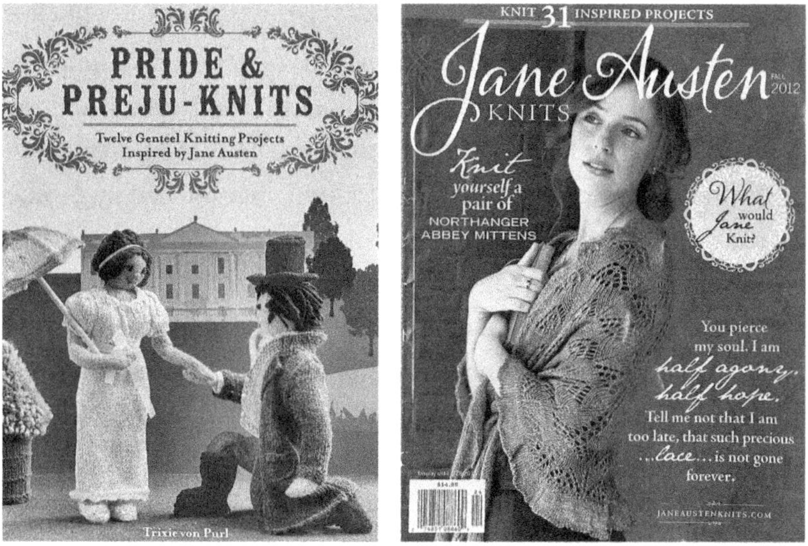

1. Cozy Austen. Covers of *Pride and Preju-knits* and *Jane Austen Knits*.

(Author's collection)

all. One might ask: Did Austen wish her readers to engage in wish fulfillment, to snuggle up in blankets by candlelight and enter a hazy state of dreamy gratification at the end of her novels? Is that what happens when one reads Austen's novels? According to Paula Byrne, an Austen historian and consultant on the television series *Sanditon*, it does: "People want to believe Jane Austen is cozy, which is just so crazy."[6] "Cozy" is not a word to describe her own life, in any case.

Popular misconceptions of the Regency contribute to the visualization of Austen's cozy happy endings. Austen's world is considered by many of her fans as genteel and mannerly, full of individuals who speak as elegantly as her wittiest characters. Edward Rothstein, in a *New York Times* review, calls this phenomenon "manners envy." Rothstein attributes manners envy in large part to images of the period that appear in Merchant Ivory films. The whitewashed aesthetic of these films, according to Rothstein, portray Austen's world with a nostalgia for and envy of lost social privileges.[7] This mannerly Regency world is annually re-created in balls, conferences, and tea parties around the world. These events contribute to idealizing the life of the landed gentry as stable, leisured, and unchanging—one long series of mannerly diversions.

In superficial ways, the countryside where Austen lived supports the sense of stability. The landscape has changed little over time: 200 years later, property lines near Chawton and especially Steventon are nearly unchanged, and most of the homes Austen visited and knew still stand, with little apparent physical alteration. The tales of human misery are often invisible, however, including the bankruptcies and the families forced to leave their estates, as happens in the opening of *Persuasion*. The stability in property boundaries and the pristine landscape come at a great cost, not only to the network of farmers and laborers directly involved, and the enslaved people at West Indian plantations who unknowingly supported this lifestyle, but also to countless younger sons and daughters of the gentry.[8]

Regency life was in fact messy, and so manners envy is likely misplaced. It was cold, brutish, and short, despite the idealizations of Austen's circumstances, such as the triviality suggested in figure 2. Twenty percent of childbirths were fatal for mothers, life expectancy was low, and life was particularly cruel for foundlings and the mentally ill. One could recite the list of statistics, but the lack of hygiene and weather-proof clothing alone would give most modern readers pause.

Austen leaves the bawdier portrayals of Georgian life to the likes of Daniel Defoe of *Moll Flanders*, Tobias Smollett of *Roderick Random*, and Henry Fielding of *Tom Jones* and *Joseph Andrews*. Her own depictions of debauchery are mostly limited to her unpublished juvenilia and sly allusions—in her novelistic treatment of

2. Horrors, according to Austen. Comic by John Atkinson.

(Used with permission of the artist, www.wronghands1.com)

the symptoms of venereal disease, for example.[9] It is important to understand that her elisions are not due to missish ignorance, as the film *Becoming Jane* would lead us to believe. In this film, Jane Austen is shocked to hear Tom Lefroy read aloud from these authors, whereas the historical teenaged Austen knew them well and wrote her own comic stories of debauchery and drunkenness. The prudish Austen is another fiction originating with her brother Henry's short account of her life and much increased by her nephew's biography, which exemplified a modest, pious, early Victorian ideal.

Austen's own world was far from peaceful, and in her own life, happy endings seemed rare indeed. Austen experienced the violence of both the French Revolution and Napoleonic Wars vicariously but vividly, and at close hand. Her first cousin Eliza was married to a

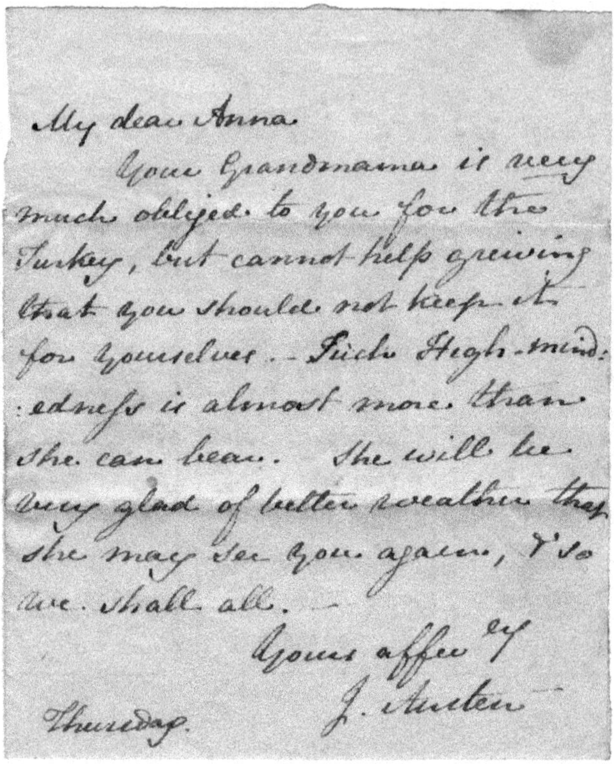

My dear Anna

Your Grandmama is very much obliged to you for the Turkey, but cannot help greiving that you should not keep it for yourselves. — Such High-mind:edness is almost more than she can bear. She will be very glad of better weather that she may see you again, & so we shall all. —

Yours affec^{ly} J. Austen

Thursday.

My dear Anna

Your Grandmama is very
much obliged to you for the
Turkey, but cannot help greiving
[sic] *that you should not keep it*
for yourselves. — Such High-mindedness
is almost more than
she can bear. She will be
very glad of better weather that
she may see you again, & so
we shall all —

Yours affec'ly
J. Austen

Thursday

3. Gifts of poultry. Letter to Anna Lefroy (December 1816).

(Courtesy of Bonhams)

French aristocrat who was beheaded in 1794, when Austen was 19. Eliza subsequently married Austen's brother Henry. Her brothers Francis and Charles fought actively in the navy against Napoleon and also against the slave trade. She read naval bulletins eagerly to hear news of their welfare. Families around her went bankrupt and moved out of their estates, never to be heard of again. After their father died suddenly, Austen and her sister Cassandra had to move from abode to abode with their mother, living an itinerant life with little privacy and less peace. At the peak of her abilities, Austen spent nearly 10 years sinking lower and lower in poverty, with neither physical nor mental space to write.

When her wealthy older brother Edward finally provided a house for the ladies, she wrote and rewrote all her major novels, publishing all six of them within the eight remaining years of her short life, including the two that appeared a few months after her death. She carefully recorded the meager earnings from each of her novels and invested some of them in her brother Henry's bank. In 1816, Henry's bank failed, and her charming but inept (and now bankrupt) brother became a clergyman instead. Austen and many of her relatives lost hard-earned savings.[10] Meanwhile, the family took little real notice of her abilities and routinely sent dozens of nieces and nephews to the maiden aunts, expecting them to babysit, further reducing her time to write.

Austen herself expresses the pain of her economic circumstances in a letter to her niece Anna, written in her last December. It is a thank-you note written on behalf of her mother for the gift of a turkey (figure 3). In light of the analogies that she must have felt with Miss Bates in the novel she published months earlier, it is a particularly sad note. The novelist of *Emma* would readily call to mind the gifts of meats, fruit, and poultry the Bateses receive, and the Austens found themselves in a similar situation. I can only think that this must have hurt her pride and reminded her of unattained ambitions. While Miss Bates had to care for her deaf mother, the dying Austen wrote letters for her hypochondriacal mother, who was deaf to others' illnesses. It is a marvel that Jane's novels are as optimistic and heartwarming as they are.

Trouble in Paradise

The popular culture surrounding Austen identifies her romantic happy endings as the key feature of her work, as John Atkinson parodies in figure 4. And yet there has been a schism in the reading of those endings. Often the "Cozy Camp" of Austen reception has little to do with the novels themselves, and more to do with the film adaptations and general cultural enthusiasm for Austen. Most adaptations are, in fact, based on fantasy readings of her endings. But not all readers of Austen are satisfied with Austen's endings. Some readers and scholars of Austen often complain about the ways Austen complicates, rushes, and destabilizes her endings.

So, what are the characteristics of these endings that have caused Austen "letdown" and have long irritated or disappointed some of her readers? Much of it comes down to expectation: Austen spends her novels building to romantic climaxes that she then suddenly undercuts in the last chapters. For one thing, the speed and pacing of her novels increase notably near the ends: Austen's conclusions feel rushed, especially in *Northanger Abbey*, *Sense and Sensibility*, *Mansfield Park*, and *Emma*. This again begs the question: If marriage is so central to Austen as novelist, why does she speed through these resolutions? The pace of her endings is not the only issue that garners frustration. Many other factors contribute to the sense of letdown.

Near the end of five of her six major novels,[11] Austen's narrator remains explicitly and stubbornly silent on the details of the happy

4. Austen spoilers. Comic by John Atkinson.

(Used with permission of the artist, www.wronghands1.com)

unions—using an annoying literary technique called "apophasis," where the narrator preemptively tells the reader what will *not be told*. The following passage from the end of *Sense and Sensibility* represents this effect: "How soon [Edward] had walked himself into the proper resolution, however, how soon an opportunity of exercising it occurred, in what manner he expressed himself, and how he was received, need not be particularly told."[12] Austen hinders the reader's luxurious enjoyment of the "proper resolution" by denying us the satisfaction of indulging in the intricate details of the long-awaited denouement.

Austen's novel *Emma* provides another famous example of Austen's cantankerous omissions. At the moment when Emma finally realizes that Mr. Knightley loves her, she wonders how to respond:

"She spoke then, on being so entreated.—What did she say?—Just what she ought, of course. A lady always does.—She said enough to shew there need not be despair—and to invite him to say more himself."[13] Readers at this moment want Emma to drop her affectations and speak from her heart as a woman rather than a "lady," yet Austen refuses to allow her to do this. She hides Emma's words at this crucial moment. Emma has never been at a loss for words, so this omission strikes the reader even more forcefully at such a critical juncture. The narrator's intrusions and pointed omissions deprive the reader of the ability to suspend disbelief, and of the ability to bask fully in the romance of the moment.[14]

Narrators also tend to come out of the shadows and intrude at the end of her novels, rather than disappearing discreetly into the background. Narrators interrupt the denouement with rhetorical questions: "Who can be in doubt of what followed?" (*Persuasion*) or "With such a confederacy against her, . . . what could [Marianne] do?" (*Sense and Sensibility*). In some cases, Austen's narrator simply drops all pretense and instead speaks as an author, using the first person: "My Fanny indeed at this very time, I have the satisfaction of knowing, must have been happy in spite of everything" (*Mansfield Park*). Austen's metafictional flourishes—where she makes us aware that we are reading a novel—also increase as we approach the end of her novels. These features all share one effect: highlighting the *fictionality* of the novel. They aren't dissimilar in effect to the sheer speed of resolution and the stubborn silence about romantic details. They seem oddly incongruous with the rest of the novel; they mark a transition to both a new mode and pace of narration; they introduce a new relationship between reader and author.

Austen uses not only speed, apophasis, intrusions, rhetorical questions, and metafictional flourishes, but also plot and coincidence to achieve this sense of the optional, artificial nature of her comic endings. She undercuts romantic happy endings through enforced symmetry of the plot, as in the case of Marianne Dashwood in *Sense and Sensibility*; through out-of-the-blue *deus ex machina* resolutions, as in both *Northanger Abbey* and *Emma*; and through a forced insistence on hyperbole and "perfection" in her resolutions, especially pronounced in *Persuasion*. The poultry thieves in *Emma* provide a particularly humorous example of *deus ex machina*: the arrival of a poultry thief into the surrounding area (on the penultimate page of the novel, no less) and his theft of Mrs. Weston's turkeys frightens Mr. Woodhouse enough to consent to Emma's marriage and to allow Mr. Knightley to move into Hartfield. In *Northanger Abbey*, a mysterious viscount suddenly materializes at nearly the same spot in the novel, only a page and a half from the end. This viscount conveniently satisfies General Tilney's vanity and greed enough to allow Henry to marry Catherine. Are these plot devices signs of lapses in Austen's invention or artistry? Or do they serve some greater purpose? What should we make of her seeming inconsistency—insisting on slow, organic, probable change throughout each novel, then suddenly resorting to external impetuses, coincidence, and luck for the final resolutions and final marriages to take place?

When you combine the increased pacing, paucity of dialogue, and all these other techniques, the endings feel particularly truncated. Consider that in the last *one to three pages* of the novels, the following obstacles are removed: Mr. Woodhouse's objection to marriage, owing to the arrival of poultry thieves (*Emma*); General Tilney's objection to Henry's marriage, owing to the sudden introduction of a titled fiancé for his daughter (*Northanger Abbey*); expectations that Fanny should marry Henry Crawford, because he has eloped adulterously with Maria (*Mansfield Park*); Edmund's infatuation with Mary Crawford, replaced by a sudden realization that he could love Fanny instead (*Mansfield Park*); and Marianne's sense that Colonel Brandon is too old and infirm to be a suitable partner in marriage (*Sense and Sensibility*). These sudden resolutions feel artificial, gratuitous, and anti-romantic. The repetition of patterns among her novels suggest that she has an overarching purpose in mind. I suggest Austen consciously separates several aspects of her marriage plots' resolutions for the sake of her didactic purpose. To put it succinctly (and alliteratively), Austen does not want her reader to conflate Romance (the romantic resolution culminating in marriage) with Recognition (the process of individual enlightenment) or with Restoration (the reestablishment of political or social order).

The complicated and anti-romantic features of Austen's endings run counter to her reputation as purveyor of delicious rom-com satisfaction. She works hard to let us know that things easily could have ended otherwise (that is, *un*happily) within the plot of her novels. Attention to these recurring techniques makes us aware of another Jane Austen—one seldom portrayed in popular culture—the Jane Austen who fidgeted, strained, and flinched at the convention of happy endings. The Jane Austen who in fact tried to refuse them to her audience.[15]

A Spinster's Impatience?

So *why* does Austen distance readers from her happy endings? Many have attempted to account for the curmudgeonly side of her endings, with explanations ranging from the psychoanalytic to the ideological. There are plenty of critics (themselves disappointed readers, perhaps) who feel that Austen goes astray in her endings, calling them "over-hasty," "botched," or formulaic."[16] In *Mansfield Park*, the narrator calls herself "*impatient* to restore every body, not greatly in fault themselves, to tolerable comfort, and to have done with all the rest."[17] Austen's narrator's impatience, according to some critics, expresses the author's own desire for separation from the novel. "Once again," John Halperin comments, Austen "cannot bear, it seems, to show us her character's happiness. That goes on offstage; her interest is chiefly in their struggles."[18] Halperin, like many other male critics, finds the source of Austen's coldness in a spinster's embitterment toward marriage: "Surely by now," he writes, "she had realised that she would never play such a scene herself; perhaps, then, it was too painful for her to invent one."[19] It is true that she was 36 at the time her first book—*Sense and Sensibility*—was published, two decades after she wrote her juvenilia and more than 10 years after she had finished her first novel, and it is certainly true that she had given up on marriage for herself by this time. Does it follow that her artistic decisions were based in frustration over her own disappointments in life?

The problem with the psychoanalytic approach to Austen is that it does not give her the credit of artistic choice.[20] It's worth considering a moral from Beth Pattillo's novel, *Jane Austen Ruined My Life*: "The truth was that a woman's romantic life could always be used to discount her professional one."[21] The protagonist speculates that the release of additional private letters might have this effect on Austen's literary legacy—that revelations of her personal unhappiness would undermine her literary reputation, but such conclusions have long since been reached by critics like Marvin Mudrick, John Halperin, and D. A. Miller.[22]

Other critics explain Austen's curious endings in more political, rather than psychological, terms, often with contradictory interpretations. Tony Tanner, for example, interprets Austen's endings as a token of her social and literary conservatism, or excessive observance of the literary expectations of romantic comedy.[23] According to this argument, Austen's social criticism and literary innovations do not extend to the endings of the novels, where she becomes *un*critical of literary and social tradition. Whatever Austen gains, in other words, in Elizabeth's courage to critique and refuse Mr. Darcy, Austen loses in her choice to have Elizabeth ultimately succumb to his offer. Mary Poovey, another influential critic, complains that succumbing to the pressures of the conventional marriage plot defeats Austen's own overall didactic and feminist aim of allowing individual choice to challenge the patriarchal order.[24] These critics both point to an uncomfortable disjunction between the moral ideals encouraged by the novel and the social facts that surround them. They claim that Austen unwittingly compromises justice in her endings, hindering her own didactic purposes. Do Austen's happy endings detract from the social satire present in the rest of the novel? Whether claiming that Austen's endings are not overtly blissful enough or that the endings are *too* happy or too "perfect," papering over life's difficulties and women's injustices, critics are responding to the strangeness of Austen's endings. Remarkably absent from the critical discourse on Austen and her endings, however, has been the possibility that these endings may have served an intentional function for Austen and her art.

Contemporary films reflect a similar difficulty in categorizing Austen: these films seem discomforted by Austen's singlehood. Many adaptations have thus either reinforced the "embittered spinster" reading, such as *Miss Austen Regrets*,[25] or tried to wash away her singlehood by sprucing up her past. In *Becoming Jane*, for example, a vastly misleading bio-flick based on Jon Spence's book by the same name, Austen (in the form of Anne Hathaway) plaintively asks, "So where is *my* happy ending?"[26] Similarly, several authors have written articles asking why the "author of happy endings" didn't herself achieve a happy ending. In these cases—as usual—the question really being asked is, Why didn't Austen marry? Yet how can we be so sure that Austen would have equated marriage with happiness?

The two sisters—Jane and her older sister Cassandra—both experienced romantic love, as far as historians can tell, but neither found a way to marry. They were both separated from their loves. Cassandra's fiancé died at 29 while working in the West Indies to provide for their marriage. Jane seems, according to several accounts, to have had at least two romances, but in one case the man's family swooped him away before he could descend to such an inferior match, and in the other case the young man may have died before a match could mature. Jane, too, was engaged, but for less than 24 hours. Harris Bigg-Wither was heir to a large estate with a lovely house; he was also brother to two of her best friends. She ultimately decided that she could not marry without love, despite all the benefits that such a match would confer. In short, when one considers all the mischances that the sisters endured, one cannot but read the following lines from the ending of *Persuasion* with a special irony: "Who can be in doubt of what followed? When any two young people take it into their heads to marry, they are pretty sure by perseverance to carry their point, be they ever so poor, or ever so imprudent, or ever so little likely to be necessary to each other's ultimate comfort."[27]

There was indeed plenty of room to doubt whether attraction and love could lead successfully to marriage and could endure travel, disease, war, inconstancy, familial pressures, economic contingencies, and the many other circumstances that get in the way of the happiness of "two young people."

The casting choice in *Becoming Jane* only intensifies this problem. Anne Hathaway, chosen to play Jane Austen in *Becoming Jane* (2007), established her fame over the previous five years playing various Cinderella-based characters: in *The Princess Diaries* (2001), *The Princess Diaries 2: Royal Engagement* (2004), and *Ella Enchanted*

5. Princess Jane? Anne Hathaway in *Princess Diaries* and *Becoming Jane.*

(*Left*, Walt Disney Pictures with BrownHouse Productions and Bottom on the Ninth Productions, 2001; *right*, Miramax Films and HanWay Films, UK Film Council in association with BBC Films, 2007)

(2004).[28] Such casting increases viewers' surprise that Austen (*cum* Anne Hathaway) has no "happy ending" of her own (figure 5). The tendency to conflate Austen's fate with her characters' fates continually fuels this flame. In fact, several modern adaptations of her novels cast the heroines as struggling novelists, furthering the displacement of Austen onto her characters.[29]

It seems unfair to reduce Austen's own "happy ending" to whether or not she married. Marriage was a precarious—and permanent—endeavor in Regency England, and hardly a recipe for Elysium. To judge from her letters, Austen was particularly dismayed at the thought of ensuing childbirth: "Poor animal, she will be worn out before she is thirty.— I am very sorry for her. [. . .] I am quite tired of so many children," she writes of her niece Anna, who just had given birth to a third child (Letter to Fanny Austen, Nov. 18, 1814). She saw two of her sisters-in-law have eleven children and four young mothers die in or shortly after childbirth. In her letters, she was frequently cruel in her depictions of marriage and childbirth. The most infamous passage is perhaps the comment on the stillbirth experienced by her neighbor: "Mrs Hall of Sherbourn was brought to bed yesterday of a dead child, some weeks before she expected, oweing [*sic*] to a fright.—I suppose she happened unawares to look at her husband" (Letter to Cassandra, Oct. 27–28, 1798). Austen clearly feared the loss of time and independence involved in marriage, particularly when younger women married much older men, as was the case with Mrs. Hall.

She writes to her niece Fanny: "Oh, what a loss it will be when you are married! You are far too agreeable in your single state—too agreeable as a niece. I shall hate you when your delicious play of mind is all settled down into conjugal and maternal affections" (Letter to Fanny, Feb. 20, 1817). Long since having given up on the prospects of motherhood, Austen transfers the language of maternal affection to her own books and career as an author. She refers to *Pride and Prejudice* as "my own darling child" (Letter to Cassandra, Jan. 29, 1813): the fruit of her mind replaced the fruit of her womb.

Happiness Reconsidered

So, what does Austen offer us in place of Hollywood-style happiness? For Austen, happy endings consist of much more than romantic love. If one takes note only of the marital endings of her novels, then her novels blend into one uniform whole, and all sense of their artistry is lost, as parodied in the cartoon shown in figure 6. As this figure suggests, this common urge to emphasize romance homogenizes the film adaptations of Austen. Hollywood is often accused of its relentless need for "happy endings," but when it comes to Austen, this phenomenon is both more uniform and more intense. Austen's novels are *defined* in public opinion by the happy conclusion of the marriage plot.[30] In pursuit of this happy ending, films create vastly expanded versions of the endings Austen writes. Sentimental and explicit film dialogue stands in for Austen's more understated words; exaggerated romantic declarations take the place of Austen's tantalizingly omitted ones; copious attention to details of dress and hair make up for the paucity of detail in Austen's descriptions; and romantic love eclipses all political, social, and ethical considerations.

In her novels, however, much more than marriage is encompassed in the comic resolution. In order for the novels to reach resolution, a variety of other difficulties, including psychological, social, and economic obstacles, must also be overcome. Some heroines face more traditional obstacles, such as separation of class or wealth; others need to learn to admit their own faults, distance themselves from their family, improve their assumptions about the world, or learn humility; still others desperately need family members to respect or understand them. Austen was keenly aware of these other challenges.

Equating marriage and happiness obscures the moral and individual growth that one can achieve *without* a marriage. We will see that for Austen, such individual growth was of paramount importance, and in fact the only thing in the heroines' control. Sophie Gilbert sums up the predicament nicely. All who love Austen, she says, must come to terms with the essential paradox of her writing: "No one did more to challenge the conventions and strictures of marriage for women in the 19th century, while simultaneously enshrining it as the ultimate happy ending" for her characters.[31] Unlike so many other novelists writing comedies of marriage, Austen builds into each of her novels the presumption that marriage is *not* the only way to achieve happiness.

For one thing, Austen attaches glamor to her charismatic bad girls who elude the traditional marriage plot, such as Mary Crawford

6. Homogenized Jane Austen. *New Yorker* comic by David Sipress.

www.CartoonStock.com

and Lady Susan. Austen's coquettes are indeed fantastically powerful: "They invent their own lives in ways that the Emmas and Elinors and Fannys never can, and in that sense they are more of a reflection of the author herself."[32] In her published novels, Austen does not give us examples of happily *un*married older women, with the exception of wealthy widows, such as Lady Russell and Lady Reynolds in *Persuasion* and *Sense and Sensibility*. She does not offer any examples of, say, women who make careers as novelists, although there were a few such women living at her time. The only reference to employment for female gentry is the descent to being a governess, the fate approaching Jane Fairfax in *Emma*. And in this instance, the fate is compared (if loosely) to slavery. Austen's utopian visions are distinctly limited as they apply to women and financial independence.

Theoretically, a happy marriage with economic stability seems the best situation for women in Regency England, even for preserving a degree of agency in shaping one's own life and the surrounding world. Austen chooses this boon in all her novels' endings. Yet such a marriage remained a fantasy for the vast majority of women, particularly after the loss of so many young men in the Napoleonic wars. In the absence of financial security, Austen herself paid dearly for her limited liberty to write.

Modern-day writers often have difficulty applying the marital happy ending to contemporary circumstances, without offering a great deal of reflexive apology. Jeffrey Eugenides has complained of the difficulty of completing a "marriage plot" in modern times without appearing naive.[33] Andrew Ahn's *Fire Island* opens with an immediate distancing from Austen's heteronormative marriage plots: "Well no offense to my girl, Jane, but that sounds like some hetero nonsense," Noah says after reciting the first line of *Pride and Prejudice*. "I don't know much about a good fortune, but not every single man is looking for a wife."[34]

Rachel Cohen's *Austen Years* is another case in point. Reviewer Tessa Carman points out the author's ambivalence about marriage. Cohen describes her own shame over wanting to share in an Austen-like happy romantic ending: "what embarrassed me was the triteness of longing for traditional happy endings, which, I now know, Austen herself is not that interested in." Carman ridicules Cohen's "jaded eye" and self-conscious distancing from happy endings. According to Carman, Cohen treats marriage as "just so much trite convention, a sign perhaps of immaturity, rather than a desire for wholeness and redemption." Carman, however, feels that "marriage is the harmonizing of different keys, a generative union, an icon of eschatological hope." The beauty here is that Carman and Cohen both have a point. Austen both critiqued and celebrated the marriage plot, whereas many of today's progressive audiences (and authors) feel that celebration of marriage is either foolishly idealistic or reactionary.[35]

The conservative, nostalgic view of Austen filtered through Victorian manners celebrates marriage unapologetically and also plays a strong role in her current popularity. Katie Roiphe suggests that "In the midst of our contemporary confusion about gender roles and sexuality, Jane Austen has come to symbolize clarity and order." Readers hanker for her "lost romantic world," and "the bright green lawns of a distant English countryside, where the virtue of marriage was a truth universally acknowledged, and love was formal, restrained, and inevitable."[36] Roiphe is not alone in choosing this nostalgic view of Austen as the key to her enduring popularity. WWJD, or "What Would Jane Do?" bumper stickers and t-shirts show a similar cultural currency: Austen has become a modern touchstone for wisdom and commonsense morality. For some, she may also have replaced religion in this role, just as the J in the slogan above is a play on "What Would Jesus Do?", a slogan that peaked in the 1990s among American Christians. As Juliette Wells has discovered, there are prolific conservative Christian adaptations of Austen, particularly the works of Sarah Arthur and Debra White Smith, contemporary evangelical Protestant writers in the United States.[37] In their own ways, scholars Devoney Looser, Juliette Wells, and Janine Barchas have all demonstrated that the Victorian ideal is still alive and well in American culture and shapes a good deal of Austen reception.[38]

Though many look at her novels nostalgically, as pretty dreams of order and harmony in our own world of chaos and loneliness, some of the critics I've mentioned are instead attracted to a savage, cynical spinster who withholds the happy ending, and they tie her to the harsh realities for women at the time. Much as Disney films were critiqued in the 1970s and '80s for supporting the damaging myth of Prince Charming and the marriage plot, Austen has been critiqued in the same way. Yet while Disney now produces "princess" films that end without marriage, and even without romance—such as *Brave* (2012), *Moana* (2016), and *Zootopia* (2016)—Austen adaptations have seen far less revision. Few adaptations of her novels omit the "happy ending" as engagement or marriage. An Austen film without marriage is rare; an Austen remake without a happy ending nearly nonexistent.[39]

Each of these perspectives (conservative and progressive feminist) isolates part of Austen's message. Austen allows her reader to eat the cake of romance and preserve feminist self-regard at the same time. The real power of Austen's endings comes from her unusual *juxtaposition* of romantic happiness and individual fulfillment, tradition and innovation, comedy and tragedy, fantasy and realism, desire for and suspicion of happy endings. She manages to provide both while showing the benefits and weaknesses of each solution without the other.

The Art of Austen's Endings

As I mentioned, there has been surprisingly little effort to analyze Austen's endings as *essential* to her artistry and her conception of the novel as a genre. In the following pages, I show that Austen creates these endings to ensure a particular effect on her readers, and to reveal a larger, philosophical point. One could say that her unusual endings are, in fact, key to her particular political philosophy. In her artistry, Austen responds to ongoing conversations about the nature of novels, marriage, and happiness. Through her endings, Austen obliquely comments upon the allure of the pursuit of perfection and reveals her skepticism regarding utopian aspirations. Through her innovative narrative techniques, Austen uses her endings to make points similar to many of those made by Mary Wollstonecraft in her *Vindication of the Rights of Woman* (1792)—foregrounding the importance of education over marriageability for women. By revealing the fictionality of her happy ending, Austen also draws attention to the actual world of economic instability that she knew so well.

In demonstrating the purposes of these anti-romantic flourishes near the end of her novels, I will argue *neither* that Austen was disappointed or embittered, *nor* that she limits these endings because she had no happy romance in her own life. Such arguments do an injustice to the complexity of her art as well as to her mastery of the novel as a genre. One can find much more in Austen's endings. By separating the elements of romance, recognition, and restoration that exist in all her endings, Austen shapes her own moral. She consistently prioritizes the individual hero or heroine's self-recognition and moral growth over the eventual romantic conclusion: for her, moral growth is essential to attain happiness, whether or not one marries. Like Shakespeare's comedies, Austen's also provide a sense of political or societal restoration of order, yet for Austen it often comprises a smaller scale, including the restoration of familial love and local community. She zooms out in her happy endings to reveal that much more than individual pairings are at stake—itself an anti-romantic move. The restoration, however, never approaches the degree one finds in Shakespeare or even Dickens.

Her oddly ambivalent endings also reveal her suspicion of extravagant enthusiasm in religion. This is where I would differ from the religious readings of her novels by critics such as Laura Mooneyham White and Alastair MacIntyre.[40] These critics describe Austen's endings as an explicit celebration of divine providence.[41] Too often, in order to make such claims about the eschatological and providential importance of her marriages, critics need to ignore the ways in which Austen undermines her happy endings. As we will see, Austen's endings are both obligatory and precarious; she makes a point of demonstrating how easily things could have ended unhappily. Her endings do manage to fulfill a general sense of providence, as with Shakespeare's comic forms, yet they give much greater weight to the value of the individual, with a stronger admixture of tragedy.

In the following chapters, I trace the craft of Austen's endings as she develops as a writer. Throughout her six published novels, Austen deliberately shapes readers' expectations and reactions by manipulating pace, ambiguity, revelation, and resolution—in no place more prominently than in her endings. Through her innovations in free indirect style, Austen carefully modulates her readers' emotional distance throughout her novels. Austen is at heart a teacher; the welfare of her readers is never far from her mind. She does not teach readers that all will be well in the best of all possible worlds; instead, she enlarges the reader's sympathy and powers of observation. For one thing, she teaches readers to expand their notions of heroism and *who* can achieve happy endings. Rather than a providential reward for virtue, happy endings are shown to belong to the marriage plot itself. With her humorously metafictional and anti-romantic craft, Austen portrays happy endings more as a (reluctant) gift from an author conforming to generic expectations, rather than as an eschatological statement about divine providence. In many of her works, Austen invokes Shakespeare to assist in her contributions to the history of the marriage plot more generally. As I understand her, Shakespeare's models play an important role in her own reformulation of courtship and comedic closure. His dramas informed her reformation of the domestic novel—her genre of choice.

I treat the novels in the sequence in which she is likely to have written them, rather than the order in which they appeared in print, beginning rather than ending with *Northanger Abbey*.[42] This chronology is important to my understanding of Austen's life and works. In my reading, Austen's artistic choices are both highly individual to each novel, and implicitly reactive to her previous successes and challenges. This book, in other words, sketches her literary life through the medium of her endings.

This volume treats not only the endings that she actually wrote, but also the cultural afterlife of those endings. All her novels have been adapted for different media—film, opera, vlogs, and theater, as well as other novels. They have spawned prequels, sequels, spin-offs, and retellings—with everything from zombies, vampires, and sea monsters to witches and dragons. These artifacts provide valuable evidence about her appeal to contemporary audiences, so I juxtapose key adaptations of each of her major novels alongside the novels themselves. I've not necessarily chosen the most popular adaptations, but rather ones that adapt her endings in either characteristic or innovative ways. Through these examples, I hope to shed a light on the myriad ways her image as "author of happy endings" has shaped her cultural capital. By considering the tendency among modern authors and screenwriters to limit Austen's purposes to the narrow goal of marriage and an even narrower understanding of the happy ending, I also invite reflection on what we consumers expect from films and novels more generally. We may differ surprisingly little from the audiences that Austen addressed more than 200 years ago.

CHAPTER 1

Commonplace Happiness

To begin perfect happiness at the respective ages of twenty-six and eighteen, is to do pretty well.

JANE AUSTEN, *Northanger Abbey*

Near the end of *Northanger Abbey*, the narrator famously invites readers to consider their own role in the happy resolution of the novel. At this crucial moment, when Catherine and Henry have declared their love but are unable to wed, the narrator playfully accuses the reader of either a lack of sympathy or a lack of affection: "The anxiety, which in this state of their attachment must be the portion of Henry and Catherine, and of all who loved either, as to its final event, can hardly extend, I fear, to the bosom of my readers, who will see in the tell-tale compression of the pages before them, that we are all hastening together to perfect felicity."[1]

Austen's narrator "fears" that our readerly "bosoms" lack the ability to share in the couple's "anxiety" for one of two reasons: either because we do not belong to "all who love [them]"[2] or because we are distracted by the "tell-tale compression of pages." This compression may make us too confident in the speedy resolution of "the final event"—namely, their marriage and "perfect felicity"—to feel the necessary concern. This passage provides a key to understanding how Austen uses the conventions of the marriage plot and the reader's psychology to achieve the desired effect of her "happy endings."

In the passage above, Austen describes a battle of desires within her reader's bosom—a battle that readers still experience today. The description bears a striking resemblance to Aristotle's depiction of the psychological power of the best tragic dramas to raise both "pity" and "fear" in the viewer; Austen's "anxiety" bears an admixture of each. Yet Austen is describing neither theater nor tragedy. Austen depicts a tension between "anxiety" and "haste" in her ideal novel reader approaching the end of *Northanger Abbey*. Austen wishes the reader to feel "anxiety" regarding the uncertain fate of the characters and also an impatient "haste" for the traditionally happy ending to occur. In this case, the narrator teasingly suggests that our *haste* for resolution might diminish our *anxiety* for the struggles of the characters. The narrator is concerned that we can be so confident in an imminent happy ending that we skip blithely over individual concerns. The irony is that the narrator's overt intrusions exacerbate this problem by denying us the possibility of suspending disbelief and immersing ourselves fully in the action. Austen's endings characteristically attempt to hold on to both the tragic and the comic, using one to puncture the other, lest the reader get too carried away. It is telling that the potential cost of readers' excessive confidence in the marriage plot is our ability to sympathize with elements of individual tragedy.

Another useful name for the reader's haste is narrative drive or "narrative lust," as C. S. Lewis calls it: "We do not enjoy a story fully at the first reading. Not till the curiosity, the sheer narrative lust, has been given its sop and laid asleep, are we at leisure to savour the real beauties. Till then, it is like wasting great wine on a ravenous natural thirst which merely wants cold wetness."[3] Austen is intently aware of our own narrative lust for discovery and resolution. She relies upon and channels this desire for her own purposes, using it to question conventional comedic closure. In anticipating the comedic closure of the novel, one can become numbed by generic expectation. Anxiety for the characters' welfare fuels narrative lust on the one hand; yet this desire can also outstrip our care for anything other than closure and resolution. We can sacrifice our humanity in the demand for the conventional resolution of the marriage plot. As a character in *Jane Austen Ruined My Life* says, "we can miss the man in looking for the hero."

Narrative Lust

It's well known that *Northanger Abbey* comments on the popular gothic novel, including the way in which readers involve themselves in gothic romances. It is less well understood that the dynamics of *Northanger Abbey*'s ending play an important role in the same critique. The gothic tradition was useful to Austen's purposes here because, even more than earlier experiments in the novel, the gothic romance and its tortured plots trained novel readers in participatory narrative lust—the longing for surprise, discovery, and resolution.[4] Narrative lust is what Catherine and Isabella wordlessly share as the basis for their friendship (the titillating suspense of reading *Mysteries of Udolpho*), yet this *anxiety* turns out to be insufficient grounds for friendship. Narrative lust is a baser, more common impulse than the kind of human empathy required to care for fictional characters—or each other.

Today we call suspenseful and engaging books "page-turners"; however, this characteristic is part of the psychology that scared eighteenth-century moralists about novels. Whereas epic poems are slow going and lyric poems are short, lust is strong and scary. The sexual overtones of Lewis's term are therefore appropriate for moralists' suspicions about the ruinous effect of novels on young women who read them in their bedrooms. Conduct books from Austen's period are full of warnings about such behavior. Consider this passage from the ominous-sounding *Evils of Adultery and Prostitution* (1792), which finds the source of the titular evils in reading novels: "Many young girls, from morning to night, hang over this pestiferous reading, to the neglect of industry, health, proper exercise, and to the ruin both of body and of soul. . . . The increase of novels will help to account for the increase of prostitution and for the numerous adulteries and elopements that we hear of in the different parts of the kingdom."[5] Novels, according to such accounts, turned women into libertines, adulterers, and prostitutes.

Novels were singled out for this moral danger. Plays are most like novels, perhaps, in their ability to create real-time suspense, but plays were considered less threatening because they were consumed publicly, not "hung over" in solitude. Musical performances are also capable of creating suspense, of course, but the pace of resolution and revelation is not controlled by the audience in any public performance. The private and solitary nature of novel reading increases its intimacy, the role of affective interplay with characters, variable speed of consumption, and the potential for generating and rewarding narrative lust. Austen's narrator teases the reader for sharing in one of Catherine's most dangerous traits, one she demonstrates both when she is immersed in *The Mysteries of Udolpho* and when she listens to Henry's own gothic tale on the way to *Northanger Abbey*. We participate in Catherine's contradictory desires—appreciating fictionality but clamoring for more: "Oh! No, no—do not say so. Well, go on."[6]

Yet Austen's narrator in the passage we began with talks of "hastening *together*" rather than alone. We are invited to think of the narrator as accompanying us in an emotional engagement in the novel. The "together" not only makes us conscious of our own desires, but also of another consciousness manipulating our desires. We likewise become aware that the author's purposes and our own can cross. We learn that we are dependent upon the author to give us what we have come to desire and expect. In order to understand how Austen and her narrator test, thwart, and reward the readers' expectations, we need to understand what Austen's readers desired and expected from the domestic novel and the marriage plot.

In *Northanger Abbey*, Austen comments on and adjusts popular expectations not only of marriage plots, but also of its ingredients, including the characteristics of the heroine and happy ending. Modern difficulties in adapting this novel to film relate directly to these purposes and demonstrate how little has changed in more than 200 years, in terms of audience expectations of heroines, marriage plots, and happy endings.

The Marriage Template

Austen's first encounter with writing the marriage plot might well be her entries into her father's parish registry. A clergyman's daughter, the teenage Austen famously inserted herself in the Steventon Church Parish *Register-Book for the Registration of All Banns and Marriages*. These playful entries into her father's parish registry are some of the earliest extant examples of Austen's handwriting. In these briefest of narratives, she "publishes and solemnizes" her own fictional marriages to men replete with Christian names. In the parish form, "Henry Frederic Howard Fitzwilliam of London" is joined to the much plainer, unadorned "Jane Austen of Steventon" (figure 7). In another entry, the same bride marries "Edmund Arthur William Mortimer of Liverpool."[7] She leaves the rest of the blanks on the form unfilled, such as dates and the presiding church official.

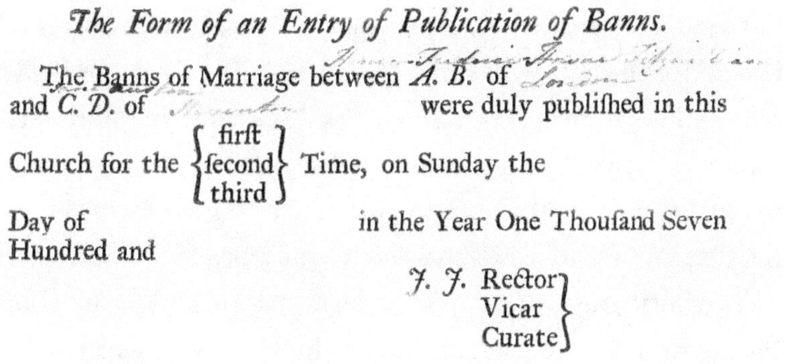

The Form of an Entry of Publication of Banns.

The Banns of Marriage between *A. B.* of and *C. D.* of were duly publiſhed in this Church for the {firſt / ſecond / third} Time, on Sunday the Day of in the Year One Thouſand Seven Hundred and

J. J. {Rector / Vicar / Curate}

7. Austen's earliest matchmaking. Register from Steventon Parish.

(Courtesy of the Hampshire Record Office: 71M82/PR3)

These entries are instructive about several aspects of Austen's sense of humor.

First of all, Austen fictionalizes the husband but leaves herself unaltered. The euphoric multiplying of his first names suggests either aristocratic standing or simply a multitude of possible future husbands. By including so many names, she avoids foreclosing possibilities. Interestingly, Austen refrains from fictionalizing date and celebrant. Perhaps such details would have made the entry too real and not sufficiently fictional to be funny. Marriage here resides firmly in the realm of imaginary fun, like possible flavors of ice cream for "The Beautiful Cassandra" of her juvenilia. She distances herself from any explicit expectation, perhaps for embarrassment or fear of disappointment. It is difficult not to associate this omission with a line from near the end of *Mansfield Park*, where the narrator quips: "I purposely abstain from dates on this occasion, that everyone may be at liberty to fix their own, aware that the cure of unconquerable passions . . . must vary much as to time in different people—I only entreat every body to believe that exactly at the time when it was quite natural that it should be so, and not a week earlier . . ."[8]

These entries are sometimes referred to as wedding registrations, but they are actually the registry of "notification of banns." The reason for the choice of "first/second/third" in the form is that law required the marriage be announced three times in public—usually three successive Sundays at church—in order to give adequate notice to anyone who might wish to object. This parish form is therefore both legalistic and anticlimactic. It proleptically announces a marriage by bringing attention to its legal criteria and to the church as the institution to officiate. It litigiously separates the romantic from the functionary. Austen's own role in filling out this form thus resembles that of an author creating a fictional character and allowing the reader to anticipate a marriage that has not yet taken place. By taking the role of the "Rector/Vicar/Curate," positions of authority that were unavailable to women, Austen also boldly assumes agency for marrying others—another urge that Georgian women might satisfy best through fictional narratives.

Finally, the fact that this is a fixed template is significant too. Not only was marriage the fixed cultural form expected for the heterosexual union of men and women above a certain socioeconomic class, but it was also a ritual that shaped literature and other societal artifacts. Marriage was the societally accepted way of satisfying the disorderly sexual passions while establishing legitimate offspring and an orderly succession of property rights. Marriage is how church and law attempt to channel passions into culturally acceptable norms. And what were the culturally acceptable norms for the novel? In English and European theater and fiction, the marriage plot had long since come to signify comic resolutions of all sorts.

Marriage is part of the Shakespearean comic template as well: in Shakespeare, weddings occur at the end of all comedies to indicate that disorderly passions have been redirected to their proper objects. There is an occasional exile (such as Don John in *Much Ado about Nothing*), but generally the comedies are consummated in the happy mixture of marriage, feasting, and dance, along with the restoration of (legitimate) political power. In *Much Ado about Nothing*, although the Prince remains single, the two final marriages nonetheless cement his moral and political authority, and the carnivalesque wedding banquet symbolizes his regenerated community/state. Even his brother has been apprehended, if not reconciled. In *A Midsummer Night's Dream*, two sets of endings occur—in the fairy world of the forest and in Athens. In both cases, marriages are either established or restored, and celebrations again mark the connubial bonds and restoration of order. Perfect children are even conceived that same evening, according to Puck. And in both these Shakespearean plays, a singular voice of authority restores order by silencing rebellious characters, including all females. Eighteenth-century literature inherits the same notions of order and comedic resolution through the marriage plot.

The Marriage Plot

Austen is a master of posing both sides of an argument, and her endings are no exception. Austen is invoked to protect tradition as much as she is invoked in favor of change; she is beloved for her romance, but she is also admired for her satirical wit. She is known for her celebrations of marriage, but she also inspires individual strength and growth. Austen both fulfills and critiques her given genres. This ability for complex envisioning of the world is, I believe, the key to her longevity as an author, perhaps even more than her style, her wit, or her three-dimensional characters. I argue that her vaunted happy endings are a particularly good place to find this double message. And *Northanger Abbey* is no exception.

Northanger Abbey contains Austen's famous digression on the defense of the novel, revealing what she particularly valued in the genre. According to this defense, the best novels display "the greatest powers of the mind [. . .], the most thorough knowledge of human nature, the happiest delineation of its varieties, [and] the liveliest effusions of wit and humour [. . .] in the best-chosen language."[9] In *Northanger Abbey*, she shows her own careful *re*definition of the genre. Most of the well-known authors of her age, including the women, were not "novelists" per se—they wrote in a wide range of genres: Frances Burney, Maria Edgeworth, and Hannah More all spanned multiple genres. Burney and More both wrote plays and poetry, for example. Edgeworth wrote many plays and letters of instruction, as well as anthologies of "extracts" for the education of the young. The popular cultural practice of publishing extracts from all genres together in one volume—a practice Austen deplores in *Northanger Abbey*—further homogenizes writings in various genres. Even within the novel itself, like advertisements for theatrical performances, there were a variety of entertainments: Jane West's *A Gossip's Story*, for example, contains a long "Legendary Tale" in verse that gets separate billing on the title page. For these reasons, one might have expected Austen to venture into other types of writing. For although she did experiment widely in her teenage writings, her published works were all novels. It was, in other words, unusual for an author of her time to focus so exclusively on novels. We need to consider what she saw in this fledgling genre.

Austen's own sense of being a novelist starts at a young age. Claudia Johnson has convincingly described Austen's short story "The Beautiful Cassandra: A Novel in Twelve Chapters" as her first novel, despite the fact that the average length of each chapter is under two sentences.[10] Austen wrote it in 1787 at age 12. Fifteen years later, in 1803, when the early version of *Northanger Abbey*, titled "Susan: A Novel," was sold to the publisher Crosby, the event marked her first entry into life as a professional author. Her choice of a title is therefore even more interesting. Of the dozens of novels published in

English in 1803, by far the most popular subtitle included the word "romance": examples include "a romance," "an original romance," "a pastoral romance," "a Gothic romance," and "an Arabian romance." Other titles suggested a putative basis in history or fact: "a history," "the adventures of . . .," "a historic tale," or "memoirs of . . .," "the history of . . .," or "the marvelous journey of . . . ." Finally, a third group of titles suggests exoticism and the intended, sentimental responses of readers, such as "a tale of mystery," "a pathetic tale," or "an interesting tale." Only three novels include the generic identifier "a novel," and all of these have a third element added—either poetry or an additional subtitle: *Human Frailties, A Novel Interspersed with Poetry*; *Frederick Montravers, or the Adopted Son, A Novel*; and *Peregrine, or the Fool of Fortune, A Novel.*[11] In this context, "Susan: A Novel" stands out for its plainness.[12]

Austen's short and simple title (one word) and subtitle (two words) suggest her ambition to purge sentimental and gothic literature of its excesses, or at least to offer an alternative form of novel. Simple as it may seem, in calling her first published book "a novel," she was proclaiming herself a novelist rather than woman of letters. Her ambitions center on reshaping the novel rather than contributing to a range of genres like most of her contemporaries. This partially accounts for the vehemence of her defense of the novel in *Northanger Abbey*: "Let us not desert one another; we [novelists] are an injured body."[13] While playful, the call to unite resembles the voice of an abolitionist or a rallying cry for oppressed workers as much as it does a literary discourse. Austen's political rallying cry calls for a revolt against the popular abuses of the novel. So, what did she write? Just what she ought, of course.

Many critics, as discussed above, look to Austen as the prototype of the marriage plot; they assume that for Austen and her reader, marriage is the *summum bonum* of life. Most historic accounts of female writers who distance themselves from the marriage plot and its conventional expectations do indeed start later than Austen. Even among those who discuss the nineteenth-century novel, such critics usually exclude Austen as a self-conscious critic of the marriage plot.[14] Rachel Blau DuPlessis, for example, takes up the topic of the marriage plot and happy ending in the history of the British novel. For DuPlessis, the dual plots of female self-improvement (the "quest plot") and the marriage plot are at war until the late twentieth century. The ending of the most important eighteenth- and nineteenth-century novels, she says, have "one main model of resolution: an ending in which one part of that contradiction, usually quest or Bildung, is set aside or repressed, whether by marriage or by death."[15] DuPlessis makes the excellent point that novels featuring women as the central character traditionally ended either in death or marriage—in either case putting the problematic, free-radical nature of an unmarried women's agency to rest. According to DuPlessis, it isn't until the twentieth century that women "have the economic, political, and legal power to sustain and return to questions of marriage law, divorce, . . . and their access to vocation," and novelists "begin to 'write beyond' the romantic ending." Yet I will argue that despite her inattention to the questions of divorce and lack of alternative careers for women, Austen nonetheless "writes beyond" the romantic ending.

Claudia Johnson has a more nuanced perspective: she notes that we do not see in Austen any great redefinition of the heterosexual marriage plot, nor any great reappraisal of the unmarried state for women. "Notably absent from Austen's plots [in relation to Mary Wollstonecraft, Ann Radcliffe, and Burney] are the ostentatious affectivity, the frantic contentiousness over suffering, and the sexual equivocality generated by male sentimentality itself that marks the plots of her (only slightly) older contemporaries." Yet I would argue that Austen recognizes that there are no other practical goals for women of the middle classes in her England. *Accepting* the marriage plot's inevitability enables Austen to focus in on the *psychological development* of her heroines within a sentimental setting. "Austen's novels can largely take for granted what is elsewhere so painfully contested. Female subjectivity is not forbidden, degraded, or displaced."[16] Paradoxically, Austen's acceptance of the nominal marriage plot and refusal for the most part to doubt its desirability allow her to form novels that enact sentimental education and take female consciousness to higher and more sophisticated levels than any author that preceded her.

DuPlessis's distinction between marriage and death as the two possible "endings" for female characters holds true for the novels of Samuel Richardson: marriage in *Pamela* and death in *Clarissa* are the only possible female resolutions. Such a divide is also true in an author that Austen particularly admired: Shakespeare. In many ways, it seems Austen defines her comedies in relation to Shakespeare's at least as much as she does in relation to the many novelists that she knew. Penny Gay and Paula Byrne have both done excellent work on establishing the commonalities between Austen's fiction and the theatrical traditions of her time.[17] Objections to the happy endings of Shakespeare's comedies are less often voiced, since they can be edited and corrected in various stagings and productions. Yet Shakespeare's comedies share in this tendency to silence the heroines through marriage, particularly his early comedies. *The Taming of the Shrew* is an excellent case in point. In what C. L. Barber calls his "festive comedies," Shakespeare, unlike Austen, tends to move away from individualism and toward the communal by denying individuality. Consider for example the resolution of the two bewildered couples in *A Midsummer Night's Dream*: The joke is that they all behave in the same way: "More sacks to the mill." . . . "Four woodcocks on a dish!"[18] While they are presented as interchangeable, the couples are nonetheless all restored to order through marriage.

The endings of novels, like plays, carry a disproportionate moral significance. Traditionally, the morality of a work is determined by the degree to which virtue is rewarded or vice punished in the final pages of the work, regardless of what preceded it. Austen consistently questions such dichotomies. Austen purposely rebels against the perfect and sanctimonious heroines that filled the pages of so many of her predecessors' novels. She gives her heroines significant faults, and the puncturing of endings adds to this redefinition of heroines and their presumed fates. Most frequently, Austen defines herself against the tear-jerking, sentimental novel, but she also reacts against the sanctimonious piety of authors like Oliver Goldsmith, Hannah More, and Samuel Richardson. Writing several decades before Radcliffe, Richardson was the king of the moralizing novel and its interface with conduct books. At the end of his novel *Pamela*, for example, Richardson closes with a last word from the author, who briefly tears off his epistolary robes to list the various moral teachings the book contains, in case we somehow missed them. Later he also published editions of alphabetized, edifying passages from his novels in duodecimo volumes so that women could carry them in their reticules and recapitulate the virtuous examples at all times.[19]

Austen does not entirely reject the Richardsonian legacy, as she maintains Richardson's interest in presenting the internal workings of a female protagonist's mind and heart, writing "to the moment, while the heart is agitated by hopes and fears, on events undecided."[20] Richardson may have inspired her initial interest in writing in the epistolary mode, but her later development of techniques like free indirect discourse stems from the shared goal of finding ways of "writing to the moment." From Henry Fielding, she inherits an enjoyment of a strong and witty central narrative voice, a voice particularly strong in *Northanger Abbey* and *Pride and Prejudice*. Such a narrator pulls her away from the epistolary mode and functions as a centripetal, animating force in her novels. One can see this compromise in "Lady Susan," which Austen wrote at 19, where she feels the need to drop the epistolary guise in the final chapter in order to take greater control of her narrative.

Through her published novels, Austen implicitly debates with these authors over what should be allowed in an ending. Austen rejects Fielding's bawdiness and Richardson's sententiousness. To get a sense of these two leading male novelists' rivalry, consider what Richardson said of Fielding. Richardson claimed that Fielding, in pursuit of more mixed and natural (a.k.a. common) characters, makes his characters coarse and vicious and creates a bad influence on his readers. In a "Concluding Note" to *Grandison*, Richardson writes:

> It has been said, in [*sic*] behalf of many modern fictitious pieces, in which authors have given success (and *happiness*, as it is called) to their heroes of vicious, if not profligate characters, that they have exhibited human nature as it *is*. Its corruption may, indeed, be exhibited in the faulty character; but need pictures of this be held out in books? Is not vice crowned with success, triumphant, and rewarded, and perhaps set off with wit and spirit, a dangerous representation? And is it not even *more* dangerous by the hasty information introduced, in contradiction to all probability, for the sake of patching up what is called a "happy ending"?[21]

In short, Richardson bemoans the fact that Fielding's charming but coarse characters are granted happy endings. Austen negotiates a middle ground between Richardson and Fielding, in addition to responding to many of the female novelists she admired.

Yet the question of happy endings that Richardson raises is not an easy problem to solve. According to the author of *The Revenger's Tragedy* (most likely Thomas Middleton), "when the bad bleed, the tragedy is good."[22] This phrase has become a touchstone for a particular approach to tragedy—one that tries to reclaim literature from charges of injustice and impiety. Such apologiae often force authors into binaries—tragedy *or* comedy, good characters *or* bad characters, reward *or* punishment. Realistically portrayed mixed characters and mixed outcomes inherently threaten this kind of evaluation. Judeo-Christian traditions have put a great deal of pressure on "endings"—salvific thinking led to so much attention in Austen's era, for example, on the death bed conversations and last utterances by famous individuals. The moral litmus test of a literary work has long been the justice of its ending. Realism is inimical to such evaluations. Then there is the question of *how* the desired resolution should come about—is worldly justice sufficient, or must one invoke providential Grace? Can amoral forces such as luck or fortune sufficiently account for characters' endings? This may seem like a quaint early modern obsession, but injustice at the end of novels with a comic tone still can rankle audiences. Modern rom-coms tend to reward all the good characters through seeming coincidences, compatible with notions of Providence, yet it is an easy justice, in a sense, as there are seldom any truly "bad" characters involved.

The Heroine of Common Life

Richardson argues against the portrayal of "common" characters; to him, the word means low and vicious. Austen seeks a middle ground between Richardson's sententious ideals and Fielding's more venal characters. At its core, *Northanger Abbey* is a novel that challenges reader expectations by celebrating the art of common life, but not in Richardson's sense of the word. In shaping the novel, Austen rejects the sentimental, the gothic, and the overly sanctimonious. According to the Austen's famous defense of the novel in *Northanger Abbey*, novels should avoid "improbable circumstances, unnatural characters, [. . .] topics of conversation which no longer concern anyone living; and [. . .] language, too, frequently so coarse as to give no very favourable idea of the age that could endure it."[23]

Northanger Abbey could be called a rumination on the common: in it, Austen teaches the beauties of and the sufficiency of common, everyday occurrences. She does this by juxtaposing the common against the exotic, the sublime, the strange, and the ideal. The "common" cannot be *too* common (in the sense of vulgarity), but it should strive to be common in the sense of being probable, recognizable, and natural. The "common" matters because it unites us as human beings: what we have *in* common. Her passion to correct the excesses of gothic romances, idealized heroines, and improbable adventures manifests itself in all her endings. There is an aspect of determined common sense about all her endings, which she inserts when she feels the audience (or she herself as author) is in danger of leaving the bounds of the common limits of feeling.

The "commonness" of Catherine Morland (*Northanger Abbey*'s heroine) is immediately apparent from the opening of the novel, particularly if one looks at her description next to the corresponding descriptions of the heroine of *The Mysteries of Udolpho*, Emily St. Aubin.[24] Austen's narrator informs us in the first line of the novel, that "No one who had ever seen Catherine Morland in her infancy would have supposed her born to be an heroine." As she grows up, Catherine is equally uninspiring: "noisy and wild, hat[-ing] confinement and cleanliness."[25] A romantic heroine might well hate confinement and enjoy the wild; however, the narrator crosses a line here. Noise—particularly dirt—destroys a romantic heroine's aura of elegance. Radcliffe's Emily, meanwhile, exhibits the rarest of characters. Emily had "discovered in her early years uncommon delicacy of mind, warm affections, and a ready benevolence; but with these was observable a degree of susceptibility too exquisite to admit of lasting peace. As she advanced in youth, this sensibility gave a pensive tone to her spirits, and a softness to her manner, which added grace to her beauty, and rendered her a very interesting object to persons of a congenial disposition." Unlike Catherine's parents, who were busy with nine other children, Emily's father "watched the unfolding of her infant character with anxious fondness," for among other things, she was his only child.

Austen's earliest readers would have understood these contrasts if they were familiar with the popular literature of the day. Radcliffe acknowledges her heroine as supremely "uncommon" and in fact exaggerates her "exquisite" perfections to the point at which a good deal of suspension of disbelief is required on the part of the reader, who certainly has never met Emily's like. In comparing the opening descriptions of these two novels, we can contrast the ways in which Radcliffe and Austen raise, challenge, and gratify their readers' expectations. Radcliffe teaches her readers to expect a heroine with unequalled beauty, grace, genius, goodness, and sensibility, who will undergo horrific trials and losses before reaching a conclusion that suits her virtue and excellence, including a marriage to a wealthy and titled soulmate. Austen parodies the "perfect heroine" trope in which Radcliffe luxuriates.

Catherine's family members are as determinedly average as she is herself. They are endowed with neither outstanding physical attractions, nor "interesting" sources of sadness, nor even tyrannical impulses: "Her father was a clergyman, without being neglected, or poor, and a very respectable man . . . and he had never been handsome. He had a considerable independence, besides two good livings—and he was not in the least addicted to locking up his daughters. Her mother was a woman of useful plain sense, and with a good temper, and, what is more remarkable, with a good constitution."

The same commonness—for better and worse—shows in Catherine's appearance and education. The Morlands "were in general very plain, and Catherine, for many years of her life, as plain as any. She had a thin, awkward figure, a sallow skin without much color, dark, lank hair, and strong features." One of the greatest triumphs of her adolescence is overhearing her parents upon one occasion remarking, "she is almost pretty today." The St. Aubin family inhabit a more celestial sphere: "In person, Emily resembled her mother; having the same elegant symmetry of form, the same delicacy of features, and the same blue eyes, full of tender sweetness. But, lovely as was her person, it was the varied expressions of her countenance . . . that threw such a captivating grace around her." Catherine, meanwhile, is far too common to "captivate," falling altogether "miserably short of true heroic height."[26]

While Catherine devours novels, Emily eschews them, preferring the sublimity of the best poets: Emily "discovered in her early years a taste for works of genius." Radcliffe is therefore implicated in the accusation that Austen levels at other novelists at the end of volume I, chapter 5: "I will not adopt that ungenerous and impolitic custom so common with novel-writers, of degrading by their contemptuous censure the very performances, to the number of which they are themselves adding—joining with their greatest enemies in bestowing the harshest epithets on such works, and scarcely ever permitting them to be read by their own heroine, who, if she accidentally take up a novel, is sure to turn over its insipid pages with disgust." What is often overlooked in *Northanger Abbey*'s defense of the novel is its metafictional aspect. Austen is referring not to historical individuals' choice of reading material, but the choice of other novelists in the depiction of *their heroines*' reading material. "Alas! If the heroine of one novel be not patronized by the heroine of another, from whom can she expect protection and regard?"[27]

Mary Brunton's heroine in *Self-Control*, for example, is ashamed of her preference for reading novels.[28] In this context, a heroine like Emily is refusing to patronize not only herself, but also the Catherine Morlands of the world. Thus the heroines themselves are enlisted in this civil war among novelists and their protagonists.

The difference between Catherine's and Emily's use of their leisure time is similarly stark. C. S. Lewis, an admirer of Austen's novels, may be paying homage to Catherine Morland in *The Horse and His Boy*, a novel where he reverses prominence between human and animal. Lewis shows the beautiful, joyful simplicity of horses rolling down hills and slopes: "'That's good. That's very good,' [Bree] said, rubbing his back on the turf and waving all four legs in the air."[29] Yet the protagonist-horse Bree develops an insecurity that any horse worth writing about would never deign to do something so undignified, nearly losing such an innocent and natural pleasure. Catherine, we are told, "loved nothing so well in the world as rolling down the green slope at the back of the house."[30] While both Catherine and Emily enjoy the outdoors, Catherine runs about in the ordinary, fresh, and typically English outdoors of ball games and grassy slopes in the company of others. Emily prefers contemplating the sublime in her solitary rambles in her remote corner of the Alps: "It was one of Emily's earliest pleasures to ramble among the scenes of nature; [. . .] she loved more the wild wood-walks, that skirted the mountain; and still more the mountain's stupendous recesses where the silence and grandeur of solitude impressed a sacred awe upon her heart and lifted her thoughts to the GOD OF HEAVEN AND EARTH." Radcliffe's use of complex sentence structure and capital letters further emphasizes the intellectual and religious sublimity of Emily's mind. Emily's pleasures are not as easily replicable nor as accessible as Catherine's, as far more people have grassy lawns than "stupendous recesses" to frolic in.

Through a long series of negations, Austen deflates the novel reader's expectations, showing that this novel, though written with sentimental and gothic novels in mind, will disappoint any reader who approaches it with similar expectations. This heroine will be much more commonplace than Radcliffe's, hardly above average in many aspects of life. And yet it remains to be seen whether Austen similarly discourages the expectation of a happy ending, including the likelihood of an advantageous marriage.

Northanger Abbey embodies a paradox at the heart of Austen's fiction: it is a novel that overtly favors the common over the "strange" and "amazing," yet it concludes with an *uncommonly* tidy, romantic ending—no less than "perfect happiness" itself.[31] We will see that finding something "strange" can be a desirable psychological step and one that she encourages in her readers. The narrator calls Catherine "strange, unaccountable" in the opening chapter,[32] and Catherine subsequently calls several characters "strange" or "unaccountable" when they act differently from how she expects. While calling Catherine "strange" seems dismissive, it also functions as an invitation to imaginative curiosity and sympathy. We as readers are called to account for Catherine as we read further, and Catherine to account for her acquaintances as she observes them and learns more about their characters. Austen wishes to estrange the reader from the psychologically improbable, just as we may need to be weaned from the exotic. In this way, choices in vocabulary foreshadow distinctions Austen makes in her conclusion.

Catherine's friend Isabella's favorite word, repeated 16 times in the course of the novel, is the intensifier "amazingly."[33] She says it so often that Catherine begins to say it as well, prompting Henry's teasing commentary. Catherine herself tends to employ the word "strange," as in, "What a strange, unaccountable character!" This word reveals Catherine's middle position for most of the novel. She is neither entirely objective as a spectator, nor entirely a participant in the events around her. She has not recognized the beauties of common sense and common cares, still hankers after the "amazingly horrid," but never falls into hypocrisy. "Strange," for Catherine, is a code word for the fact that something she is experiencing doesn't make sense to her. As Henry remarks, she attributes to others her own innocent motives, and only gradually does she become able to understand duplicity in others. Her heroism consists in this intellectual growth and in the fact that she does not become dishonest herself. Her simplicity allows her to observe follies around her and (sometimes unknowingly) poke fun at examples of excess—like linguistic nonsense: "I do not speak well enough to be unintelligible."[34] In this novel, the horrid and amazing are set up as opposites of the common. She possesses, along with the rest of her family, "a degree of moderation and composure, which seemed rather consistent with the common feelings of common life, than with the refined susceptibilities, the tender emotions which the first separation of a heroine from her family ought always to excite."[35] "The common feelings of common life" are by definition that which we have *in* common, unless we choose to delude ourselves. Austen's goal is for the novel to celebrate our shared existence in opposition to the exceptionalism and solitude of sentimental heroines and heroes. This is particularly unattractive for film adaptations of Austen, which instinctively resist "commonness" and Austen's progressive redefinition of heroines.

While rejecting gothic fantasies, Austen paradoxically reveals how "common" gothic violence is. In mock gothic mode—in imitation, perhaps, of Alexander Pope's *Rape of the Lock*—there is indeed abduction, imprisonment, and solitary expulsion in *Northanger Abbey*; however, its forms are comically subdued. The abduction and imprisonment consist of an unwilling carriage ride with her brother and two others, undertaken under false premises; the solitary expulsion from Northanger Abbey involves an unaccompanied trip home. In making these events so ordinary, Austen might be said to diminish their terror. And yet one could equally well say that Austen instead reveals their ubiquity, long before a #MeToo movement.

Northanger Abbey uniquely includes *all* of the telltale characteristics of her speedy and intrusive endings—features that she uses more sparingly in her other novels. *Northanger Abbey* is also her most consistently metafictional novel: the one that plays most overtly with levels of reality, frequently outing the narrator as author and the plot as fiction. The joyful transport of metafictional ploys—intrusive comments, playful asides in first person, reminders to the reader about the "volume" in their hands, and so on—runs throughout the novel, so the ending itself comes more as a continuation of this playfully self-conscious mode, rather than the startling shift in tone in many of her other novels.

The Reader's Sagacity

How does Austen test the expectations of her readers in *Northanger Abbey*? She ruptures the marriage plot, downplays romantic elements, and emphasizes the commonplace when readers are expecting remarkable heroines with exotic experiences who face grave dangers and are rewarded by illustrious marriages. When the narrator of Austen's endings suddenly draws attention to the artificiality of plot and to the power of the author to construct or control it, she drastically changes the social dynamic between author, narrator, and reader.

> *I leave it to my reader's sagacity* to determine how much of all this it was possible for Henry to communicate at this time to Catherine, how much of it he could have learnt from his father,

> in what points his own conjectures might assist him, and what portion must yet remain to be told in a letter from James. *I have united for their ease what they must divide for mine.*[36]

This passage ends with a striking division of labor between reader and narrator-*qua*-author, made even more remarkable by the list of enticing questions that the narrator teasingly poses, only to refuse to address. We might think that the implied narrator gloatingly indulges in her power here or is unspecific for her "ease," as the passage suggests; if such were the case, readers could feel at the author's arbitrary mercy. But such a reaction would be more likely in a novel such as Laurence Sterne's *Tristram Shandy*, where it is difficult to anticipate the narrator-protagonist's next move, or in Henry Fielding's *Tom Jones*, where the reader has agreed from the opening pages of the novel not to question the author's authority. Austen's narrator is neither so quixotic nor so tyrannical and achieves a different (more democratic) dynamic with the reader.

Rather than finding ourselves at the mercy of a despotic narrator, we in fact find ourselves in a sudden vacuum of authority. The reader's shock results from the fact that Austen's narrator simultaneously announces her authority (that is, her authorship) and abdicates it. Consider the word "leave" in the following similar passage: "I *leave* it to be settled by whomsoever it may concern, whether the tendency of this work be altogether to recommend parental tyranny, or reward filial disobedience."[37] What appears in these passages to be an abdication, a withdrawal or denial of authority, is, however, really a self-conscious transfer of authority to the reader, along with a lesson about the abuses of authority. The point at which the fiction is heightened, when the narrator exposes her powers of construction or control, and rhetorical questions such as those above are introduced to the text, is also the point at which the reader's freedom (and obligation) to interpret or to participate in the construction of the fiction is also announced. The division of labor that I mentioned above entails an imaginative participation in the fleshing out of concluding details on the part of the sympathetic reader.

Rhetorical questions explicitly invite the reader's response: "[W]hat probable circumstance could work upon a temper like the General's?" asks the narrator when she enlists the reader's help in devising the speedy conclusion of *Northanger Abbey*.[38] This technique is most apparent in *Northanger Abbey* and *Mansfield Park*, but for different reasons. In *Northanger Abbey*, it is more organic, as this ironic narrator is the central character of the novel. From the very start of this novel, the reader is training in self-awareness of the effects of reading; drawing attention to the reader's feelings and expectations therefore seems much less incongruous.

For Austen, the art of the commonplace is a cornerstone of her characterization and her own style of happy ending. Part of the significance of the common comes down to the fact that, literally, it is what we have *in common*. Without reducing her art to the lowest common denominator, she can still focus on individuals who are believable and match readers' experiences more closely than those of Fanny Burney, Oliver Goldsmith, Ann Radcliffe, or Samuel Richardson. At the same time, she makes sure that readers recognize domestic felicity and successful marriages as—dare I say—rather *uncommon*. To consider such happiness as a common or natural outcome, rather than the product of effort and superlatively good fortune, is to fall into the rom-com trap. Austen particularly wants to avoid this "dangerous moral."

Along with withholding romantic details and increasing narrative pace, Austen indulges in similar narrative intrusions (and retreats) at the end of most of her novels. Consider the following example from *Northanger Abbey*:

> A heroine returning, at the close of her career, to her native village, in all the triumph of recovered reputation, and all the dignity of a countess, with a long train of noble relations in their several phaetons, and three waiting-maids in a travelling chaise and four, behind her, is an event on which *the pen of the contriver may well delight to dwell*; it gives credit to every conclusion, and the author must share in the glory she so liberally bestows.—But my affair is widely different; I bring back my heroine to her home in solitude and disgrace; and *no sweet elation of spirits can lead me into minuteness*. A heroine in a hack post-chaise is *such a blow upon sentiment, as no attempt at grandeur or pathos can withstand*. Swiftly therefore shall her post-boy drive through the village, amid the gaze of Sunday groups, and speedy shall be her descent from it.[39]

In this passage near the end of *Northanger Abbey*, Austen draws attention to her own pen by means of an alternative pen that might hypothetically write a different ending. Her alternative "contriver" feels "delight," "a sweet elation of sprits," and "a share in the glory" of the successful and wealthy heroine with a long retinue. In fact, the other "contriver" writes the first several lines of the opening of this paragraph—a scene that does not occur in this novel. The contriver of the grander and more pathetic scene feels tempted "into minuteness" of detail. Austen closes the paragraph with apophasis—claiming not to narrate while still giving us details of Catherine's disgraceful return. Instead of in grandeur, Catherine returns in a hack post-chaise, alone, on a Sunday, driven by a post-boy, and gawked at by residents. In the case of *Northanger Abbey*, Austen frequently appears to belittle her own account by comparing it to the grander portrayals of authors like Edgeworth and Burney. Yet this doubling—of her version with the other contriver's version—creates the special magic of her endings.

Austen's Extra Chapter

Austen paid meticulous attention to details regarding symmetry in this novel. When *Northanger Abbey* appears in its intended two volumes, we can better detect some of the parallel scenes. In chapter 2 of each volume, for example, Catherine receives invitations to go to a new location (Bath and Northanger Abbey, respectively). In chapter 5 of each volume, Catherine is introduced to and intoxicated by a new novel (*Udolpho* and Henry's spoken gothic story). In both chapters 7, Catherine is monopolized by vain bullies talking about themselves at length (John Thorpe on his horses and gigs, and General Tilney on his house and gardens). Both chapters 8 center on Miss Tilney (Catherine's first introduction to her in Bath and the intimate tour of Northanger with her). Both chapters 10 feature Catherine's determination to reform herself and take charge (in Bath she is determined to defy her brother and avoid the Thorpes, and at Northanger she is abashed at her error and resolves to keep a check on her imagination). In both chapters 11, Catherine is trapped by bad weather, and there is talk of escape to a romantic destination (a foiled trip to Blaize Castle and a successful trip to Woodston). Both chapters 14 include Catherine's best and worst journeys (the walking trip with Henry and Eleanor, and the ignominious trip home to her parents). And finally, in both chapters 15, romances culminate into engagements (Isabella and James announce theirs but wait for the Morlands' approval; Henry and Catherine announce to her parents and wait for the General's approval).

Unlike her usual penchant for the same number of chapters in each volume, Austen added an additional chapter to volume II, bringing it to 16 chapters.[40] Adding an "extra chapter" to the otherwise symmetrical structure of *Northanger Abbey* enables Austen to separate the marital resolution from the rest of her novel. Austen can emphasize her point that the actual marriage is not essential to the novel as a whole—it is a bonus, a gift, and far from inevitable. Appropriately, it is the extra chapter that provides the happy resolution for Catherine and Henry, for though they viewed the possibility of gaining the General's consent as "almost impossible,"[41] this chapter clears the path for his consent through the sudden (for the reader) appearance of a viscount who marries Eleanor. This marriage pleases the General so much that Eleanor convinces him to forgive Henry and give his consent to his marriage. Individual growth and corrected vision are within our own powers, and therefore fall within the symmetrical form of the novel. They are anticipated results of time and growth, barring great disaster. In contrast, the asymmetry highlights that the fortune of finding a perfect mate and having circumstances align to allow marriage with that individual. This romantic resolution is so far outside the common that Austen markedly breaches the symmetry of her novel to allow it. The extra chapter is a somewhat less organic part of the novel: it gives us a sense that the marriage was also not organic, not the probable conclusion of the story. The happy romantic resolution is a gift given not to please the reader, but to fulfill the conventions of "romance," to use the narrator's own word.

Austen directly addresses the artificiality of this "gift" to the reader after introducing the viscount and refusing to describe him any further: "Concerning the one in question [the viscount], therefore, I have only to add—*aware that the rules of composition forbid the introduction of a character not connected with my fable*—that this was the very gentleman whose negligent servant left behind him that collection of washing-bills."[42]

Such comments heighten the reader's awareness of Austen's deviation from the norms established by the rest of the novel. Such self-referentiality, overt fictionality, and *deus ex machina* techniques seem, among other things, to contradict Aristotle's (and Samuel

Johnson's) demand for the organicism of action that traditionally allows the reader to feel, at the conclusion of a work of art, that it could *not* have ended otherwise.

Austen also uses other techniques to separate this final marital resolution from the rest of the novel, and to downplay its importance. Most notably, she picks up the pace of narration, emphasizes improbability, and limits the "glory" that Catherine attains through the marriage.[43]

First, the narrator/author presents this *deus ex machina* resolution in the first person with apparent self-consciousness: "aware that the rules of composition forbid the introduction of a character not connected with my fable." Second, Catherine must share the limelight with Eleanor. The final chapter includes not one, but two marriages in a scant few pages. Eleanor's was entirely unlooked for by the reader. And when the narrator says, "My own joy on the occasion [of the marriage] is very sincere. I know no one more entitled . . . to receive and enjoy felicity," she is referring not to Catherine, but Eleanor Tilney![44] The narrator never expressly states her joy about Catherine and Henry's wedding.

After receiving consent from the General, the actual marriage is extremely understated. Austen describes it as follows: "the event which it authorized soon followed: Henry and Catherine were married, the bells rang and every body smiled."[45] Austen omits the actual wedding, just as she excludes all dialogue involved in their proposal or other confessions of love. Catherine is not heard to speak a word from halfway through chapter 15. This could seem to support the view that marriage permanently silences the heroine and deprives her of her individuality, just as the institution itself deprives her of economic and legal rights. It is tempting to see this as analogous to Shakespeare's silencing of the loquacious Beatrice upon her marriage in *Much Ado about Nothing*, but this comparison risks losing sight of the irony of Austen's portrayal here. Catherine's words are also playfully elided in Henry's avowal of his love because "they pretty well knew [her heart] was already entirely his own."[46] To make the situation even less glorious for Catherine, the narrator explains: "I must confess that [. . .] a persuasion of her partiality for him had been the only cause of giving her a serious thought. It is a new circumstance in romance, I acknowledge, and dreadfully derogatory of an heroine's dignity; but if it be as new in common life, the credit of a wild imagination will at least be all my own."[47] The many omissions and other anti-romantic rhetorical strategies force the reader to recognize the essential superfluity of the final romantic resolution.

Far from presenting the marriage as the deserved conclusion and reward for extensive romantic suffering, the narrator herself minimizes any suffering on the part of the central pair, herself limiting the "anxiety" that the reader can feel for them: "as this took place within a twelvemonth from the first day of their meeting, it will not appear, after all the dreadful delays occasioned by the General's cruelty, that they were essentially hurt by it. To begin perfect happiness at the respective ages of twenty-six and eighteen, is to do pretty well."[48] The ending of *Northanger Abbey* indirectly celebrates the unjust actions that postponed and could have prevented their marriage. Their pain, according to the narrator, helps the ending be happier. While there is no doubt truth in this statement, in terms of narrative sympathy, it prevents the narrator from expressing "proper" outrage at the obstacles thrown in the way of the happy couple: "[I] profess[-] myself moreover convinced, that the General's unjust interference, so far from being really injurious to their felicity, was perhaps rather conducive to it, by improving their knowledge of each other, and adding to their strength of attachment."[49]

Adding to the puncturing of the romance here is also that almost *no one* around Catherine ever suspects her of being involved in a courtship: neither the Allens, nor her siblings, nor her parents.

This is especially remarkable in these last pages. Her mother suspects nothing romantic, even *after* Henry arrives at their house and asks Catherine to go on a walk to the Allens' house. When he asks for their permission to marry, "Mr. and Mrs. Morland's surprise on being applied to by Mr. Tilney, for their consent to his marrying their daughter, was, for a few minutes considerable: it having never entered their head to suspect an attachment on either side."[50] Austen in this way bookends her adventures: in the beginning, "No one who had ever seen Catherine Morland in her infancy, would have supposed her born to be an heroine."[51] And at the end, no one suspects her of it either. One effect of this device is to make Catherine's adventure less probable, more like a fairy tale.

We must also consider the final line of the novel: "I leave it to be settled by whomsoever it may concern, whether the tendency of this work be altogether to recommend parental tyranny, or reward filial disobedience."[52] The last sentence with its pseudo-moral appears to fulfill the traditional role of the epilogue in theater, negotiating the liminal space between performance and the reentry into real life. The narrator's statement both reduces the reader's choices to either obedience or rebellion and isolates the moral to encompass only one single action vis-à-vis his father. Austen thus overtly shrinks the moral scale of the novel. In lines such as this one, the narrator takes on a rather parental (if not tyrannical) relation to the reader as we near the end of the novel. Readers may suddenly feel aware of the limitations of what Austen will reveal and when she will reveal it, rather than just enjoying the progress of an evolving relationship. This dynamic contributes to the impression that neither Catherine nor the reader has earned the happy resolution. It is a gift consciously presented by the proud and recalcitrant author.

This teasing manipulation of the reader, as it occurs in her forcedly happy endings, might give a second account for the annoyance or frustration some readers feel at Austen's endings. Austen's artistic but manipulative use of anticlimax alters the social dynamic between reader and author. Teasingly, the narrator of *Northanger Abbey* tells readers that we could neither *possibly* understand nor care about the anxiety that the hero and heroine feel as they wait for permission to marry. She tempts readers to care about the internal workings of the plot, only to jar us out of our suspension of disbelief in the subsequent phrase by overtly asserting the fictionality of the ending (and playfully suggesting the reader's conventionality). Just as she did as a teenager, writing entries in her father's wedding registry, Austen draws attention to templates and conventional expectations of marriage. But while Austen thwarts the reader *as* a reader of novels/marriage plots, she teaches us to laugh at both literary and societal expectations, to recognize them for ourselves and in ourselves, but not to reject them. She teaches readers to love novels while recognizing their potential dangers and abuses.

Her elaborate treatment of the final, extra chapter recalls the central theme of *Northanger Abbey*—the benefits of the "common." In her chastisement of the gothic novel, Austen exposes our readerly tendencies to enjoy, even seek, the suffering of our heroines. She pokes fun at the conventional need for heroines to be exotic, beautiful, "interesting"—demands that distance readers from their own surroundings. She takes part of the argument that some moralists of her time made about novels per se and wields it against the reader, in order to show that she is writing a different kind of novel—one that may invoke the gothic but does so for the sake of the common.

So, each time she awakens her readers out of a gothic horror and lurid desire for disaster, or out of a desire to see all difficulties swept conveniently away at the end, she reveals a psychology often associated with novels (and perhaps life in general). She reveals the heart of her critique of the culture of sensibility as well as the gothic novel—its withholding of sympathy for the exclusively "interesting" and the indulgence in the pleasures of grief.[53] The magic of her solution is to give us the happy ending, while also reminding us of its *evitability*—leaving the price tag attached. She turns the lights on in the theater a bit earlier than we would like, so that we can be self-reflective about what we have witnessed.

Filming Irony

Northanger Abbey has been particularly challenging to adapt to film with any degree of adherence to the original tone and purpose of the novel. Part of this difficulty comes from challenges inherent to filming dramatic irony, as well as the problem of what to do with the narrator's voice. In the absence of a narrator commenting on Catherine's actions and assumptions, it is difficult for film to convey the metafictional tone of the novel. In most cases, the adaptations have responded by simply giving up on the irony and embracing the gothic romance within *Northanger Abbey*. The cover of one edition of the novel, pictured in figure 8, demonstrates this gothic *Northanger Abbey*, taking Catherine's fears as founded in real dangers: "The terror of Northanger Abbey had no name, no shape—yet it menaced Catherine Morland in the dead of night!"

The filmic equivalent to this paperback edition is the 1987 adaptation directed by Giles Foster, with a screenplay by Maggie Wadey.[54] This film includes fantasy insets—a renaissance Catherine receives help from a French maid, for example—but the problem is that the non-fantasy images are just as strange. Whether it's an eerie tête-à-tête by a canary, the General flirting with a horrifically made-up "marchioness," or Henry Tilney arriving through a misty haze on horseback to visit and propose to Catherine (figure 9), the "real scenes" are almost as strange as the fantasy insets. With the possible exception of a scene where a disheveled General Tilney leans over

8. Mock gothic. Cover, *Northanger Abbey*.

(Paperback Library Gothic; author's collection)

a stone basin with blood dripping from his hands, this film consistently interprets the "strangeness" that Catherine encounters as belonging to the situations themselves rather than to the disjunction between her expectations and the real world. All sense of dramatic irony is thereby lost.

The vaguely monastic, eerie music plays indiscriminately through both types of scenes, further undermining any contrast. The music suggests gothic mystery and danger when Catherine is immersed in reading the *Mysteries of Udolpho*, yet the music melds into *all* scenes, regardless of whether they are exaggerated or not. It even plays as Catherine is arriving home. The Bath of this film is even stranger than the one that inhabits Catherine's imagination, and as a result, the viewer is led to conclude that Catherine is right to compare her life to Emily St. Aubin's. The Catherine of this film is conventionally beautiful (Katherine Schlesinger) and appears born to be a heroine: all satire is lost from the start. This film is meant to appeal to an audience that requires beauty and exceptionalism in its heroines and who want exotic, gothic plots for entertainment. Foster and Wadey seem to assume that contemporary audiences would be bored by the commonness of the original. This phenomenon suggests that audience expectations have changed surprisingly little in more than 200 years, despite intervening political movements and developments in women's opportunities.

Catherine in Paradise

There are at least two films that succeed in creatively upsetting the traditional marriage plot in their adaptations of *Northanger Abbey*, each for different ends.[55] The clearest exception to the distortions described above is *Ruby in Paradise*, which ultimately makes the claim that female friendship, education, and careers are superior

9. Gothic in all the wrong places. Scenes from *Northanger Abbey*.

(BBC TV Production in association with A&E Network, 1987)

to courtship and marriage. *Ruby in Paradise* falls into the category of film that is an homage to an Austen novel rather than a slavish retelling. Insofar as it transfers the plot of *Northanger Abbey* into a twentieth-century setting in Florida, it is a loose retelling. Ruby Lee Gissing leaves her home in Tennessee and travels alone to a resort haven on the coast of Florida, where tourists gather in the spring and summer to bathe, frolic, and flirt. This is the approximation of Catherine's journey to Bath. Ruby/Catherine leaves behind a troubled family existence of abuse and poverty, although these issues continue to haunt her in "paradise." Austen seems far from the content of the film until Ruby's boyfriend Mike suggests that she read *Northanger Abbey*. She takes the book off the shelf and reads from the description, noting (slightly bitterly) that she has little in common with the life that it describes. Ruby nonetheless reads the novel and makes overt comparisons as she does so between her life and Catherine's. The sense is that Austen's world is too far from hers to be relevant—Austen's seeming too chaste, orderly, innocent, and pastoral. But the viewer who knows *Northanger Abbey* is invited to make further comparisons, and the voiceover of Ruby's thoughts as she writes in her journal enables us to obtain a more detached and ironic approach to the plot.

There is a clear analogy to John Thorpe in Ricky, a rake who sexually assaults Ruby and is inordinately proud of the motorcycle (gig) that he drives. The son of the owner of the store where she works, the rake's responses to her refusals jeopardize her job and her fragile financial security. Yet in this story, Ruby eventually sleeps with him. Given this comparison, Ruby's contrasting boyfriend Mike seems vastly better: he is chivalrous, gentle, moral, has a beautiful home, and seems to want a permanent relationship with her. Yet his didactic religion makes her angry, and he is too possessive or controlling, suggesting different things about her future that she rejects. Victor Nunez, the director, here seems to take direct issue with the eighteenth- and nineteenth-century marriage plot's "mentor-lover" convention. Ruby refuses to be bullied by Ricky, but also to be domesticated by Mike.

As in *Northanger Abbey*, there are contrasting female candidates for Ruby's friendship. The more mature Rochelle (Eleanor Tilney?) announces at the end that she will "finish [her] degree" and her boss won't be able to afford her anymore: her happy ending is that she is going to promote her own career through further education. The two friends make plans for future education and careers, while watching a romantic couple stroll on the beach. Ruby breaks up with Mike, pays off her debts, and decides that female friendship is a better basis for a happy ending. At the end, she is inspired by the strength and resilience of a neighbor in her trailer park, who sings a song of praise to Shiva while scrubbing floors. Her last journal entry reconciles herself to her own, modest—common, perhaps?—style of heroism: "[I] suppose it means more, making it in some big, great city somewhere, but this is the world I found, and I guess the questions stay the same: [. . .] Can we ever know our true desires? and Why are we—all of us—so often lonely and afraid?" She finds her own answers in the resilience and stability of holding down a job, reentering the gift shop where she works in the final scenes. For many, the film suggests, this is heroism enough.

Roger Ebert's commentary on the film suggests his awareness of twentieth-century audiences who expected different—seemingly more gothic—entertainment from films. He points out that while unemployed, Ruby briefly considers becoming a stripper, and unlike countless films where women become strippers or prostitutes, Ruby rejects that more gothic and degrading outcome. He also suggests that the audience might find the events of the film a little too boring or common: "My description of *Ruby in Paradise* may make it sound like events in a boring everyday world. Nothing could be further from the truth. The greatest adventures in life don't take place in bizarre places with fantasy people. They take place as we size up the world and take our chances with it. And here is a young woman, on her own, smart and capable but still feeling her way, who makes some discoveries about what she can achieve, and what makes her happy."[56] Ebert's apology for *Ruby in Paradise* recalls Austen's defense of the novel in *Northanger Abbey*, and once again, it is striking that this defense still needed to be made in the final decade of the twentieth century.

Atoning for Happiness

Ian McEwan calls *Atonement* his "Jane Austen novel." Even without such an explicit, extratextual commentary, a reader might make connections to Austen. McEwan invokes Austen from the start of this novel, with an epigraph from *Northanger Abbey*—the "Dear Miss Morland, consider the dreadful nature of the suspicions you have entertained . . ." passage, where Henry Tilney chides the heroine, Catherine Morland, for leaping on extremely thin evidence to the shocking conclusion that General Tilney murdered his wife.[57] Catherine's overactive imagination has been trained by the gothic novels that she loves to read. The film adaptation of *Atonement* reunited the same director (Joe Wright) and star (Kiera Knightley) who collaborated on *Pride and Prejudice* only two years earlier. The adaptation of *Atonement* was his second feature film, coming on the heels of his successful *Pride and Prejudice.* A look at McEwan's novel and Joe Wright's film adaptation will help identify aspects of the twenty-first-century reception of Austen's happy endings. In *Atonement,* the analogous character to Catherine would be Briony Tallis, an adolescent girl who spies on her older sister Cecilia's romantic encounters with the housekeeper's son, Robbie. Briony is an aspiring novelist and tends to see the world in romantically exaggerated terms. She is also 13, keenly aware of sexuality and extremely discomfited by two scenes that she witnesses—one romantic, the other a rape.

On one tragic day, Briony delivers and reads an explicit note that Robbie sends to Cecilia. (He sends it as a sort of Freudian slip, at some level fully meaning the lewd proposition it contains but having consciously intended to send a more formal apology to Cecilia instead.) We learn that Robbie was also Briony's first crush, and that she once, at age 10, jumped into a lake to see if he would save her life, forcing him to conform to her idea of romance. This earlier escapade is an indicator of the life-and-death stakes of her romantic indulgences and conflation of reality and make-believe. The same proclivities also cause her, like Catherine Morland at her worst, to be insensible to what is really occurring around her. Briony has a more worldly and sexually aware cousin named Lola, analogous to Isabella Thorpe. Lola is temporarily staying at the estate as her parents undergo a painful divorce. Lola has a secret: a wealthy young man, brought to the estate by Briony's older brother, is secretly trying to seduce and eventually rapes her. The much more sexually aware Lola tries to confide in Briony of her anxiety before the rape, but instead Briony prefers immersing herself in her own stories, both real and imagined.

On the fateful day, Briony delivers the explicit letter, and at dinner she sees Cecilia and Robbie make love in the library. Fascinated, horrified, and jealous, she grows angry at both of them. During dinner, a search is undertaken outside in the dark for Lola's twin brothers, who have run away. In the course of this search, Lola is raped. Briony thinks she has seen the face of the rapist and accuses Robbie. (It was actually Leon's friend.) Robbie's life is ruined, as is Cecilia's, as war also breaks out. Not only did Briony's actions prevent a happy ending for the two lovers, but she also indirectly causes their deaths, by estranging them from their families and forcing them into dangerous occupations they would not otherwise have undertaken. Just as Austen shows the dangers of such romantic separation from reality, McEwan shows even worse ramifications, but creates a more explicitly Freudian rationale for the imagined facts. Or to put it another way, he exposes the Freudian underpinnings of the gothic fantasies in which Isabella and Catherine indulge.

The film also has family theatricals, written by Briony. They star "Arabella," and the cousins vie for who will play this part—the name no doubt an allusion to the heroine of Charlotte Lennox's *Female Quixote*, an inspiration for Austen's Catherine Morland.[58] The theatricals never occur, yet the events taking place in the house are far more sensational anyway. Lola does get the central part, as it were, of the suffering romantic heroine (both in the intended play and in the larger plot), so Briony is once again left out of the limelight; however, her critical testimony that she saw Robbie rape Lola gives her importance at a moment when the world around her is disintegrating into violence and the sexual desires that she finds so threatening. After immense suffering, Robbie and Cecilia are eventually united, and Briony makes a wartime visit to them to make a much-overdue apology.

In this film, the protagonist-author Briony Tallis plays a metafictional trick and fills a role similar to Austen's or her narrator. We eventually learn that Briony has grown up and has become a successful author of 21 novels. The 21st novel (a number indicating maturity) is the novel within *Atonement*, by the same name. In an interview at the end of our novel, she explains that the events and names of the novel are unchanged, and that the novel is, in a sense, a confession. Like *Northanger Abbey* is to Austen, it is also both her first and her last novel. Briony reveals that the last part of her novel—the resolution / happy ending—*never occurred*: the happy ending was the only part of the novel that was fictitious. She explains that she never had the courage to go and apologize to her sister; instead, both Cecilia and Robbie died terrible deaths in 1940. Just as in Austen's novels, Briony the author fictionalizes her happy ending. Briony does so organically, allowing her reader to suspend disbelief and enjoy the resolution, but McEwen the author punctures it for his reader. The happy ending is thus embedded within a much more tragic novel.

Yet here the motives for providing a happy ending are also fictionalized. The narrative structure of *Atonement*—the novel within the novel—mirrors Austen's technique in giving a happy ending with a significant price attached. In *Atonement*, the reality belongs to what in Austen would have been the alternate ending. Whereas Austen's motives are harder to decode, Briony's are explicit: she gives a happy ending as a gift, "an act of kindness." She speculates that there would have been no purpose, no point in telling the true, sad story of such failed lives and spoilt love. The reader is given the happy ending first, and then shocked to discover that it never "happened." The first-time viewer of the film enjoys what appears to be a conventional marriage plot starring Cecilia and Robbie, with the manor-house setting and class conflict that we have come to expect, only to be shocked into a self-conscious level of metafiction when we discover that we were witnessing a "fictional" account of a fictional story, rather than the story for which we had suspended disbelief. The individual who was the principal obstacle to the marriage plot is instead catapulted to a position not only as central protagonist but also as the author of the story we have invested ourselves in. Briony, in a sense, betrays the audience after betraying Cecilia and Robbie.

Whereas Austen provides the happy ending and the price tag—the rose and thorn—simultaneously, *Atonement* follows the rose with the thorn. It is ultimately a tragic, rather than a comic, ending. It is similar in that the heroine comes to know herself in the absence of requited love; however, in McEwan's reversal, the tragic ending of the romance plot comes before the enlightenment of the heroine.

The fact that Briony, the fictional author, is dying also supports the Freudian reading of narrative that Peter Brooks promotes in his explanation of the importance of endings. Brooks aligns the structural function of narrative closure with the death drive: "All narrative may be in essence obituary in that . . . the retrospective knowledge that it seeks, the knowledge that comes after, stands on the far side of the end, in human terms on the far side of death."[59] In hastening together, readers are in a sense hastening to our own earthly conclusions. If we follow the logic of the Judeo-Christian valuation of endings, then "Only the end can finally determine meaning, close the sentence as a signifying totality. . . . Plot is the internal logic of the discourse of mortality."[60] And yet, as Austen demonstrates through her narrator, our narrative drive to know and to conclude can be fundamentally *in*humane. The trick, for Austen's "sagacious reader," is to temper our narrative drive with appreciation of the exercise in imaginative sympathy that novels, better than any other medium, allow us to attain.

CHAPTER 2

Expecting Literary Justice

[T]hey were neither of them quite enough in love
to think that three hundred and fifty pounds a-year
would supply them with the comforts of life.

JANE AUSTEN, *Sense and Sensibility*

Jack shall have Jill;
Naught shall go ill;
The man shall have his mare again, and all shall be well.

SHAKESPEARE, *A Midsummer Night's Dream*

Sense and Sensibility has possibly the most disappointing romantic closure of any Austen novel. When I teach this novel, many students see themselves in Marianne, grow impatient with Elinor, and complain that neither heroine gets the right man in the end. Its "happy ending" doesn't seem terribly happy. Edward appears a sorry reward for long-suffering Elinor, and at more than twice her age, Colonel Brandon seems too old and somber for Marianne. Both are, as Susan Allen Ford notes, "unswoonworthy."[1] In fact, the first time I ever spoke at any Jane Austen Society meeting was when I was invited to speak at a public debate for the Greater Chicago Region chapter titled "Did Marianne Dashwood Marry the Wrong Man?" A large percentage of individuals present felt Marianne "should have" married Willoughby, while Elinor should have married Colonel Brandon, leaving the depressive Edward to his own misery. Film adaptations of *Sense and Sensibility*—while plentiful—also tend to make major plot, age, or character adjustments to please their intended audiences. With the exception of *Mansfield Park*, no other Austen novel invites this degree of romantic dissatisfaction.

Austen uses several techniques to puncture or lessen the romance in *Sense and Sensibility*'s ending. Even though Elinor's final courtship is more leisurely than Catherine's, having a full two chapters to resolve itself, Austen still pointedly wields her pesky apophasis, taunting the reader with the things that she refuses to reveal: "How soon [Edward] had walked himself into the proper resolution, however, how soon an opportunity of exercising it occurred, in what manner he expressed himself, and how he was received, need not be particularly told."[2] While there are no first-person intrusions in this novel, Austen nonetheless makes us aware of our lot as readers of fiction as surely as in *Northanger Abbey*. The coup de grâce, Marianne's sudden and much abbreviated courtship with Colonel Brandon, is reduced to a scant four paragraphs in the final chapter, two pages from the end of the novel.

In the ending of *Sense and Sensibility*, we see a curious alternation between jubilant excesses of mischievously dark humor reminiscent of the juvenilia and more idealistic, optimistic expressions that are then immediately dampened with snide remarks or quotidian intrusions. The jubilant celebration of folly is most marked in relation to Lucy Steele and her future husband Robert Ferrars. For example, Lucy tricks Robert into courting her, and

> the rest followed in course. Instead of talking of Edward, they came gradually to talk only of Robert,—a subject on which he had always more to say than on any other, and in which she

> soon betrayed an interest even equal to his own; and in short, it became speedily evident to both, that he had entirely supplanted his brother. He was proud of his conquest, proud of tricking Edward, and very proud of marrying privately without his mother's consent. [. . .] They passed some months in Dawlish; for she had many relations and old acquaintance to cut—and he drew several plans for magnificent cottages;—and from thence returning to town, procured the forgiveness of Mrs. Ferrars, by the simple expedient of asking it.[3]

This rollicking account of selfish mischief draws heavily on Austen's style in "Love and Friendship."[4] One can also draw a line from the gloriously mischievous day on the town in "The Beautiful Cassandra" to Sophia's hilarious self-absorption in "Love and Friendship" to Lucy Steele's wickedly successful manipulations of the Ferrars family. This same trajectory of delight in female transgression later extends and morphs into Elizabeth and Lydia's respective "wildness," Lady Susan's more venal self-indulgence, and Mary Crawford's wit and world-weary cynicism. Austen explicitly connects Lucy Ferrars and Lydia Wickham, the vulgar new brides from two separate novels, in certain repeated gestures. Both deliberately show their rings to passersby and send similarly frivolous letters upon their marriages. Austen's endings are generally colored by at least one such character who makes an art form out of self-interest.

Only a few pages earlier we have an example of the more idealistic expressions that are cut short by the narrator. The following statement expresses the family's newfound happiness after Edward's proposal: "The change which a few hours had wrought in the minds and the happiness of the Dashwoods, was such—so great—as promised them all, the satisfaction of a sleepless night."[5] The sentence comes as a culmination to the happy changes at Barton Cottage and at the end of a crescendo. As the sentence progresses, we aspire to greater heights of idyll, only to be instantly deflated by the trivial culmination of the last three words. We want to hear about the achievement of lifelong happiness rather than one night of poor sleep.

Similarly, the only account of Elinor's response to Edward's proposal of marriage is presented thus:

> [Edward] could do nothing till he were assured of his fate with Miss Dashwood; and by his rapidity in seeking *that* fate, it is to be supposed, in spite of the jealousy with which he had once thought of Colonel Brandon, in spite of the modesty with which he rated his own deserts, and the politeness with which he talked of his doubts, he did not, upon the whole, expect a very cruel reception. It was his business, however, to say that he *did*, and he said it very prettily. What he might say on the subject a twelvemonth after, must be referred to the imagination of husbands and wives.[6]

The description of Edward's feigned doubt is reminiscent of Henry Tilney's self-assurance in *Northanger Abbey* but doesn't sit as comfortably in this novel. And the suggestion that his joy or gratitude will deteriorate within a year, albeit humorous, feels "dreadfully derogatory of an heroine's dignity."[7] Whereas the narrator of *Northanger Abbey* makes such indignities explicit and self-conscious, Austen enacts them more indirectly in *Sense and Sensibility*, and her intention is less clear. There is an inherent and unstable tension between the humor and the romance in *Sense and Sensibility*.

Beyond Elinor and Marianne, or "They Only Wanted Something to Live On"

It is difficult to unravel the complicated history of the composition and revision of Austen's earlier novels. "Susan" (the early version of *Northanger Abbey*) was the first manuscript to be sold to a publisher, but *Sense and Sensibility* was the first to be published. Together they show the negotiation of Austen's changing ideas about novel writing. In *Northanger Abbey*, Austen's narrator is almost drunk on the notion of authorship, figuratively waving her quill in the face of her readers. Metafiction colors the entire novel, and the most important character by far is the narrator. For this reason, the ending of *Northanger Abbey*, full of literary techniques to draw attention to its brevity and artificiality, doesn't detract from the novel as a whole. The ending is of a piece with the tone of the rest of the novel, and the character that we love most—the narrator—seems delighted with her own conclusion.

In *Sense and Sensibility*, Austen tries for a more transparent use of narrative voice. She builds the third-person view much less obviously into the novel, and the narrative voice changes in style depending upon whether it depicts events from Marianne's or Elinor's point of view.[8] According to Austen family tradition, the original version of *Sense and Sensibility* ("Elinor and Marianne") was epistolary. In revising the novel to the shape we are acquainted with, Austen found a middle ground between the absence of narrative voice altogether (as in epistolary fiction, composed entirely of letters) and the intrusive metafictional narrator of *Northanger Abbey*. In *Sense and Sensibility*, Austen finds a new way of exerting control over her narrative and attempting to shape her reader's attachments and emotions. So, when it comes to endings, Austen also needed to develop different techniques to convey her desired degree of happy ending. In *Northanger Abbey* she overtly gift wraps the happy ending for us in an "extra" chapter, but in *Sense and Sensibility* there is an attempt at a more organic ending with fewer intrusions and more romantic investment allowed. *Sense and Sensibility* has more emphasis on romantic sadness—both in attachment and loss—than *Northanger Abbey*, where all romantic attachment is either slight or pretended. Austen nonetheless punctures the romantic conclusion of *Sense and Sensibility* in several of her characteristic ways to ensure a separation between the non-romantic resolutions and the romantic ones. Contrary to readings of her endings as Providential, she ensures that her happy endings *do not* satisfy all expectations of worldly justice. Austen consistently holds utopia at arm's length.

Another tremendous difference between *Northanger Abbey* and *Sense and Sensibility* is the tone. *Northanger Abbey* is ebullient and all about new beginnings, despite the vice and mischief to be found in certain families. Catherine is in quest of becoming a heroine in her own story, and the author, readers can sense, is enjoying her own entry into the world of published authors. *Sense and Sensibility* has a much sadder and more world-weary tone. The first chapter opens with a telescoping story of two successive generations of poor decisions and unjust or unwise legacies. The marvelous second chapter gives us a vivid close-up of a third generation following suit. We watch the blow-by-blow enactment of yet another unjust division of fortune, as Fanny gradually persuades her husband John Dashwood to ignore the deathbed wish of his father. It is perhaps fitting, then, that financial injustice remains such a strong theme in *Sense and Sensibility*. We will never know how much of this theme was present in "Elinor and Marianne," the early, epistolary version; however, I think it is likely that the theme was strengthened by Austen's own experience of financial decline and her itinerant years after her father died, where she wandered among relatives' homes without any financial or material stability.

The selfishness permeating most of the actors, particularly those who hold the purse strings, heightens the already strong threat of financial insecurity in *Sense and Sensibility*. Even at the point of greatest happiness, just after the engagement of Elinor and Edward, the narrative doesn't let us forget this financial threat to their future plans:

> One question after this only remained undecided, between them, one difficulty only was to be overcome. They were brought together by mutual affection, with the warmest approbation of their real friends; their intimate knowledge of each other seemed to make their happiness certain—and they only wanted something to live on. [. . .] [T]hey were neither of them quite enough in love to think that three hundred and fifty pounds a-year would supply them with the comforts of life.[9]

The prominence of the theme of injustice, particularly financial injustice, from the opening of the novel, places higher pressure on the novel's ending. While Marianne does become "patroness of a village," Edward, who was born to inherit a great estate, makes a meager livelihood as a curate. He is by far the poorest of Austen's heroes, with no reversal in sight.[10]

Critics of *Sense and Sensibility* usually complain of its ending on both these accounts—both romantic and financial injustice. Distributive justice falls short in several ways. It is ethically outrageous that the villains in the novel retain their ill-gotten material gains while the most admirable couple are wrongfully disinherited and struggle for enough money to marry. For some, this injustice threatens to make the novel tragic rather than comic, or at the very least a "problem novel."

The "Confederacy Against" Marianne

Austen generally adopts the understanding of comedy as being both by definition and by tradition about restoring order: marriage serves as a microcosm of the reestablishment of societal harmony and justice. As we saw in *Northanger Abbey*, Austen portrays her narrator *qua* author as enjoying this role of rewarding the good. On the occasion of Eleanor Tilney's illustrious marriage at the end, the narrator says: "My own joy on the occasion is very sincere. I know no one more entitled, by unpretending merit, or better prepared by habitual suffering, to receive and enjoy felicity" (NA, 260). Even when the fates are *not* doled out in accordance with justice, Austen's narrators tend to admit their deviation from the traditional comic role. At the end of "Lady Susan," for example, the narrator proclaims: "Sir James may seem to have drawn an harder Lot than mere Folly merited.—I leave him therefore to all the Pity that any body can give him. For myself, I confess that *I* can pity only Miss Manwaring."[11]

Later, in *Mansfield Park*, Austen's narrator similarly desires to "let other pens dwell on guilt and misery." Austen, in other words, does not question the traditional idea that comic endings should provide marriages, restoration of peace, and distribution of justice, but she does impose new qualifications. The narrator in "Lady Susan" above extends the invitation to the *reader* for a *shared* responsibility for a just outcome of the story. As we saw with *Northanger Abbey*, Austen manipulates the traditional expectations of the comic ending both to shape the reader's response and to convey her own didactic purpose and political "philosophy." Austen differs with Shakespeare in the degree to which such comic restoration takes place within the fiction, and the world of *Sense and Sensibility* is much darker than the world of *Northanger Abbey*.

In a Shakespearean comedy, one would expect "unnatural" insurrections to be rectified by the end of the play, yet they are never corrected in this novel. Edward, the eldest, is deprived of his seniority in favor of his foolish younger brother for threatening to marry the same woman that the younger brother eventually marries. And Lucy, the woman who shares this abundance, becomes a favorite with her mother-in-law, while Elinor, "though her superior in fortune and birth, [is] spoken of as an intruder."[12] Mrs. Ferrars never receives a comeuppance, and Fanny and John Dashwood never fulfill the father's deathbed wish of supporting Elinor and Marianne. Lucy, the most low-bred and wickedly cunning of the characters, rises to great wealth and power, while the single most admirable character doesn't receive recognition—even from her mother—until late in the novel. Elinor does get what she wants at the end of the novel, in recognition from her mother, renewed friendship with her sister, and a happy marriage to Edward, but the happy resolutions of the novel are nearly overwhelmed by the vastly unjust hierarchies that remain unchallenged. There may well be a rare Malvolio or Don John who is excluded from the happy resolution of Shakespeare's comedies, but all other order is restored—rightful rulers are pronounced, and virtuous love is rewarded with marriage, wealth, and even perfect children. Not so for Jane Austen.[13]

Marianne's "Extraordinary Fate" and the Curious Case of Willoughby

The ending of *Sense and Sensibility* resembles the hurried tidying of one of the epilogues traditionally attached to comedies performed in Austen's day. I have already mentioned the scant four paragraphs that are allotted to Marianne's courtship and to her falling sufficiently in love with Colonel Brandon. Even more striking to me on rereading *Sense and Sensibility* is the sheer *duration* of the treatment of Willoughby, long after he has married Miss Sophia Grey. By extending the discussion of Willoughby and elaborating upon the strong influence of his charms on both Elinor and Mrs. Dashwood, Austen diminishes the chance for the reader's affections to transfer along with Marianne's. In the final volume, Austen allots a long chapter 8 to Willoughby's return and extensive nocturnal confession to Elinor. This extended appearance alone would have been worth noting, but added to that, Austen dedicates the *subsequent three chapters* to the three women's processing of his charms. In chapter 9, Elinor mulls over his words and his surprising attractions; in chapter 10, Marianne follows suit; and in chapter 11, even Mrs. Dashwood takes time and effort to set her infatuations aside. This leaves only three chapters for the resolution of both Elinor's and Marianne's marriage plots. I will return below to the importance of this unusual narrative strategy.

The speedy resolution and forced symmetry of *Sense and Sensibility* are reminiscent of the restoration of order in *A Midsummer Night's Dream*. Near the end of the forest confusion, Puck applies the love potion remedy to Lysander, returning him to his previous lover. Puck's words underscore the restored order of things, yet also suggest the arbitrary nature of the comic conclusion.

> When thou wakest,
> Thou takest,
> True delight
> In the sight
> Of thy former lady's eye:
> And the country proverb known,
> That every man should take his own,
> In your waking shall be shown:
> Jack shall have Jill;
> Nought shall go ill;
> The man shall have his mare again, and all shall be well.[14]

Tony Tanner complains that Marianne Dashwood "is married off to Brandon to complete a pattern, to satisfy that instinct for harmonious arranging which is a part of the structure both of that society and the book itself. Her energy is sacrificed to the overriding geometry."[15] The "overriding geometry" that Tanner complains of reminds me of the lines spoken by Puck above.

Puck is teasing the foolish lover, of course, but the reference to the proverbial Jack and Jill suggests that any heterosexual coupling might be equally satisfactory. The last line about "the man" and "his mare" further emphasizes the lack of individuality in the young lovers of this play, even reducing the woman to a possession or commodity for the man, equivalent to his favorite horse. Shakespeare diminishes the "dignity" of the young couples; their interchangeability removes any possibility of romantic investment in their comic conclusion. All Shakespeare's comic plays (even the plays within the plays, like *Pyramus* and *Thisbe*) have such epilogues, and indeed the comic plays performed during Austen's life had epilogues with a similar purpose. Explicitly, they often beg for the audience's approval, but implicitly, they also claim that a new order has been attained, and disharmony dispelled.

The main source of readerly annoyance in *Sense and Sensibility* tends to be Marianne's "happy ending," which can seem either artificial, rushed, unbelievable, and/or to the wrong man. In each case, readers dislike the ending because it does not feel sufficiently *happy*. Feminist critiques of the novel frequently come down to an argument about Marianne's objectification. Elinor is granted a (somewhat) happier ending, but the narrator nonetheless teases her with snide comments; Marianne's treatment is much more slighting, if also effected humorously. Again, the role of irony seems at odds with the romantic content.

Although there is no first-person narrator waving a quill in our faces in *Sense and Sensibility*, narrative intrusion remains an important vehicle for Austen's irony. Take for example the famous passage about Marianne's "extraordinary fate":

> Marianne Dashwood was born to an extraordinary fate. She was born to discover the falsehood of her own opinions, and to counteract, by her conduct, her most favorite maxims. She was born to overcome affection formed so late in life as at seventeen, and with no sentiment superior to strong esteem and lively friendship, voluntarily to give her hand to another!—and *that* other, a man who had suffered no less than herself under the event of a former attachment, whom, two years before, she had considered too old to be married,—and who still sought the constitutional safeguard of a flannel waistcoat![16]

While the reversal in Marianne's situation and opinions is humorous, the passage also feels a bit punitive. Colonel Brandon's reward, in contrast, is treated with unironic, heartfelt approval: "Colonel Brandon was now as happy, as all those who best loved him, believed he deserved to be;—in Marianne he was consoled for every past affliction;—her regard and her society restored his mind to animation, and his spirits to cheerfulness; and that Marianne found her own happiness in forming his, was equally the persuasion and delight of each observing friend."[17] There is a sense that the narrator is carefully titrating degrees of sympathy according to the characters' deserts, yet most readers would rank Marianne's deserts much higher. Readers thus often come away with an intuited sense of injustice, as Marianne receives so little narrative generosity.

A good deal of bartering of "Marianne's heart" goes on among the characters, rather than Marianne's choosing for herself. Mrs. Dashwood says, "Marianne's heart is not to be wasted for ever on such a man as Willoughby," for example, and nearly offers Colonel Brandon Marianne's "heart" while traveling with him. Marianne is treated as an object or prize for good behavior by several characters.[18] Ruminating about Willoughby's visit, Elinor is in doubt about whether

Willoughby or Colonel Brandon should be the fortunate winner of Marianne's heart: "[F]or a moment [Elinor] wished Willoughby a widower. Then remembering Colonel Brandon, reproved herself, felt that to *his* sufferings and *his* constancy far more than to his rival's, the reward of her sister was due."[19] Marianne's fate is wrapped up by the whole team, according to the narrator: "With such a confederacy against her—with a knowledge so intimate of [Colonel Brandon's] goodness—with a convection of his fond attachment to herself, [. . .] what could she do?"[20] Finally, Elinor, Edward, and Mrs. Dashwood "each felt [Colonel Brandon's] sorrows, and their own obligations, and Marianne, by general consent, was to be the reward of all."[21] Not only do they base their interpretation on their sense of Brandon's merit, but they are also conferring Marianne in payment for his good deeds to themselves: his giving the parish to Edward, and his driving Mrs. Dashwood to see Marianne on her sickbed. Their rationale makes Marianne's marriage seem even more like a contractual bargain. Even in the final climax, Marianne seems to have no choice: "Marianne could never love by halves; and her whole heart became, in time, as much devoted to her husband, as it had once been to Willoughby."[22] Jack shall have Jill; Brandon shall have Marianne.

Why would Austen so carefully develop her characters and their dilemmas, only blithely to arrange a happy ending in the last few pages of the novel, pairing characters according to plan or "geometry," even when, in cases such as the rapid, final changes in and marriage of Marianne Dashwood in the last few pages of *Sense and Sensibility*, the author seems to sacrifice character and agency for the sake of symmetry? One of Austen's earlier reviewers stands out for understanding this anti-romantic aspect of Austen's work. Writing in 1870, the Shakespeare scholar Richard Simpson finds Austen not seriously committed to the romantic ideal: he suggests that for Austen, "the most ill-assorted couples may get used to one another,"[23] giving Mr. and Mrs. Willoughby from *Sense and Sensibility* as an example.

Simpson thinks that Austen's satiric detachment intentionally undercuts the romantic plots (not that he minds):

> Thus the great coil Miss Austen makes to bring the right people together is really much ado about nothing. . . . [S]he of course devotes all the machinery of the novel to bring together the true hero and heroine. Now, what is this other than taking a humourist's view of that which as a novelist she was treating as the summum bonum of human existence? That predestination of love, that preordained fitness, which decreed that one and one only should be the complement and fulfilment of another's being—that except in union with each other each must live miserably, and that no other solace could be found for either than the other's society—she treated as mere moonshine, while she at the same time founded her novels on the assumption of it as a hypothesis.[24]

Simpson's Austen may be too unromantic for twenty-first-century readers, as Linda Troost and Sayre Greenfield note: "We doubt that many picture Austen as Simpson does: 'She sat apart on her rocky tower, and watched the poor souls struggling in the waves beneath. And her sympathies were not too painfully engaged.'"[25] A picture of the author icily detached from her literary creations does not entice modern readers who want more than satire in their reading. Such a view, though, was not uncommon in the nineteenth century. Simpson's reading shows how difficult it is to account for the tensions within Austen's happy ending, with critics and readers tending either to call all romance to question or to deny any check to it.

I have argued elsewhere that in order to understand Austen's purposes in this novel, one must first recognize Austen's subtle jokes about Colonel Brandon sprinkled throughout the novel.[26] Austen endows Colonel Brandon with many of the traditional accoutrements of the man of feeling but does so humorously—moving his duel off stage, revealing his romantic past only indirectly, making subtle allusions to dovecotes, and placing Marianne's objections about his waistcoat in doubt. But it is easy to miss these details particularly because the irony is not as clearly marked in this novel.[27] The joke is that Colonel Brandon, despite lacking Willoughby's overt charms, abides most closely to Marianne's cherished romantic notions, even while 19 years her senior.

The ending of *Sense and Sensibility* reveals other aspects of Austen's pursuit of the right degree of happiness and of the proper role of the novel. Let us return for a moment to Willoughby's unusual prominence in this novel after he has not only rejected Marianne but also definitively married another woman. Willoughby stands out among Austen's sexy men whose names start with W. Like Wickham, he acts initially like a wanton rake. Unlike Wickham, he is capable of both love and repentance, but unlike Wentworth, he doesn't ultimately marry a heroine. Willoughby's repentance scene is unusual in Austen's oeuvre. His nighttime drunken visit and manic pursuit of Elinor's forgiveness is also an act of vanity—of concern not for others' happiness, but for how they think of him. "Let me be able to fancy that a better knowledge of my heart, and of my present feelings, will draw from her . . . forgiveness," he says.[28] Throughout this scene, Willoughby cares most about how the Dashwoods envision him, and his effect on Elinor is stunning. Elinor strives to rationalize and moralize his unhappy ending: "each faulty propensity in leading him to evil, had led him likewise to punishment," yet she clearly struggles to keep him at an emotional distance.[29]

Another narrative intrusion informs the reader of Willoughby's subsequent life. With dispassionate candor, the narrator informs us of both what he felt and didn't feel about his loss of Marianne. The forgiveness of Mrs. Smith

> gave him reason for believing that had he behaved with honor towards Marianne, he might at once have been happy and rich. That his repentance of misconduct, which thus brought its own punishment, was sincere, need not be doubted;—nor that he long thought of Colonel Brandon with envy, and of Marianne with regret. But that *he was for ever inconsolable, that he fled from society, or contracted an habitual gloom of temper, or died for broken heart, must not be depended upon*—for he did neither. He lived to exert, and frequently to enjoy himself. His wife was not always out of humor, nor his home always uncomfortable; and in his breed of horses and dogs, and in sporting of every kind, he found no inconsiderable degree of domestic felicity.[30]

In including such an extensive alternate conclusion, "that he was for ever inconsolable, that he fled from society, or contracted an habitual gloom of temper, or died for broken heart," the narrator resurrects the fashions of sensibility that Willoughby had encouraged in Marianne. The italicized description is conventionally desirable, but she describes it only to reject it apophatically. The relationship of Marianne and Willoughby is, for Austen, based in the excess of the culture of sensibility and the fad of self-victimization that nearly destroys Marianne. Wickham's future quotidian enjoyments are not only realistic—they also further disprove the romantic excesses that Willoughby touted and Marianne vainly believed. In this way, Austen explicitly denies both Marianne and the reader the conventionally romantic degree of reward that they might have desired, even at the price of perceived distributive justice.

There is another reason why Austen could not have allowed Marianne to marry the reformed Willoughby (other than that he was already married). Austen takes a strong stance against the trope of the virtuous woman marrying the reformed rake, so common in her predecessors' and contemporaries' novels. Austen's perceived injurious treatment of Marianne relates to her proto-feminist wish to protect Marianne and her readers from such a resolution. The most famous example from the literature that Austen read would have been Samuel Richardson's *Pamela, or Virtue Rewarded.* The bulk of this epistolary novel concerns a modest servant's attempts to avoid rape and/or abduction by her master, Mr. B. At the end, Mr. B decides he must marry her to satisfy his desires, and she experiences an unusually rapid rise in station and wealth. Her virtue consists mostly of an energetic preservation of her virginity, and her "reward" is marriage to the lecherous master who tried to seduce and rape her. Austen surely saw the absurdity and harm in such a reward structure and avoided marriage to reformed rakes in her novels. It is also fitting that only Elinor is allowed the romance of marrying her first attachment.

Bovine Intrusions and the Trampling of Perfection

There are additional ways Austen punctures the happy ending of *Sense and Sensibility.* I have mentioned that Austen gives us a peek at Edward and Elinor's married life and impecunity one month into their marriage. Let us look more closely at the description: "They had in fact nothing to wish for, but the marriage of Colonel Brandon and Marianne, and rather better pasturage for their cows."[31]

The description is particularly cutting in a couple of different ways. Austen's well-loved use of anticlimax reappears here in a list where the last item is not as important as those that precede it. Austen uses this technique for comic effect in her juvenilia: "What probability," asks a character in "Love and Friendship," "is there of my ever tasting the Dissipations of London, the Luxuries of Bath, or the stinking Fish of Southampton?" The stinking fish here are an anticlimax after the high-flown considerations of the previous two experiences. Turning back to the sentence from *Sense and Sensibility*, the reader concerned about "the marriage of Colonel Brandon and Marianne" will be put out of countenance by the concern for "rather better pasturage for their cows," so incongruous with the marriage. The passage carries even further indignities for Marianne. The juxtaposition suggests that Marianne's marriage is a commodity or an afterthought equivalent to their menial farm tasks. Finally, the parallelism between the two items they are wishing for—"the marriage of Colonel Brandon and Marianne, and rather better pasturage for their cows"—associates Brandon with the better pasturage, and Marianne—worse yet—with the cows.

To explain the other effects of this passage, I'll draw a comparison to a similar porcine passage from Gustave Flaubert's *Madame Bovary*, written several decades later but arguably influenced by Austen.[32] At the high point of Emma Bovary's seduction by her aristocratic neighbor Rodolphe, Flaubert uses the setting of an agricultural fair to puncture Emma's romantic imaginings of the occasion. In this sad but also hilarious scene, Flaubert alternates the intimate dialogue between the lovers with the judgments of the president of the agricultural society, who is overseeing the judging of pigs, manure, and general farming. Here is a small section of the scene (with the judge's comments in italics):

> "Thus we," [Rodolphe] said, "why did we come to know one another? What chance willed it? It was because across the infinite, like two streams that flow but to unite; our special bents of mind had driven us towards each other."
>
> And he seized [Emma's] hand; she did not withdraw it.
>
> "*For good farming generally!*" cried the president.

"Just now, for example, when I went to your house."

"*To Monsieur Bizat of Quincampoix.*"

"Did I know I should accompany you?"

"*Seventy francs.*"

"A hundred times I wished to go; and I followed you—I remained."

"*Manures!*"

"And I shall remain to-night, to-morrow, all other days, all my life!"

[. . .]

"And I shall carry away with me the remembrance of you."

"*For a merino ram!*"[33]

And so it continues. In the longer excerpt, Flaubert first alternates sections, then paragraphs, then sentences, mentioning manure three times, until manure obscures the lovers' last promises. Rodolphe indulges in abstract (and insincere) language: "across the infinite, like two streams that flow but to unite . . . ," while he only wants a quick affair with Emma and has just previously compared her to a "carp on a cutting board panting for love." Emma Bovary is, in fact, a former farm girl with aristocratic aspirations. The dialogue alternates quickly between their overblown sentiments and the rough-and-tumble realism of prizes for pigs, manure, and filthy lucre. The juxtaposition shows the earthy desires that they disguise with fine language as well as the blindness (Emma) and deception (Rodolphe) involved in the scene:

"A hundred times I wished to go; and I followed you—I remained."

"*Manures!*"

"And I shall remain to-night, to-morrow, all other days, all my life!"

Through this technique, Flaubert places the narrator and the reader outside of Emma's romantic delusion and punctures the romantic story in which she believes she is playing the main part. Clearly, Austen doesn't take the bovine or porcine intrusion to the same length as Flaubert, but the humorous and romance-puncturing effect is similar to Austen's deflations at the end of her novels: "And I shall carry away with me the remembrance of you. [. . .] *For a merino ram!*"

The reader of *Sense and Sensibility*, like Emma Bovary, may wish to forget the dependence of romantic heroes and heroines upon such lowly details as the quality of their pastures and the health of their cows, but such self-deception is a romanticization that pulls one apart from reality. Love and marriage have earthy sides to them, as do finances. And it is folly to ignore these or to feel oneself above them. The climactic resolution of *Sense and Sensibility*, in the midst of speaking of "perfection" and the like, pulls us out of the romance into the fields by remarking that "all Elinor and Edward had to wish for was rather better pasturage for their cows."[34] Austen once again, as in *Northanger Abbey*, wields the quotidian like a weapon against those who substitute fantasy for reality.

Just as Edward doesn't share Marianne's "passion for dead leaves" early in the novel[35] and teasingly throws a damper on her romantic enthusiasm for the picturesque, the author analogously throws a playful damper on readers tempted to indulge in Elinor's romantic ending by referring to something as quotidian and earthly as cow pasturage at a key moment. The bovine interruption reminds us of the necessities of their subsistence and deflates ethereal fantasies.

Jack shall have Jill;
Brandon shall have Marianne,
Edward shall have Elinor again,

They shall all have better pasturage for their cows,
And all shall be well.

Limiting Utopia

So, *did* Jane Austen match the wrong characters in her ending of *Sense and Sensibility*?

A critique of the culture of sensibility and its excesses underlies her choices and the reasons why readers misunderstand them. Austen's endings juggle several different goals: didactic correction; social criticism; romantic dampening; ironic humor; and traditional comic resolution, including the marriage plot. Part of the difficulty is the complex interplay among these goals. She provides the traditional happy ending—in a literal sense—abiding by this generic prescription; however, she values individual growth—both in her characters and her readers—above the romantic conclusion. Her characters must grow intellectually and ethically before any romantic resolutions take place.

The several chapters devoted to processing Willoughby near the end of *Sense and Sensibility* are particularly important for this reason. Through mulling over Willoughby's power, each of the characters learns something important about herself: Elinor learns her own susceptibility; Marianne gains independence and wisdom; and Mrs. Dashwood gets a glimpse of her former folly. Through this processing, both Marianne and Mrs. Dashwood learn to appreciate Elinor much more, and to understand their former blindness to the difference between representation and reality. Part of the great sadness in this novel is the difficulty of self-representation and how easily one can be misunderstood, even among one's closest connections:

> [Mrs. Dashwood] now found that she had erred in relying on Elinor's representation of herself [. . .]. She found that she had been

> misled by the careful, the considerate attention of her daughter, to think the attachment, which once she had so well understood, much slighter in reality, than she had been wont to believe, or than it was now proved to be. She feared that under this persuasion she had been unjust, inattentive, nay, almost unkind, to her Elinor;—that Marianne's affliction, because more acknowledged, more immediately before her, had too much engrossed her tenderness, and led her away to forget that in Elinor she might have a daughter suffering almost as much, certainly with less self-provocation, and greater fortitude.[36]

In a sense, the reader has to learn the same lessons alongside Mrs. Dashwood. Just as she gives Elinor short shrift in her sympathy, many readers are tempted to do the same, largely because Marianne conforms more clearly to conventional expectations of the romantic heroine from the start. Learning about the ethics of self-representation prepares Marianne for a happier life as an adult, regardless of her eventual marriage to Colonel Brandon. The real triumphs are Marianne's growth, Elinor's delivery from self-disguise, the reunion of the sisters, and Mrs. Dashwood's recognition of Elinor, rather than the marriages they achieve. In a sense, by making the marriages in this novel less attractive, Austen emphasizes her heroines' individual growth much further.

Austen also uses familial attachment to diminish the ultimate importance of marriage in this novel. One of the most striking aspects of the ending is the final tribute to sisterhood, where the proximal relationship of the two sisters seems to be posited as the best part of the happy ending: "Between Barton and Delaford, there was that constant communication which strong family affection would naturally dictate;—and among the merits and the happiness of Elinor and Marianne, let it not be ranked as the least considerable, that though sisters, and living almost within sight of each other, they could live without disagreement between themselves, or producing coolness between their husbands."[37] According to this passage, the restoration of the good rapport and "constant communication" between the sisters are the *most important* aspects of its comic/happy ending.

There are many ways in which the world depicted here falls short of utopia. In *Sense and Sensibility*, the society is peopled by deceitful, selfish creatures, and selfless love and affection are the rare exception. In this sense, the open communication and cheerful affection among the two couples are utopian in themselves. One of the secrets of Austen's happy endings is that they are often brought about by the folly and vice of other characters. While such a mechanism provides long-sought resolutions, it does so without claiming more of society's goodness than scrutiny can withstand. Simultaneously, it helps provide organic outcomes in the plot. It is tempting to connect such an approach with debates within moral and economic theories of the eighteenth century. The Anglo-Dutch Bernard Mandeville argued in his provocative *Fable of the Bees: Private Vice, Publick Benefits* (1714, 1723) that individual vice translates in practice into societal virtue and a well-functioning society.[38] His dramatic claims inspired countless responses, including Adam Smith's extremely influential *Theory of Moral Sentiments* (1756). Smith tried to describe a mechanism by which our selfish natures could be translated into *both* private morality *and* public virtue, and his mechanisms included the "impartial spectator" and the "invisible hand." Austen does not provide any mechanism for either justifying or transforming private vice. She merely acknowledges its presence, which is consistent with notions of the fallen world common to Christian orthodoxy. The ubiquity of vice and folly also helps describe the odd mixture of happiness and sadness, celebration and restraint, romance and cold showers of reason that characterize Austen's endings.

Yet to what extent do the happy endings always depend on other characters' weaknesses? Just to consider a few examples of this phenomenon: in *Northanger Abbey*, General Tilney's obsession with rank garners the final permission to marry; in *Sense and Sensibility*, Lucy's passion for money removes Edward from her clutches; in *Pride and Prejudice*, Lady Catherine's bossy provocations to Elizabeth reveal to Darcy that he still has a chance; Henry's adulterous affair with Maria and Mary's complicity cure Edmund of his infatuations in *Mansfield Park*; poultry thieves and Mr. Woodhouse's self-interest indirectly lead to his acceptance of his daughter's marriage in *Emma*; and in *Persuasion*, Louisa and Captain Benwick's neediness and quickly shifting attachments open the way for a more lasting romantic resolution. Whereas in Charles Dickens's novels, final restorations are often the result of a magnanimous action by a single individual, in Austen's, they tend to benefit from the selfishness of others.

This desire to juxtapose happiness with self-interested limits to happiness shows itself even in the narrative syntax of *Sense and Sensibility*, where the nasty truth is often hidden among ironic expressions of good fortune:

> [Lucy and Robert Ferrars] settled in town, received very liberal assistance from Mrs. Ferrars, were on the best terms imaginable with the [John and Fanny] Dashwoods; and setting aside the *jealousies and ill-will* continually subsisting between Fanny and Lucy, in which their husbands of course took a part, as well as the *frequent domestic disagreements* between Robert and Lucy themselves, nothing could exceed the harmony in which they all lived together.[39]

Self-interest thus punctures not only any pretense of a happy ending, but also the very narrative of the ending as well. Conversely, good news is also similarly hidden within layers of clauses:

> What Edward had done to forfeit the right of eldest son, might have puzzled many people to find out; and what Robert had done

> to succeed to it, might have puzzled them still more. It was an arrangement, however, justified in its effects, if not in its cause; for nothing ever appeared in Robert's style of living or of talking, to give a suspicion of his regretting the extent of his income, as either leaving his brother too little, or bringing himself too much;—and if Edward might be judged from the *ready discharge of his duties in every particular, from an increasing attachment to his wife and his home, and from the regular cheerfulness of his spirits,* he might be supposed no less contented with his lot, no less free from every wish of an exchange.[40]

Robert and Edward are both satisfied with their lots—Robert with his money and Edward with responsibility and love. Edward is set apart from Robert by his "regular cheerfulness" rather than his complete satisfaction with his life.

Is Austen redefining marriage in this novel, or just putting it in its place? In some ways, her work here is similar to Mary Wollstonecraft's in *Vindication of the Rights of Woman* (1792), where she raises the significance of moral education over that of marriage. Whereas Wollstonecraft is ambivalent about the institution of marriage, Austen's skepticism does not go as far. Like Wollstonecraft, she sees that romance can be channeled into moral education for the betterment of both sexes. Austen redefines the marriage plot so that its romantic aspects do not overshadow aspects that are within the agency of almost all would-be heroines. Most individuals are responsible for their own degree of insight and moral growth, and romantic motivations can help lead to this growth, especially through disappointment. Yet such internal growth is necessary but not sufficient to achieve external manifestations of this wisdom. Better relations with one's family are, generally speaking, more readily available than proposals from an ideal mate.

This theory of Austen's happy endings works more clearly for heroines who begin their novels with faulty understanding, like Marianne. These heroines consistently develop internally and achieve a sort of enlightenment around the time when their lovers have rejected them. Their romantic loss fuels self-discovery, but in Austen's case, this is a didactic move because she wants to be sure that her readers understand what is of primary importance. The case is less clear with heroines like Elinor, who face external obstacles more than internal ones. In the case of Austen's quieter, more introverted, and less mistaken heroines, the main lesson seems to be the growth necessary to manage disappointment with cheer. This may be sad morality to conclude with, but Austen does not conceive of a name for it until she writes *Persuasion*: "resources for solitude." Where one's individual power is not strong enough to overcome the power of external and corruptive forces, the heroines learn tolerance for their inability to get what they want.

Somewhere between the opinions of Alistair Duckworth's and Marilyn Butler's Burkean conservatism and Helena Kelly's and Mary Poovey's more radical reading of Austen, one can find an explanation of the political philosophy behind Austen's endings. Critics like Duckworth and Butler claim that the central import for Austen is that is impossible to "improve" the world. Critics like Helena Kelly and Mary Poovey meanwhile claim that Austen's characters "must" improve the world.[41] Are these two exhortations compatible? How does Austen both keep her readers hoping for and desiring improvement, perhaps even forming utopian resolutions, while at the same time dousing them with cold reminders of the banal and very real pains of a highly imperfect world? How does she combine romance and realism?

Of all her novels, *Sense and Sensibility* (followed closely by *Mansfield Park* and *Persuasion*) may deal most explicitly with distributive justice and the inability of the happy ending to create utopia. Limits to utopian improvement are clear. Austen, however, like St. Augustine, tries to find a balance between free will and Providence. Her heroines are free enough to take responsibility for their actions, but not so free that they can blame God and grow embittered at the injustices that are all around them. Austen believes in the importance of self-amelioration, but her hope for how much can be achieved by an individual female in her society is indeed not high, and the room for luck, fortune, or Providence is—for better or worse—enormous. Even coincidence, such a friend to the unfortunate in Dickens, often serves to limit the opportunities for Austen's main characters. In the ending of *Sense and Sensibility*, Austen seems torn between the desire (1) playfully to dismiss readers' attachment to her characters and (2) to encourage their delight over the joyful resolution. One could say that she is torn between an Elinor-like restraint and a Marianne-like overexuberance. Austen provides the happy conclusion of the marriage plot but makes it clear that her novels are not only about marriage plots. Her authorship is more than that. Austen often zooms out near the end of her endings, showing the married or marrying couple in a larger context. This more distant perspective lets her reader consider the marriage in light of larger moral and political issues.

Filming Sensible Endings

Next to *Pride and Prejudice*, *Sense and Sensibility* has elicited the most film adaptations of Austen's novels. Apart from titles identical to Austen's, films like the Tamil film *Kandukondain, Kandukondain* (2000) and *Prada to Nada* (2011) speak to the novel's global appeal. More remotely, *Material Girls* (2006) and *Frozen* (2013) can also be seen to bear resemblances to the novel.[42] Adaptations of *Sense and*

Sensibility that try to approximate the novel have struggled to find a middle ground between the novel's cold, ironic realism and its exuberant romance. Almost without fail, adaptations have overemphasized the romantic and underplayed the ironic. They turn Marianne into a romantic heroine and diminish Elinor into an anti-Marianne.[43] In the case of Disney's *Frozen*, the film takes Marianne's invective "Cold-hearted Elinor! Oh! worse than cold-hearted!" (SS, 24) as the key to Elinor's character and the inspiration for its plot set in Scandinavian climes. And whereas Austen perpetuates Edward's poverty to establish a clear distinction between financial success and happiness, most film versions of *Sense and Sensibility* either omit Edward's financial fall altogether (like *Prada to Nada*) or they aggrandize the wealth of Colonel Brandon in the film's conclusion (like Ang Lee's otherwise excellent *Sense and Sensibility*).

Of the period adaptations, the Ang Lee version (1995) stands out for excellence in visuals and acting—a gorgeous film, with a script lovingly written by Emma Thompson herself.[44] Yet while the Ang Lee adaptation is masterful on its own terms, Thompson and Lee choose to elide Austen's irony and her critique of excesses of sensibility. In comparison to the experience of reading the novel, the viewer gets no ironic detachment from Marianne's excesses (which are also less excessive); instead, Marianne can laugh at her own excesses, and Elinor becomes a secondary observer to Marianne's more gripping drama. In the context of Austen's endings, however, there are even more important issues to consider. The filmmakers used casting to overcome some of the anti-romantic aspects of the novel. Colonel Brandon is made much more riveting through the casting of Alan Rickman, and his courtship much grander and more explicit through the gift of a pianoforte (a gesture borrowed from Frank Churchill of *Emma*). Hugh Grant is similarly used to correct some of the blandness of Edward. Grant is good at the bumbling inarticulateness, and his long association with romantic comedies evokes generic expectations of happy endings and marriage by his very appearance. Edward's proposal is more explicitly romantic than anything in the novel: "My heart is, and always will be, yours." Willoughby watches the wedding from afar as a reminder of what might have been, appropriately casting a distant shadow on the felicity of the wedding, rather than haunting multiple chapters near its end. Nonetheless, there are multiple eloquent and dashing men competing for the Dashwood sisters in the film, whereas two out of three suitors in the novel are stifled, inarticulate, and silent.

Ang Lee and Emma Thompson's version stays true to many aspects of the plot but takes a bold step with the final wedding. It is Marianne's wedding; Elinor's is entirely omitted. For a long time, I refused to believe this, thinking it was a double wedding, but the screenplay is clear. The more modest Ferrars couple appears near the doorway in the background, dressed rather drably. Presumably they are already married; the screenplay refers to Elinor as matron of honor, which might account for her bouquet. The film's ending continues Mrs. Dashwood's error and the trend of assigning the principal attention and romance to Marianne, without a hint of irony. The last several cuts focus—rather oddly—on Colonel Brandon riotously throwing two bags of coins in the air in a sort of golden ejaculation. The viewer shares a low-angle view of the coins falling, as though we too are among the audience being showered with coins (figure 10). While the gesture certainly conveys his long pent-up emotions suddenly being released in joy, the choice is a rather odd one when one considers the role of money and financial insecurity in the original novel.[45] Yes, it is joyful in the novel as well, that the Dashwoods as a family are no longer suffering from want; however, the film's conclusions makes the acquisition of money dangerously central to the happy ending itself.

10. A golden effusion. *Sense and Sensibility.*

(Columbia Pictures and Mirage, 1995)

Wealth is indeed difficult to untangle from love in the traditional happy ending. Is Cinderella happy at the end of her fairy tale primarily because she marries a man she loves, because she marries a wealthy man, because she becomes a princess, or because she can finally leave her abusive home? Whereas Austen purposely tests the separation of love and finances in her novels, particularly *Sense and Sensibility*, adaptations of this same film generally return to the traditional, unquestioned association between the two.

The Price of Prada

Prada to Nada, a 2011 film adaptation of *Sense and Sensibility* by Angel Garcia set in Beverly Hills, emphasizes the arrival of riches in the end even more explicitly than Ang Lee's film. As the title suggests, consumerism and brand names are central to this adaptation. This time it is Nora (the Elinor character) who is showered with wealth in the final scenes. The Edward in this version has never suffered a financial reversal, so the poignancy of their marriage is much reduced. He is still a successful lawyer, and his only "sacrifice" is agreeing to live in her lower-middle-class Latino neighborhood rather than his uptown luxury.[46]

Edward's proposal itself is highly unusual: he presents Nora with a moving truck, shrink-wrapped furniture, house contract, key to their new house, and engagement ring all in one grand gesture. In fact, the engagement ring is attached to the key chain as though it were just another key. Rather than bending on one knee, he holds a pen with the house contract on a clipboard for her to sign. When the viewer first sees the key, we do not know the ring is there too, so we experience Nora's confusion, in thinking this is a financial rather than a romantic transaction. Even when we do see the ring, it is on top of the real estate deed, complete with specific numbers including house price ($450,000) and amount of earnest money ($90,000) (figure 11). The suddenness of the event is particularly striking in a twentieth-century adaptation, as the two have kissed only once. She accepts his offer, they hug and kiss, and the next frame is their wedding. In this film adaptation, it is Elinor's romance that is abbreviated instead of Marianne's, which Garcia gives the greater screen

11. Contractual love. *Prada to Nada.*

(Lionsgate, 2011)

time. The Garcia version does, however, allow Edward to propose: after asking her to sign the deed, he uses almost the exact words from Emma Thompson's screenplay: "Nora, I love you. My heart is, and always has been, yours." One could say that this happy ending for Nora successfully re-creates the strange mixture of romance and hard-nosed realism of Austen's own ending. While one could say that the key and contract detract from Nora's romantic happy ending, it is still not in the spirit of Austen's didactic message.

The emphasis on materialism says more, perhaps, about our contemporary definitions of happy endings than it does about Austen's. In any case, the emphasis on the balm of material goods ultimately doesn't sit well with the social criticism in Austen's novel. One danger is making the story one of the sisters' regaining their former glory rather than facing obstacles and becoming better people, capable of greater happiness in the future. Even though *Prada to Nada* depicts a lower-middle-class neighborhood, it is hardly a picture of want. By avoiding any depiction of real poverty or need, both

12. Legal marriage. *Prada to Nada.*

(Lionsgate, 2011)

these adaptations diminish the emphasis on financial injustice that Austen has built into her novel. The Ang Lee version offers no other ethical issue in its stead. Garcia does include Nora's commitment to pro bono work as a lawyer, helping immigrants with work-related claims. They are, in fact, married from her new office, and Edward's decision to live in the family neighborhood is an implicit acceptance of this mission. (See figure 12 and the sign for "Consuelo Legal Gratis," or "Free Legal Counsel," over their heads.) The film also tackles the problem of self-representation through Nora and Mary's shared Latina heritage. Mary's weakness throughout the film is related to her ignorance and dislike of her own cultural heritage. The sisters' eventual move to be closer to their Hispanic relatives is also a move to learn and embrace their Spanish-speaking culture. The mural captured in the wedding scenes evokes this broader social issue for Mary (figure 13). The mural, presumably painted by the Colonel Brandon character, poses a political and existential question: "Soy Mexicano? Soy Americano? Soy?" ("Am I Mexican? Am I American? Am I?"). Overall, the Garcia version does a better job than most in

13. Identity crises. *Prada to Nada.*

(Lionsgate, 2011)

puncturing the happy ending with issues of social and ethical import, even though it chooses not to do so in the way of Austen's novel.

Austen tends to treat emotional inequity as she treats financial inequity. And the greatest inequities in this novel are not the heterosexual or romantic ones. The single most important bond in the novel is the bond between Marianne and Elinor. The most important restoration, therefore, is the mutual understanding among the Dashwood women. The balms of friendship and sympathy thus overshadow the financial injustices in the end. Even where financial relations remain unjust or tragic, Austen indirectly counters them through the currency of sympathy. Readers, like other characters in the novel, can still extend sympathy to the most deserving characters. By the end of the novel, many emotional inequities are overcome, and *emotional* rather than financial justice is restored. Austen enacts this restoration through her implied reader's feelings. We readers are thus crucial agents in the restoration of Elinor's recognition and in her happy ending itself.

CHAPTER 3

The Limits of Romance

I wonder who first discovered the power
of poetry in driving away love.

ELIZABETH BENNET in *Pride and Prejudice*

Jane Austen ruined my life. I blame her entirely.
Well, I also blame my mother for filling my head with
an unshakeable belief in happy endings.

BETH PATTILLO, *Jane Austen Ruined My Life*

In composing this book about Austen's endings, I've been tempted to treat *Pride and Prejudice* as an exception to the rule. Is *Pride and Prejudice* free of the anti-romantic elements that Austen uses to undercut her other happy endings? I used to think so. Unlike with *Sense and Sensibility*, one does not encounter too many readers who are dissatisfied with the matches created at the end of *Pride and Prejudice*. There are, however, those who complain that the novel encourages a fairy-tale-like view of marriage—or that it encourages women to rely on men to come to their rescue. Such critics might complain that in giving Elizabeth wealth, a happy marriage, and the ability to maintain her independence of mind, Austen is giving

Elizabeth *too* happy an ending. Readers growing up reading *Pride and Prejudice* might form unrealistic expectations of life. In the past 15 years, several new novels based on Austen have begun precisely from this premise. This chapter will analyze less noticed aspects of *Pride and Prejudice* that resist the conventional happy ending, as well as some of the varied contemporary adaptations of the novel that either accept or reject such limitations on romance.

I'm tempted to agree with Austen, as she declared in a letter, that *Pride and Prejudice* is "rather too light & bright & sparkling" in comparison with her other novels (Letter to Cassandra, Feb. 4, 1813). The happy ending of *Pride and Prejudice* seems unpunctured and idyllic: there are no memorable narrative intrusions, no frustrating omissions of poignant conversations, and no ironic smirkings to give alloy to the happy romantic conclusion or tarnish the sense of utopia at Pemberley. Surely this is part of the reason for the countless sequels written for readers suffering from Darcymania. *Pride and Prejudice* doesn't seem to fit into the same category of novels that willfully undermine the reader's self-indulgent suspension of disbelief.

Yet surely Austen's own comments about *Pride and Prejudice* in her letters show that the situation is more complex than it seems. It is worth taking the oft-quoted statement above in its larger context. Writing to her sister Cassandra on January 29, 1813, a few days before the criticism above, Austen playfully calls *Pride and Prejudice* her "own darling child," delights on having a copy in her own hands, resents the other two copies *not* being in her own hands, and praises her protagonist rather shamelessly: "I must confess that *I* think [Elizabeth] as delightful a creature as ever appeared in print, & how I shall be able to tolerate those who do not like *her* at least, I do not know" (Letter to Cassandra, Jan. 29, 1813).

A few days later, on February 4th, Austen writes again to her sister. In the meantime, *Pride and Prejudice* has been read aloud at Chawton Cottage, with performances by her mother and "Miss Benn." Austen has soured a bit over readings of *Pride and Prejudice* that don't meet her standards: "Our 2d evening's reading to Miss Benn had not pleased me so well, but I beleive [*sic*] something must be attributed to my Mother's too rapid way of getting on—& tho' she perfectly understands the Characters herself, she cannot speak as they ought.—Upon the whole however I am quite vain enough & well satisfied enough." It is not the tone of an author who has lost faith in her own work. Her dissatisfaction, in fact, must be read in light of her own pride in her achievement. It is also an indicator of how much she longed to write in a way that would generate performances in sync with her mind's eye and well-tuned ear.

She continues the same letter with a playful, self-mocking tone: "The work is rather too light & bright & sparkling;—it wants shade;—it wants to be stretched out here & there with a long Chapter—of sense if it could be had, if not of solemn specious nonsense—about something unconnected with the story; an Essay on Writing, a critique on Walter Scott, or the history of Buonaparté—or anything that would form a contrast & bring the reader with increased delight to the playfulness & Epigrammatism of the general stile." When taken in context, it becomes clear that she is not complaining that her work is too sparkling, but rather that one might better *appreciate* how sparkling it is, were there more passages to give contrast. She uses the language of the picturesque, describing how best to set off the beauty of the landscape, rather than identifying any flaws in the landscape itself.

This illuminating pair of letters to her sister underscores the duality that we have been tracing—a central aspect of Austen's goals as an author. In her endings, we witness her efforts to balance her seemingly contradictory goals for her comedies of marriage: the sentimental investment of the reader checked by metafictional ploys and ironic social commentary, a belief in the power of love tempered with knowledge of the realities of economic existence, a hope for happiness in marriage with a recognition of the hazards and limits for women in this state, and a wish for distributive justice at the end, even if only awarded fictitiously.

Before Darcymania

The romantic view of *Pride and Prejudice* is so pervasive that it is difficult to conceive of a time when the novel had a different reputation. Comparing the early reviews of *Pride and Prejudice*, Linda Troost and Sayre Greenfield have demonstrated that nineteenth-century reviewers (all by men, as far as we know) praise her work primarily "for its comedic and natural characters, as well for the elegance of its style." As their overview shows, there was little emphasis placed on romance (and hardly any mention of Mr. Darcy) in these reviews: "[Austen] did not go unnoticed for her romance of course. Early reception of her novels by people like [Maria] Edgeworth and [Mary] Mitford, show their appreciation of the romantic aspects and poignant feelings in her novels. But these opinions appeared in letters, not published reviews." Greenfield and Troost point out that her identification as a romance novelist, or novelist exclusively dedicated to romance, is much more recent. Earlier readers saw different emphases, even in relation to *Pride and Prejudice*.[1]

Many would agree with Austen's own comment about Elizabeth: "as delightful a creature as ever appeared in print." It seems to be the novel in which Austen's ability to create charm receives the least check from its author. In fact, she indulges it to such a degree in *Pride and Prejudice* that she dedicates *Mansfield Park*, which she is writing concurrently with her final revisions to *Pride and Prejudice*, to its antidote: the dangers of charm. In *Mansfield Park*, Austen pays penance for the self-indulgence of her wit in *Pride and Prejudice.* She provides the "shade" that she playfully had suggested lacking in *Pride and Prejudice*: "it wants to be stretched out here and there with a long chapter of sense." This she gives us in *Mansfield Park.*

While *Pride and Prejudice* is dissimilar to *Northanger Abbey*, there are still aspects of metafiction that they share. When Jane and Bingley finally reach an understanding, the narrator tells us: "Elizabeth, who was left by herself, now smiled at the rapidity and ease with which an affair was finally settled, that had given them so many previous months of suspense and vexation. And this [. . .] is the end of all his friend's anxious circumspection! of all his sister's falsehood and contrivance! the happiest, wisest, most reasonable end!"[2] Elizabeth's thoughts encourage the reader to consider the dwindling pages and to evaluate the plot itself, especially whether it need have been so complicated. In general, the metafictional devices that Austen uses via the narrator in *Northanger Abbey* are in *Pride and Prejudice* converted into Elizabeth's thoughts and words.

In the last two chapters in particular, Elizabeth speaks as though she is comparing her life and her romance against the standards of the conventional marriage plot. For example, whereas in *Northanger Abbey* the narrator conveys her doubts about the appropriate moral for the novel, Elizabeth too is concerned about the "moral" established by the resolution of her romance. "My thanking you for your kindness to Lydia had certainly great effect," she says to Darcy. "*Too much*, I'm afraid; for what becomes of the moral, if our comfort springs from a breach of promise, for I ought not to have mentioned the subject? This will never do."[3] While much milder than the metafiction in *Northanger Abbey*, such passages nonetheless increase a sense of irony and detachment. The metafiction or self-consciousness in *Pride and Prejudice* serves as a mild self-parody of what a reader might want from a happy ending. Elizabeth herself announces her intended happy ending: "It is settled between us already, that we are to be the happiest couple in the world."[4] The magic is that *Pride and Prejudice* both satisfies and pokes fun at the desire for happy endings.

Many of Austen's other characteristic antidotes to romance are also present in *Pride and Prejudice*, as we shall see in this chapter. Not only does she make it clear that individual development occurs in the absence of a romantic resolution, but she also zooms out to emphasize larger societal and moral issues even in the last happy pages of the novel. In lieu of an epilogue, she shows that the resolutions have far-reaching effects beyond the individuals most directly—and romantically—connected to it. She also adds shade to her ending by showing the threat of cynicism and near misses. She questions the central importance of romantic happiness by emphasizing false sentimentality, the importance of civility, the limitations even Darcy and Elizabeth see to their happiness, and the *summum bonum* of sisterhood. In these ways, even in *Pride and Prejudice*, Austen offers checks to readers who might see finding the perfect mate as the answer to their own utopian aspirations.

Self-Knowledge and Cynicism

Elizabeth Bennet, like her lively counterparts Emma Woodhouse and Marianne Dashwood, achieves her growth and self-knowledge at a moment when she thinks she has *lost* her ideal romantic partner. Austen times these moments of epiphany to make it clear that the heroines' personal growth does not depend upon marriage or the presence of a romantic partner. Marianne Dashwood doesn't really come to know herself until after she recovers from the physical illness that her sadness at the loss of Willoughby provoked. Emma Woodhouse doesn't fully recognize herself until she thinks that Mr.

Knightley may love another. And Elizabeth Bennet comes to recognize her errors in judgment gradually only after refusing Mr. Darcy's proposal of marriage and receiving his letter of explanation. Their education is sentimental: romantic attachment and especially its (perceived) loss helps stimulate these heroines' growth. The importance here is that within the logic of the novels, the heroines gain the enlightenment regardless of their future situation.

Symbolically, this tactic shows that self-knowledge is necessary but not sufficient for the romantic resolution, but also that self-knowledge may be sufficient for a full and useful life. The marriage itself is more the stuff of fairy tales. The hope for such a union can remain in her readers, as long as it is checked by the knowledge that they are exceedingly rare and really a gift rather than something to be expected. They can only occur, though, with the aid of self-knowledge. This lesson is conveyed through one of the alternate endings imbedded in the novel: we are to infer that had Elizabeth and Darcy married after his first proposal, the marriage would not have been as happy as the union that occurs after their enlightenment.

In the preceding chapters, I have argued that it is important for Austen to draw attention to the transition from the heroine's enlightenment to the romantic resolution. She shows the fictionality of this resolution in order to indicate that things easily *could have ended otherwise*—that the individual stories portrayed in the novels could easily have ended *un*happily. In *Pride and Prejudice*, she does not do so through an abrupt change of pace in the ending nor through the intrusions of a narrator. Instead, the humor itself, from the novel's opening line, both enhances and interrupts the marriage plot.

Austen also uses humor to undercut sentimental romance in the course of her novel. One case in point is Elizabeth's commentary on romantic poetry. When Mrs. Bennet starts bragging about a young suitor who composed poems for Jane, Elizabeth makes the memorable remark, "I wonder who first discovered the efficacy of poetry in driving away love."[5] In such moments, Elizabeth expresses Austen's own dislike of false sentimentalism, as strong perhaps as her dislike of false piety. In allowing her heroine to make such expressions, she undercuts traditional gender roles in novels, where men were allowed to express unconventional statements much more than young women. It also raises the stakes for the novel, suggesting that if it fulfills the romantic marriage plot, it will do so on its own terms, not by relying on clichés.

Perhaps the strongest anti-romantic trait that threatens the happy ending of *Pride and Prejudice* is the attractive temptation of cynicism. Wit, what Aristotle called the freest and therefore most dangerous of the social virtues, tends to thrive on disdain. And for the disappointed, witty commentary gives clever minds an alternative to anger. This kind of wit is of course most memorably depicted in the delightful humor of Mr. Bennet. For my sons, for example, Mr. Bennet is by far the favorite character in the novel. It takes many readers a long time to see the dark undertones of Mr. Bennet's humor, library retreats, and general abstention from parental duties. He reveals the psychology of disappointed wit in a closing speech to Elizabeth, the child who most resembles him in personality: "I know your disposition, Lizzy. I know that you could be neither happy nor respectable, unless you truly esteemed your husband, unless you looked up to him as a superior. Your lively talents would place you in the greatest *danger* in an unequal marriage. My child, let me not have the grief of seeing *you* unable to respect your partner in life."[6] The italicized "you" underscores the potential similarity of their situation and comes close to Mr. Bennet's direct acknowledgment that he can be neither "happy nor respectable" in his disappointment because of his own "lively talents."[7]

When Elizabeth is at a low point of the novel, disappointed at the events around her—her confused feelings about Darcy, her shame over the folly of her family, her recognition of Wickham's lies, her pain at Jane's continued absence, and her anger over Bingley's avoidance of Jane—her aunt remarks: "Take care, Lizzy; that speech savors strongly of disappointment" (PP, 174). The word "disappointment" here means more than a momentary dissatisfaction. It connotes a deeper, more lasting bitterness—the "danger" in Mr. Bennet's warning above. Such cynicism provides a built-in alternative ending for Elizabeth. When her aunt offers her a temporary escape via a tour of the Lake Country, she is delighted to accept, but not entirely out of joy. She quips to her aunt, "What are men to rocks and mountains?"[8] This line shows much more than Elizabeth's wit. It shows that she too is capable of falling prey to cynicism and the temptation to withdraw from society. If Elizabeth does not find contentment in her surroundings, she may well follow her father—but without the benefit of an income and a library of her own.

When most people think of cynicism in *Pride and Prejudice*, they may think of Charlotte Lucas's statements on marriage rather than Elizabeth's temptations. Charlotte's early expression of her anti-romantic beliefs are so stark that Elizabeth herself does not believe them: "Happiness in marriage is entirely a matter of chance. [. . .] It is better to know as little as possible of the defects of the person with whom you are to pass your life."[9] Charlotte's is the anti-romantic voice of the novel, proclaiming that she does not believe in happy endings, at least for herself. Here as in other Austen novels, chance does indeed play a major role in the happy endings, but not at the moment or in the way that Charlotte asserts. Charlotte is not really a cynic, in the sense of having experienced bitter disappointment; she is rather rationalizing her pragmatic approach to her socioeconomic situation. It is difficult to draw the line between realistic expectations and cynicism, just as Elizabeth wonders in relation to Charlotte, "Where does discretion end and avarice begin?"

Charlotte might better be described by the absence of hope. Hope is implicit in Elizabeth's rejection of her suitors, in favor of an unknown alternative, matrimonial or otherwise. Mr. Bennet would not have been so disappointed by his wife had he not hoped for a higher level of companionship. Could it be then that Charlotte, having immunized herself against hope, has a greater chance for serenity, if not happiness?[10] Austen clearly learned from Samuel Johnson about the dangers of hope, that the "understanding of man, naturally sanguine, may, indeed, be easily vitiated by the luxurious indulgence of hope"; and yet that hope is also, in the same essay, "necessary to the production of every thing great or excellent."[11] Hope for a happy ending can motivate us to try to shape our lives to the best of our abilities; however, excessive reliance on future outcomes will generally lead to disappointment or cynical detachment. It is at the moment that Elizabeth's hope falters that she is most tempted to devolve into cynicism. Yet Charlotte's alternative seems impoverished by her lack of hope.[12] By showing both the beauty and hazards of hope, Austen teaches her readers to hope to become heroines (or heroes), and to tolerate their fate in the absence of a happy ending.

Civility and Love

When Elizabeth Bennet teasingly asks, "Is not general incivility the very essence of love?" she introduces an important theme that resurfaces strongly at the end of the novel.[13] The culture of sensibility and much of sentimental literature would suggest that love elicits feelings that naturally exclude others. Austen shows extremes of this behavior in "Love and Friendship," where the characters regularly spurn family members and old friends in favor of instant kinship with lovers. Austen challenges this aspect of sensibility in the otherwise romantic ending of *Pride and Prejudice* by subordinating the romantic to the social.

The gesture to the broader social and political world comes most overtly through the use of the word "civility." The word appears incongruous in the most private conversation between Elizabeth and Darcy when they become engaged. In speaking of the first proposal, Elizabeth remarks: "We will not quarrel for the greater share of blame annexed to that evening [. . .]. The conduct of neither, if strictly examined, will be irreproachable; but since then, we have both, I hope, improved in *civility*."[14] This word comes across as strikingly public in the very private, romantic context. It seems concerned with manners at a moment when readers are more involved with avowals of authentic feelings. The topic thus serves to puncture the romance, at least as romance is conventionally structured.

We see this civility in action in the following pages: with effort, Darcy tolerates her family, and Elizabeth restrains her wit. She knows that romantic love is far from pure expression of feeling. She withholds witty commentary because Darcy has not yet learned to be a target of her laughter: "Elizabeth longed to observe that Mr. Bingley had been a most delightful friend; so easily guided that his worth was invaluable; but she checked herself. She remembered that he had yet to learn to be laughed at, and it was rather too early to begin."[15] Martin Amis comments on a similar phenomenon: "The final paragraph gives us the extraordinary spectacle of Darcy opening his house, and his arms, to Elizabeth's aunt and uncle, who made what money they have through *trade*. Darcy, Jane Austen writes, 'really loved them.' This is the wildest romantic extravagance in the entire corpus: a man like Mr. Darcy, chastened, deepened, and finally democratized by the force of love."[16] Seemingly, civility is the very essence of love.

The interplay between individual and community inhabits the very core of this novel. The marriage presented at the end of *Pride and Prejudice* is more than just a companionate marriage. In the older Shakespearean tradition of marriages reestablishing order, like the restoration of order in *A Midsummer Night's Dream*, it corrects faults in both families. Every indication at the end is that the two couples who marry will establish a new and superior community. But in zooming out at the end of the novel to issues of broader interest, Austen shows that marriages shape more than just the individuals being wed, whether they are exemplary or not. Even in this romantic novel, social concerns are paramount.

Bewitched, Body and Soul

The various film adaptations of this novel have struggled with how to balance its satire and romance. The 1980 *Pride and Prejudice* starring Elizabeth Garvie and David Rintoul emphasized the intellectual aspects more than many; the 2005 film starring Kiera Knightley and Matthew Macfadyen went to the opposite extreme in its sensational romanticism. The 1995 miniseries with Jennifer Ehle and Colin Firth is somewhere in the middle, but with the strongest emphasis on physicality of the three, most memorably Darcy's diving into a lake and emerging in a clinging white shirt.[17] The endings of these films are consistent with these tendencies.

Compared with Austen's other novels, *Pride and Prejudice*'s ending seems on the surface to indulge in romantic sentiment. One of the most striking differences in its ending compared with her other novels is the number of pages that follow the successful engagement of the principal couple. Not only do we get some of the actual conversation involved in the proposal, but we also get a full three chapters to witness their interactions after the engagement.

Nonetheless, even here, Austen is somewhat reticent about details. What do they say in their actual avowals of love? Elizabeth is at first "too much embarrassed to say a word." She is silent at first, and out of concern for "the anxiety of his situation" forces herself to speak: "though not very fluently, [she gives] him to understand that her sentiments had undergone so material a change . . . as to make her receive with gratitude and pleasure his present assurances."[18] This is not only formal language, but it is also summary rather than direct quotation. We do not know what she said.

Darcy's response is even more enigmatic, and it has inspired a great deal of creativity among the screenwriters of adaptations. One of the most famous examples, written by Andrew Davies, is spoken by Matthew Macfadyen to Keira Knightley in the 2005 adaptation. Following a fairly faithful rendition of the words that Austen included in the proposal scene, Macfadyen elaborates: "You have bewitched me body and soul and I love, I love, I love you. I never wish to be parted from you from this day on." These words have been emblazoned on jewelry and home furnishings, and many a veteran Janeite has scoured the novel for this passage. Yet none of these words were written by Austen. Instead she informs us: "The happiness which this reply produced was such as he had probably never felt before, and he expressed himself on the occasion as sensibly and as warmly as a man violently in love can be supposed to do."[19] Rather than dampening the romance of this scene in the novel, however, the elision here only adds to the reader's participation in the fantasy, especially as the narrator indulges in what she in other circumstances calls a hackneyed expression, "violently in love." (The only other place Austen uses it is in "Love and Friendship," from her teenage writings.) How does Kiera Knightley respond to this extravagant speech by Mathew Macfadyen? Not the four words one might have expected. Instead she says, "Your hands are cold."

The American release of this film included an additional two minutes at the end: in an outdoor, flame-lit terrace scene, a postcoital Darcy and Elizabeth are giddy *en déshabille*. This was too much for British audiences, who reportedly laughed at the preview. The British version was released without the last minutes. The American film nonetheless ends with intimate, romantic banter about what terms of endearment Darcy is allowed to call Elizabeth. When he suggests that he call her "Mrs Darcy" when he is cross, she replies: "No. You may only call me Mrs Darcy when you are completely and perfectly and incandescently happy." He follows this by saying "Mrs Darcy" no less than five times while kissing her gently between utterances.[20] Instead of zooming out to broader communal and societal issues, as the novel does, this ending seems to return to the kind of "general incivility" embraced by the sentimental novels that Austen critiqued. The film as a whole is visually more Brontë than Austen, with cliff-top solitary profiles, large expanses of foggy moor, and a strong tendency to focus on solitary individuals in large outdoor expanses, the very reverse of Austen's claustrophobic village surroundings and her careful emphasis on the social effects of romance.

Romance Is a Category, Not an Insult

The "Mollywood" (Mormon Hollywood) *Pride and Prejudice* directed by Andrew Black in 2003, originally titled *Pride and Prejudice: A Latter-Day Comedy*, deserves much more attention than it has received.[21] It is of particular interest here because it adds several anti-romantic elements that enable the film to imitate the tone and ending of the original novel more successfully than the more romanticized versions. Set in Provo, Utah, in the early 2000s, this film relies on the social culture of the Church of Jesus Christ of Latter-Day Saints as a stand-in for the religious traditions, social restraints, and tight-knit communities of Austen's villages. It also uses something called the "Pink Bible" as a replacement for the strong socioeconomic pressures to marry. The fictional Pink Bible is modeled after a mid-nineties blockbuster called *The Rules: Time-Tested Secrets for Capturing the Heart of Mr. Right.*[22] Predictably, the Elizabeth character rolls her eyes at such a volume, while Lydia and Kitty are in its thrall—or, rather, Lydia is in its thrall and Kitty is in Lydia's. The sisters are college housemates in this film, with Elizabeth and Jane unrelated tenants of the boy-crazy Lydia and Kitty. Mary is their awkward friend. Elizabeth is an aspiring novelist, the character adopting aspects of Austen herself, and works at a bookstore while taking classes, revising her novel, and sending it to publishers.

Given its religious foundation, one might think that a Mollywood *Pride and Prejudice* would emphasize marriage; however, the film's approach shares Austen's skepticism about religiously motivated proposals. Through the conceit of the Pink Bible, and some extremely patriarchal and sexist speeches by Collins, the film does a good job of satirizing the folly of pursuing marriage out of duty and particularly without mutual respect. The viewer gains, alongside the film's Liz, a sense of the paucity of eligible men and the near impossibility of finding a good partner in life. Elizabeth Bennet's limited options and claustrophobia are transferred to the modern world through a 26-year-old graduate student's limited financial resources, the sense of waning time to have children, and her dependence on the approval of a publishing house to get her book published. This latter constraint is much worsened when the only press that has shown interest in her novel turns out to be owned by Will Darcy.

A good deal of the tension between Liz and Will in this film is worked out through discussions of her novel, *The Iron Carriage, by E. L. Bennet* (an androgynous name, rather than anonymous like Austen). Her best friend Jane keeps secretly sending inquiries to

14. Sexy Austen? "Jane Austen Comic," by Kate Beaton.

(Used with permission of the artist, harkavagrant.com)

Harlequin-type romance novel publishers on her behalf, such as "White Knight Books." Liz, fiercely independent, rankles at the very thought of this, much like the Austen portrayed in the comic strip in figure 14, who wants her book taken seriously and feels that focusing only on the romantic or erotic is demeaning. When confronting Jane about the submission to White Knight Books, she explains:

> Liz: "Jane, they publish historical romance novels. You know, ripped bodices, heaving bosoms. That's not my novel."
>
> Jane: "It *is* a romance."
>
> Liz: "She's a mechanical engineer!"
>
> Jane: ". . . who finds true love in the end, which is my favorite part."

Liz does not want to be rescued by a "white knight" and prefers to consider her novel a "Napoleonic techno-fantasy" rather than a "romance," whether historical or not. In this, the film extends its parody much further than most adaptations—directly addressing the twentieth-century *reception* of Austen as chick lit. Liz and Will's debate over the genre of her book is analogous to contemporary debates over Austen's opus. Elizabeth rankles at the diminution of her work to "mere romance" in the way some Austen scholars feel about Austen's reception in popular culture, particularly in film adaptations. On a macro level, scholars of romance literature still frequently face an uphill battle arguing that romance novels deserve the same kind of generic respect as more high-brow genres of literature.

This dispute over novel subgenres continues elsewhere in this film adaptation. The first proposal scene is divided into two parts: Will rudely asks Liz out in the bookstore where she works, but the second half is conducted vis-à-vis the acquisition of her novel. Meeting at a restaurant called Pemberley, Will offers to purchase the book from Elizabeth but says it needs considerable revision—"by a more experienced author." The conversation flows at multiple levels, with Elizabeth bristling at the power he—of all people—currently wields over her future career. Like Jane, Will debates with Liz over the genre of her novel:

> Will: "Generically, I'd call it a romance."
> Elizabeth (annoyed): "Ok, ok. It's *not* a romance."
> Will: "That's not a put-down, Miss Bennet. That's a category."

After more discussion of its weaknesses, including its being "immature, naive, cliche, weak," Elizabeth abruptly asks, "Is this about me turning you down?" Negotiations over the ownership of her book stand in for ownership of her body and herself. Little is more personal than one's words and ideas, and here Liz is unwilling to give Will power over any part of herself, even if it means giving up a rare chance for publication and the start to a successful career. There is an undercurrent of Austen's own difficulties getting published. Part of the adaptation's power comes from the multiple levels of meaning, with the heroine enacting aspects of Austen alongside aspects of Elizabeth. The scene echoes the irritation that one might imagine on the part of Austen herself, when her novels were neglected in favor of lesser, sensational works, or anachronistically, to see the Harlequinization of her novels and their denigration to chick flicks, where social criticism is erased in the passion for the love story and erotic titillation.

The Pemberley restaurant scene is a particularly good modern rendition for conveying some of the desperation and dependence a Regency woman might have felt to receive a proposal of marriage, and the drastic step it was for an Elizabeth Bennet (or a Jane Austen) to refuse not only a Mr. Darcy but even a Mr. Collins. We are accustomed to women working and having careers, so it is much harder to imagine the sense of limited options for a woman in Austen's time. Liz is a struggling graduate student with a car that is constantly breaking down and no money to fix it, let alone a clear path to financial independence. Advances by a wealthy, intelligent man who also happens to be co-owner of a publishing firm are a double whammy. Elizabeth's indignation rises with her sense of powerlessness and vulnerability. As Darcy utters the critical words above, we see only an extreme close-up of his lips (figure 15). The sense is that this patriarchal system of publishing is pronouncing her judgment, and she focuses excruciatingly on his words. While her defiance of him is not as stylish as the inset fantasy version of it (she knocks over a glass of water rather than throwing it in his face), she nonetheless rejects him decisively as man and publisher: "You are the most sorry, sad man I've ever met, and I don't want you anywhere near my book."

The imbedded fantasy scenes in this adaptation also work well to separate the ideal fantasy from the disappointingly real. Each time

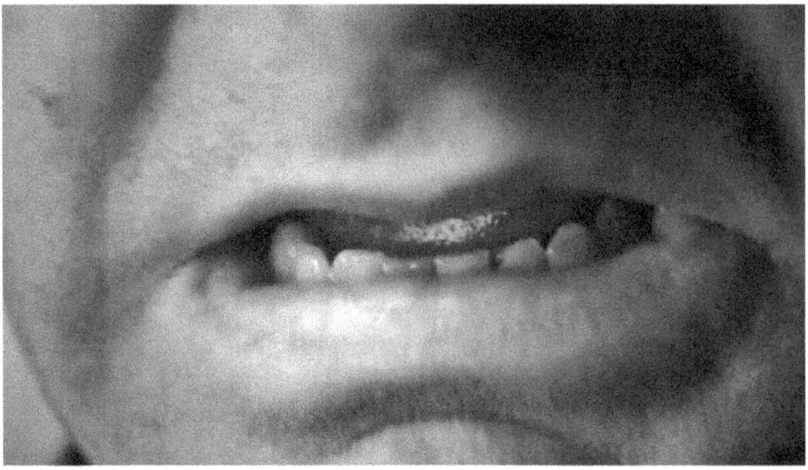

15. Lips of patriarchy. *Pride and Prejudice: A Latter-Day Comedy.* (Excel Entertainment Group, 2003)

we are enjoying with the heroine a much-deserved comeuppance for the men around her—splashing water in Will's face, throwing a prayer book at the Collins figure, or imagining a violent death for the Bingley equivalent for deserting Jane—the insert abruptly ends, and we realize it was a personal fantasy (or her novelistic tendencies) rather than an actual event. The inset scenes combine Elizabeth's heroic spirit with her much more limited, humorous actions in a doubling reminiscent of Austen's techniques. In fact, this film excels at the anti-romantic and humbling details that puncture but do not ruin the romance. The equivalent of Darcy's second proposal, for example, occurs while Will is handcuffed, bleeding, and lying on asphalt, having nearly been run over by a police car (figure 16). The situation adds humor and anti-romantic aspects to the romantic climax, and at the same time, the high-angle shot and Will's (literal) imprisonment reverses the power hierarchy between Liz and Will.

The ultimate, happy ending of the film liberates Liz in several ways: she publishes her book, visits England, sees a portrait of Jane

16. High-angle kiss. *Pride and Prejudice: A Latter-Day Comedy.* (Excel Entertainment Group, 2003)

Austen, and becomes engaged to Will. To the merit of the film, it is not *entirely* clear which of those is most important. Lydia and Kitty both find fulfilling careers focused on female empowerment, and Mary finally marries Collins, after they discover a common love of historical reenactment.

The Many Lives of Mary Bennet

Of the characters excluded from a traditional happy ending in *Pride and Prejudice,* Mary Bennet has perhaps invited the most attention in both fictional and theatrical adaptations. In the novel, Mary has few lines and is generally ignored by her family, yet her presence in adaptations far exceeds her role in Austen's fiction. The third daughter of five, stuck between two bonded pairs, she is a solitary figure. Mary is also the only member of the family who admires Mr. Collins. And as Mr. Collins transfers his conjugal aspirations down the line of sisters from Jane to Elizabeth, Mary would naturally have been the next object of his admiration had it not been for the intruding attentions of Charlotte Lucas. At least such is the alternate ending that the novel suggests to many readers.

In the past decade in particular, Mary has become an important character for adaptors of Austen's novel, and her single state—the only Bennet girl who doesn't have an admirer and doesn't want to dance at balls—provides an opportunity for alternative modern narratives and sequels that give Mary a romantic happy ending. Mary has also become an important character for authors and playwrights who wish to challenge conventional strictures on female beauty, female intellectualism, binary genders, and the heterosexual marriage plot itself. A few of the novels that feature Mary as principal character include Patrice Sarath's *The Unexpected Miss Bennet* (2011), Virginia Aitken's *Mary Bennet's Chance* (2011), Shanon Winslow's *Return to Longbourn* (2013), Pamela Mingle's *The Pursuit of Mary Bennet: A Pride and Prejudice Novel* (2013), Jennifer Paynter's *The Forgotten Sister: Mary Bennet's Pride and Prejudice* (2014), and Amy Street's *Becoming Mary: A Pride and Prejudice Sequel* (2015).[23]

Most commonly, Mary is provided a revisionist plot with a conventional happy ending. No longer in the shadow of her beautiful older sisters, and relieved of her mother's desperate obsession with marriages, Mary is free to be herself and can find her own love story. These versions are often highly erotic in ways that exceed the boundaries of Regency novels, yet they are conventional in other ways, with little distinction between her marriage and her happy ending. Eucharista Ward's *A Match for Mary Bennet: Can a Serious Young Lady Ever Find Her Way to Love?* (2009) is a tamer example of this type of adaptation, written by a Franciscan nun.[24] In it, Mary remains devout, interested in books, and has the choice among multiple suitors.

A second category of retelling takes advantage of the fact that Mary is described as "plain." Some authors use this opportunity to challenge the traditional aesthetics of beauty and attraction. *The Other Bennet Sister* by Janice Hadlow (2020) develops the theme of spectacles—based purely on the cinematic tradition of giving the bookish Mary glasses—and turns a romance around a man who finds her attractive, even with spectacles.[25] Hadlow gives Mary's story an arc that resembles Elizabeth's in *Pride and Prejudice*, including two contrasting suitors. At one point in this sequel, Mary has the opportunity to marry the heir to Rosings but declines him. The novel includes extended discussions of beauty and finery, as well as the nature of happiness.

A third category consists of adaptations where Mary finds her intellectual equal. *Miss Bennet: Christmas at Pemberley*, a popular play by Lauren Gunderson and Margot Melco,[26] takes advantage of Mary's bookish tendencies to give her a friend and potential mate who is similarly bookish, awkward, and fascinated by maps. In *Pride and Prometheus*, John Kessel combines a number of these approaches.[27] He gives Mary a passion for science and geology, and involves her in interesting discussions with Dr. Frankenstein himself. Love and marriage are still at the forefront in these novels, but Mary's life has a satisfying intellectual component as well. Mr. Collins teaches Mary to read and write Greek in *The Other Bennet Sister*, and the poems of Wordsworth gain central importance in the novel, along with Aristotle's definition of happiness from the *Nicomachean Ethics*.

Finally, several of the adaptations of Mary's story challenge the tradition of the heterosexual marriage plot, revealing Mary as gay or non-binary, sometimes providing her with another woman as a life partner. A play by Kelsey Hercs that opened in New York in 2018, *Threadbare Morality: The Queer Musings of Miss Mary Bennet*, "depicts the spinster Mary as a closeted lesbian, embracing her off-putting qualities precisely by imagining a rich and complex inner life for a woman for whom social awkwardness is the only way to

17. *Threadbare Morality* poster. Photography by Harry Pocius.

(Reproduced with permission of photographer and playwright, HarryPocius.com)

fend off the gentleman callers who fill her with dread."[28] The striking poster for *Threadbare Morality* in figure 17 picks up on the film convention of always portraying Mary with glasses, yet challenges the stereotype through her marked confidence and poise. Kessel's *Pride and Prometheus* similarly provides Mary with a live-in companion who shares her love for seashells, fossils, and science.

The Hazards of Happy Endings

In the popular imagination, exposure to Austen's novels—particularly *Pride and Prejudice*—can be dangerous. Several works of fiction build on the idea that reading Austen too early or too often builds excessively high expectations. The danger is that readers of Austen might expect happy endings of their own. These novels portray contemporary *readers* as heroines whose fondness for Austen has led to great disappointment in life. They have suffered because they have taken Austen's (romantic) happy endings, particularly in *Pride and Prejudice*, too much to heart. They have hoped for a Mr. Darcy of their own and have not found him. Examples include Beth Pattillo's *Jane Austen Ruined My Life* (2009 novel), Shannon Hale's *Austenland* (2007 novel and 2013 film) and its sequel *Midnight in Austenland* (2012 novel), Guy Andrews' *Lost in Austen* (2008 TV miniseries), Laurie Viera Rigler's *Confessions of an Austen Addict* (2008 novel) and *Rude Awakenings of an Austen Addict* (2010 novel), and Paula Marantz Cohen's *Suzanne Davis Gets a Life* (2014 novel).[29] These works are useful for assessing the popular view of Austen's happy endings, particularly as exemplified by *Pride and Prejudice.*

Austen therapy here takes on a radically new meaning: *needing* therapy as a *result* of reading Austen rather than reading Austen for consolation. They respond less to individual novels than to the popular reception and cult status of Austen's entire oeuvre. The subgenre was probably inspired by Helen Fielding's blockbuster *Bridget Jones's Diary* (1996 novel and 2001 film).[30] Fielding returns to the epistolary origins of Austen's first novels in this journal written by a thirty-something working for "Pemberley Press." The plot loosely follows *Pride and Prejudice.* The subsequent screenplay by Andrew Davies and the film's casting emphasize the Austen connections further by casting Colin Firth (who played Darcy in the popular 1995 *Pride and Prejudice* miniseries) as the "Mark Darcy" character of the novel.

The subsequent novels in this subgenre retain some aspects of *Bridget Jones's Diary*: the heroine who is in her thirties, struggling in her career, and concerned about finding a husband in time to have a family of her own. These heroines feel like misfits and tend to have deadbeat, long-term boyfriends with disgusting habits, who create a drastic contrast to the manners and speech of Austen's heroes. These novels perpetuate several fictions about Austen: that she wrote principally for women, that she cared primarily about romance, and that Regency life was mannerly and prim. Most of them attempt to include feminist ideals about moving past the importance Austen places on marriage by living well without finding Mr. Right; however, most of the novels nonetheless feature happy endings with romantically satisfying plots. It isn't clear at all, however, whether they pose examples that are better or more liberating than Austen's own novels, particularly allowing for the dumbing down and self-denigration of the Elizabeth characters.

In *Jane Austen Ruined My Life,* the heroine, a divorced Austen scholar, was born in the southern United States to a Janeite mother and a pastor father. She negotiates the competing worldviews of her parents, similar to Elizabeth Bennet; however, she, the heroine, married too precipitately in pursuit of an Austenian happy ending. Looking back on her life, Emma tries to unravel the happy endings promised by her mother's Austen novels from the "divine plans" and Providential care promised by her father's creed. At times they are confused: "[A]ll my life I had been taught that if you did the right thing, acted with integrity, and didn't make a fool of yourself, not only would Mr. Right come along, but he also would arrive with full financing and a lifetime guarantee of fidelity. I believed this until I was thirty-three years old and found my husband in a compromising position that involved my teaching assistant and our kitchen table."[31] Because of this conflation, Emma at times sounds more like she is responding to Samuel Richardson's *Pamela, Virtue Rewarded* than to Austen's oeuvre: be virtuous, and you earn a husband.

Emma goes to England "to get my revenge on Jane Austen. And my parents. Not to mention my cheating ex-husband. Most of all, I'm going to England to prove that there's no such thing as a happy ending. And that I was a fool to think that I could ever have one." The novel also includes aspects of A. S. Byatt's *Possession*, in that there is a scholarly pursuit of an unknown trove of Austen's letters that Cassandra hid rather than destroyed. Emma has to undergo various tests before she can be judged worthy of admittance to the select group of caretakers of these precious papers. The plot is perhaps excessively elaborate, but the heroine travels among Austen-related destinations, searching for clues about Austen's own failed romance. In this novel, it turns out that in the third entry into the church registries from Austen's youth, "Jack Smith" refers to an actual man that she loved. Jack, the heroine discovers, died before they could marry.

Emma wants to wreak vengeance on Austen for having deluded her into wasting her life: "It was definitely Jane Austen's fault. She had sucked me in, with her Darcys and Wentworths and Knightleys. She had tricked me into believing that such men really existed."[32] Emma's cousin, Anne-Elise, tends to blame Emma more than Austen for Emma's unrealistic expectations of life: "You were so certain that you had to have a hero that you forgot to look for a man . . . Who could live up to your Jane Austen fantasies? No mortal could satisfy you."[33] Emma thinks that Austen, in portraying something in her fiction that Austen herself knew did not exist, was guilty of misleading generations of young women. By revealing Austen's own unhappy life, she hopes to "expose Jane Austen as a fraud, to use those lost letters to illuminate the gap between [Austen's] own painful single state and the fantasy-laced happy endings of her novels"—the "promise of a happy ending [that] had led me into torment and trouble."[34] She calls Austen a mass swindler and compares her novels to "snake oil."[35]

Gradually, as Emma finds letters indicating Austen's own near-marriage and lost love, she comes to recognize her own blindness. She has bought into the idea that "our world revolved around securing a commitment from a man" and that once the commitment was achieved, the happy ending was won.[36] Emma says that this kind of thinking is in one sense too controlling and in another a denial of responsibility: "attempting to know the future, to predict the outcome of love, would always negate the possibility of a happy ending,"[37] and yet "I wasn't going to be a patsy any more. The time had come to stand on my own two feet."[38]

Yet for all its feminist ambitions, this novel still defines Austen's "happiness" according to romantic love, when presumably there are other contributors to happiness, including having the time, comfort, and good health to complete her novels. Pattillo's happy ending differs only in the expression of the romantic resolution: marriage is determined but merely postponed. These novels that begin with complaints about the expectations raised by Austen's novels and their happy endings nonetheless end with similarly resolved romances with highly eligible men.

Lost in Austen's Amanda Price suffers from "manners envy" and longs for the elegance of Jane Austen's world; she reads *Pride and Prejudice* whenever she is depressed about her life.[39] This miniseries continues in the thirty-something-woman-with-deadbeat-boyfriends tradition, with a magical twist: Amanda Price and Elizabeth

Bennet are able to change places through mysterious doorways in their respective homes. This adaptation manages to split the romance and satire onto the two heroines: Amanda Price ends up marrying Mr. Darcy, while Elizabeth Bennet is much happier staying in the modern world and gaining a career. (She shows a particular aptitude for technology and computing.) Amanda's story is a reader's fantasy fulfillment, while the Elizabeth Bennet arc satisfies more feminist ideas. Through the dual heroines, it simultaneously embraces and rejects the traditional marriage plot, although the emphasis is still on an Austen fantasy world that is gorgeous, mannerly, and idyllic.[40]

Austenland, a hilarious comedy written by Shannon Hale and subsequently made into a film, focuses on the commercialization of the Austen fantasy life that motivates characters like Amanda Price.[41] In *Austenland,* the heroine is paralyzed by her obsession with Austen's world and is unable to find love (or even grow up) in her own surroundings. She spends her life savings buying a trip to an Austen-themed immersive Regency week in England, surrounded by actors playing assigned parts. Eventually, art and life become deeply intertwined, and only through disappointment can she leave her prefabricated fantasy behind. The film capitalizes on this intertextual doubling by casting J. J. Feild, who played Henry Tilney five years earlier in the 2007 *Northanger Abbey,* as Henry Nobley.[42] Within the fiction, Nobley is hired to play a part, but only to please his aunt: he is really a history professor, not an actor. The didactic lesson of the film has more to do with a *Bridget Jones*–style "every girl deserves a hero" resolution than any anti-romantic puncturing. The only disappointment is that neither novel nor film acknowledges its own role in Austen's commercialization and commodification. These adaptations all contribute to the cult surrounding Austen and happiness; they encourage the idea of romance as the most important part of her novels, to the exclusion of satire, social commentary, and even irony.

The Austen Cancer

From wartime editions read in the trenches of World War I to consolation during the COVID-19 pandemic, readers have turned to Austen's novels as therapy, especially in difficult times. Paula Marantz Cohen's *Suzanne Davis Gets a Life* (2014) also deals with healing. Suzanne Davis suffers from two illnesses: breast cancer and Austen-itis. Whereas the cancer overtakes your body and your life, she implies, Austen's ideas overtake your mind and your expectations. Nearly all of the adaptations with readers as heroine either explicitly titrate expectations of romantic happy endings, or they make a point of providing ecstatically happy romance to "ordinary" women. Most somehow in actuality do both of these things, occasionally causing hypocritical results. One of Suzanne's major lessons in the course of this novel is to look for Mr. Good Enough, rather than Mr. Right.

In this novel, the heroine is almost 35, has a loudly ticking biological clock, and trails a history of bad relationships. She decides to narrow her pool of candidates from all of New York City to her apartment building, which she claims is her version of Austen's "three or four families in a country village."[43] She acknowledges that she has:

> [A] lot of unresolved anger toward Jane Austen, the result of having been given her complete works for my fourteenth birthday and thereby conditioned to believe, at an impressionable age, that Mr. Darcy was out there, waiting to be charmed by my sarcastic wit and to carry me off to Pemberley (or at least a mock-Tudor in Scarsdale). Jane Austen raised my expectations, so that I was fated to be continually disappointed.[44]

Austen recurs more subtly through the rest of the novel. When her book club finally discusses *Pride and Prejudice*, Suzanne tells the others what she thinks: "My problem with Jane Austen [. . .] is that she misleads her more impressionable readers. She gives women unrealistic expectations. What do her heroines do except wait around for Mr. Right to come along and recognize their worth? It's an unhealthy model for young women to follow."[45] Her novels, she says, don't teach young women "to question whether their expectations are realistic or what they should do if they don't get what they think they deserve." She recommends female readers therefore wait until their thirties to read Austen.[46]

Many of the novels in this category end with Mr. Right anyway, but Paula Marantz Cohen characteristically understands Austen even more deeply. Suzanne comes to understand herself at a moment when there is no man in her life: "cancer [. . .] made me see Jane Austen differently. Elizabeth got Mr. Darcy at the end of the novel; [. . .] but that wasn't really the point. Being a heroine meant being decent even if you *didn't* get Mr. Darcy. [. . .] I wanted a life where I would be my best self, even if I never married or had a child or lived in an apartment bigger than a shoebox. Even if my life ended sooner rather than later."[47] Suzanne Davis "gets a life" here in the sense of avoiding death from cancer, but also through finding a new start. A brush with mortality wields a powerful anti-romantic punch: it re-centers this heroine on the prerequisites for a happy and successful life.

The Fantasy Marriage

This chapter has not touched on the countless other *Pride and Prejudice* adaptations, including fantasy, sci-fi, and the voluminous fan fiction. As we have seen, many recent adaptations have striven to achieve a middle ground between romance and feminist social criticism. And yet, with the transposition of Austen's *Pride and Prejudice* into magical and paranormal tropes—particularly zombies, vampires, and dragons—the original novel and its deeper themes are often nearly erased, the original text simply alluded to through character names and a few plot points. One interesting trend, however, is casting Elizabeth and Darcy in glamorous and politically important roles. More than Pemberley is at stake: they are often saving an entire nation.

Pride and Prejudice and Zombies (2009) and *Jane and the Damned* (2010), along with several other vampire-, zombie-, and dragon-themed adaptations, embed either Elizabeth or Austen herself in an apocalyptic military war to save England (or all of humanity) from destruction.[48] The happy endings of these military and political struggles provide a simple way to deemphasize the romantic. Often there is no romantic resolution for the heroine, or one is implicitly postponed owing to the plan for sequels.

These adaptations satisfyingly include women in naval, army, and other military exploits that Austen's brothers would have known firsthand. These novels hybridize Austen and the "bow-wow strain" of Sir Walter Scott yet ultimately do justice to neither. True, these heroines' world is less claustrophobic, their options less limited. Their world, however, is so fantastical as to bear small resemblance to the "common" existence that Austen chose to depict. These novels do, in a sense, emphasize societal and political issues over romance in their endings. Yet, disappointingly, the societal issues that are addressed are also fantasy rather than reality: England is overrun by zombies or vampires—sometimes by the French as well—rather than plagued by the more perpetual issues of social class, implicit prejudice, misrepresentation, ethical dilemmas, or financial injustice that Austen addresses. As a result, these novels are both more epic and more trivial than the original.

The *Pride and Prejudice* plotline transports remarkably well across time and culture. There are successful transpositions to a Muslim community in Toronto (Uzma Jalaluddin), a Black/ Hispanic neighborhood in New Jersey (Ibi Zoboi), contemporary Pakistan (Soniah Kamal), Indian immigrant communities in California (Sonali Dev), Asian American immigrant experience (Karen Tai Yamashita), and a Black Baptist church in Atlanta (Rhonda Baraka), to name a few.[49] While these films and novels vary widely in geographical setting, they all use *Pride and Prejudice* as a vehicle to make valuable commentary on class struggles, prejudices of various kinds, and perennial women's issues, as well as to approach the marriage plot from new angles. Afro-Latino teens in New Jersey deal with issues of gentrification and loss of local culture in Ibi Zoboi's *Pride*, for example. Significantly, Zoboi transforms the marriage plot for her young adult audience to encompass education as well as finding a boyfriend. Instead of Elizabeth arriving at Pemberley, Zuri arrives and glories at Howard University.

To take another example, the international film *Bride and Prejudice*, set in India, the United Kingdom, and the United States, takes moral and psychological issues of bias, love, and prejudice into international politics and postcolonial disputes about globalization.[50] The DeBourgh-Darcys are a hotel-owning American family, and the aristocratic snobbery of the novel becomes material greed in the film. Lalita (the Elizabeth character) fiercely defends not only her family and village, but also India as a young nation. Part of Wickham's attraction is that the young Australian appreciates Indian heritage and history. The disgust associated with Kholi (the Mr. Collins figure) stems largely from his having emigrated to the United States for entirely materialistic reasons. The Bingleys gain prestige because they live in England "near the Queen," yet there is nothing threatening in the worshipful, Anglophilic tendencies of Mrs. Bakshi (Mrs. Bennet).

The British colonial venture has been erased, and the threat, according to this film, is American commercial colonization. The final wedding shows a humbled and acculturated Darcy wearing Indian clothes, riding an elephant, and playing Indian instruments. His assimilation of Indian culture indicates his choice to accept India as it is, rather than judging it according to outsider standards or attempting to buy more prime Indian real estate to turn into American hotels. While not without its charms, the danger in this adaptation, as with so many others, is that the political message tends to diminish the moral significance of Austen's work. Effectually, Lalita has nothing to learn because she is already on the right side of the postcolonial conflict and champions her local culture. There is little left for irony to do. *Pride and Prejudice* has once again shown its malleability, but what is really left of the original novel in these adaptations? It has, as Maria Biajoli puts it, been consumed by its popularity.[51] The happy ending that people associate with the novel is largely one that Austen never wrote.

CHAPTER 4

The Thin Veil of Comedy

Let other pens dwell on guilt and misery. I quit such odious subjects as soon as I can, impatient to restore every body, not greatly at fault themselves, to tolerable comfort, and to have done with all the rest.

JANE AUSTEN, *Mansfield Park*

Liked it, in many parts, very much indeed, delighted with Fanny;—but not satisfied with the end—wanted more Love between her & Edmund—

FANNY KNIGHT'S OPINION OF *MANSFIELD PARK*, transcribed by Jane Austen

Despite the anti-romantic elements identified in the previous chapter, *Pride and Prejudice* is indeed the most "light and bright and sparkling" of her novels, and had Austen wished to, she most likely could have written many similar novels, each as light and bright as the previous. Instead, Austen writes *Mansfield Park* almost as an antidote to *Pride and Prejudice.* Whereas comedy takes central stage in *Pride and Prejudice*, in *Mansfield Park*, only a thin veil of comedy separates us from grimmer truths. The reversal is reflected in the heroines as well. In Mary Crawford, Austen creates a lively and charming character who bears a strong resemblance to Elizabeth Bennet in wit and playful willfulness. For one thing, they both love to laugh. Yet in *Mansfield Park*, which she begins while still revising *Pride and Prejudice*, Mary becomes the antagonist and Austen chooses her opposite—someone awkward, quiet, and introverted—as her heroine. Austen undercuts both the security of comedy and the allure of charm for the reader as well as for the novelist herself.[1] Austen also, once again, reminds readers of their unspoken biases in literature.

In *Northanger Abbey*, the narrator teases the reader about expecting beauty, brilliance, and sublime feelings in the heroine of a novel. In *Mansfield Park*, Austen chooses a more organic mode to continue this critique of readerly expectations, homing in on the issue of charm.[2] In *Mansfield Park*, Austen also adjusts a prominent theme from *Pride and Prejudice*—injudicious prepossession—and applies it metafictionally to the readers themselves. In her new challenge, Austen will teach readers about the dangers of charm by encouraging them to be charmed by the wrong characters. This type of dialectic between novels is characteristic of Austen as a restless artist. As she completes one project, rather than building on the most successful aspects of it, she finds a way of taking on a new project that contrasts with it as much as possible while remaining within the marriage plot genre. As a result, her novels alternate between the bright and witty heroines whose primary obstacles are internal, and the more understated, misunderstood, and wiser heroines whose primary obstacles are external.

In the case of the transition from Elizabeth Bennet to Fanny Price, the contrast is unusually strong. And modern readers are not the only ones that feel its impact. In her "Opinions of *Mansfield Park*," Austen took the trouble to record all the reader opinions she could discover, and one senses that many readers of her time were also jarred by the difference between the two novels, generally to Fanny's detriment. Austen's brother Edward remarks, "Not so clever as P. & P." His sons Edward and George were split on the topic of Fanny, one "admired" her and the other "disliked her," and both preferred the Crawfords. Her niece Anna Lefroy "could not bear Fanny." Austen's mother "thought Fanny insipid." Mr. J. Plumptre regretted "the want of some character more striking & interesting to the generality of Readers, than Fanny was likely to be." Others regretted the lack of romance at the end: Fanny Knight, although enjoying her namesake, was "not satisfied with the end—wanted more Love between her & Edmund"; similarly, Benjamin Lefroy was "angry with Edmund for not being in love with [Fanny]."[3] Austen does not seem disappointed by these responses, as there were plenty of positive responses to counter them, but perhaps more so because she was confident in her choices as artist, and saw these negative comments as indications that she had succeeded in challenging the conventions of the marriage plot in the way that she intended.

I recall reading *Mansfield Park* as a young teenager, having had it recommended to me by my college-aged brother. I devoured the novel, slightly surprised by its difference in tone from other Austen novels that I loved. I remember being struck by the meticulously detailed and nuanced character building, heavy uses of symbolism, and the different style—much denser language than in her first three novels. But as I approached the ending, I became nervous. I remember glancing furtively at the compression of pages and wondering how on earth she was going to reach a satisfactory conclusion in so short a space, after such a leisurely pace in the rest of the novel. When I read the last few chapters, I was incensed. Stomping into my brother's room I asked, "*Why*? Why would she do this? Why develop everything so carefully only to rush the conclusion like that? Was this her last novel? Did she die writing it?" Excusing for a moment the teenage hyperbole—imminent death being the only conceivable excuse for such literary travesty—let me note a few of the aspects of the ending of *Mansfield Park* that make it so striking.

Novel's Grander Scale

Mansfield Park has an epic scope that distinguishes it from Austen's other novels. *Sense and Sensibility* does start with a chapter that reaches back two generations, but otherwise the scope of the action is under two years. *Mansfield Park* reaches back "Thirty years ago" in its opening chapter, but it also begins with her youngest heroine by far.[4] We first encounter Fanny at age 9, and the ending also telescopes indeterminately into the future. The title *Mansfield Park* refers to an estate, itself spanning generations and inviting analogies with the state of the nation. The novel spans greater geographical regions than any other novel as well, with characters traveling to Antigua and Portsmouth among other places during the action. *Mansfield Park* thus has epic pretensions, while it still shares the intimate connection with a single heroine like all of Austen's other novels. Against this epic background, we learn to care for Fanny, or at least feel we know her intimately, over the course of 10 years.

The language is far denser and the syntax more complex than in Austen's previous novels. Sometimes one sentence will encompass half a printed page. Here is a sample sentence from *Mansfield Park*:

> "Advise" was his word, but it was the advice of absolute power, and she only had to rise and, with Mr. Crawford's very cordial adieus, pass quietly away; stopping at the entrance door, like the Lady of Branxholm Hall, "one moment and no more," view the happy scene, and take a last look at the five or six determined couple, who were still hard at work—and then, creeping slowly up the principal staircase, pursued by the ceaseless country-dance,

> feverish with hopes and fears, soup and negus, sore footed and fatigued, restless and agitated, yet feeling, in spite of every thing, that a ball was indeed delightful.[5]

This sentence captures the many nuances of Fanny's feelings as she departs from the ball in her honor, including the contradictory impulses of joy and reluctance, excitement and exhaustion, in an almost stream-of-consciousness style.[6] Passing recollection of a scene from Sir Walter Scott's *Lay of the Last Minstrel* weaves into the many complex strands of thought moving through her head. In this and other passages we see Fanny simultaneously as subject and as a mock heroine, herself casting her own actions upon an epic scale as teenagers are want to do. The references to the coded term "advise" when it comes from the mouth of absolute power is indicative of the deeper political philosophical strains that run through this novel as well.

Sense of an Ending

Despite its temporally and geographically epic pretensions, *Mansfield Park*'s most important action and drama is internal, psychological. After hundreds of pages of such complex and nuanced psychological and philosophical treatment, however, the pace changes suddenly and dramatically in the novel's last three chapters. The novel's grander scale makes the abrupt ending all the more jarring.

The final events and obstacles to romance are wrapped up in record speed, even faster when taken in context than those of *Northanger Abbey* and *Sense and Sensibility*. In volume III, chapter 15 (out of 17), Fanny's father learns of the adulterous affair between Henry and Sir Thomas's daughter Maria from a newspaper in Portsmouth. A letter from Mary attempts to dismiss the scandal, and a sad letter from Edmund reveals that his other sister, Julia, has eloped shamefully and that the events have shown him Mary Crawford's true character. These events conveniently put an end to Henry's courtship of Fanny and open the way for Edmund to fill the vacuum left by Henry. Both Crawford suitors have thus been disqualified by adultery (or acceptance of it) within a chapter. Yet the disappointed Edmund arrives in Portsmouth saying just the wrong thing—calling Fanny his "only sister."[7] This is *not* encouraging in relation to a final marriage, as we have only two more chapters to achieve a romantic resolution.

In chapter 16, we hear at great length of Sir Thomas's negotiations in London and the travails of Mrs. Norris and the deserted Mr. Rushworth, but nothing of Fanny's and Edmund's feelings until halfway through the chapter. At this point, with one and a half chapters to go (MP, 524), Fanny is wishing that Edmund would speak of his feelings about Mary. We wait and speculate alongside Fanny as to the state of his heart: Fanny "seldom saw him—never alone—he probably avoided being alone with her. What was to be inferred? That his judgment submitted to all his own peculiar and bitter share of this family affliction, but that it was too keenly felt to be a subject of the slightest communication. This must be his state. He yielded but it was with agonies, which did not admit of speech. Long, long would it be ere Miss Crawford's name passed his lips again."[8]

The narrator, speaking entirely from Fanny's point of view here, cannot be trusted in this overblown estimation of time, as the following paragraph confirms: "It *was* long, They reached Mansfield on Thursday, and it was not till Sunday evening that Edmund began to talk to her on the subject."[9] The narration shares the youthful anxiety that feels three days to be an eternity, and the whole narrative thus joins in the suspense that the few remaining pages causes for the reader. Having expressed doubt as to the reader's sufficient anxiety in *Northanger Abbey*, here Austen ensures it. There is a rush, an urgency to conclude the romantic ending. Yet Edmund spends pages recounting his last meeting with Fanny's rival Mary, lamenting the "perversion of mind" of "a woman whom nature had so richly endowed."[10] Fanny listens to his account of Mary and in the last line of the penultimate chapter we are assured that "Fanny's friendship was all that he had to cling to."[11]

The final chapter of *Mansfield Park* must thus do all the work, not only of tidying the many sad threads of the story, but also the entire courtship for a hero and heroine who up to this point are more like sister and brother or best friends. Austen begins her chapter with self-conscious allusions to her own artistry and explicit control over the content of her novel—wielding "absolute power" much like Sir Thomas.[12] Like him, she claims to sweep all mischief under the carpet: "Let other pens dwell on guilt and misery. I quit such odious subjects as soon as I can, impatient to restore every body, not greatly in fault themselves, to tolerable comfort, and to have done with all the rest."[13] As in *Northanger Abbey* and *Sense and Sensibility*, Austen's narrator directly engages the question of distributive justice at her conclusion, highlighting her own power and control over the narrative. She further prevents us from suspending disbelief by referring to Fanny in the first-person possessive and drawing attention to her own artistry: "My Fanny indeed at this very time, I have the satisfaction of knowing, must have been happy in spite of everything," for among other things, "Edmund was no longer the dupe of Mary Crawford."[14] Yet Edmund is "suffering from disappointment . . . and wishing for what could never be." After "wandering about and sitting under trees with Fanny all the summer evenings," Edmund's spirits finally begin to be "very tolerably cheerful again."[15] And *still* Edmund has not discovered a potential mate in Fanny.

With four and a half pages to go in the Cambridge edition, Edmund finally begins to wonder (in an annoyingly hypothetical mode) "whether a very different kind of woman might not do just as well—or a great deal better" than Mary.[16] *Still* not understanding Fanny's feelings, he hopes to convince her that "her warm and sisterly regard for him would be foundation enough for wedded love."[17] Is this the "tolerable comfort" that the narrator has vowed to "restore to every body, not greatly in fault themselves"?[18] After such a tortuous wait for Edmund to come to his senses, the reader might reasonably expect to celebrate joyfully with Fanny. Yet, using her characteristic narrative techniques—in this case apophasis, narrative intrusion, romantic hyperbole, rhetorical questions, and narrative reticence—Austen wields the ultimate insult to her heroine. How long did it take Edmund to transfer his romantic affections from Mary to Fanny?

> I purposely abstain from dates on this occasion, that every one may be at liberty to fix their own, aware of the cure of unconquerable passions, and the transfer of unchanging attachments, must vary much as to time in different people.—I only entreat every body to believe that exactly at the time when it was quite natural that it should be so, and not a week earlier, Edmund did cease to care about Miss Crawford, and become as anxious to marry Fanny, as Fanny herself could desire.[19]

The narrator's abstention works against romance in this case, partly because of the hyperbolic "unconquerable passions" and "unchanging attachments"—cant phrases from the cult of sensibility or a teenage romantic, which make the narrator sound insincere at this crucial moment. Adding salt to the wound of this transfer of affection, she writes that Edmund "learn[s] to prefer soft light eyes to sparkling dark ones."[20] Isolating the characters' eyes is unusual for Austen, who seldom describes physical traits, but in this case the synecdoche makes the two women seem like interchangeable commodities—analogous to the choice between a dark and a light waistcoat. Never have Austen's anti-romantic techniques packed as strong a punch as in this ending.

Subsequently, the final two paragraphs are written with no apparent irony, simply extolling the happiness of their union, as though it had never been questioned, and performing the happy ending that her readers must be expecting (and by this point feel is their due): "With so much true merit and true love, and no want of fortune or friends, the happiness of the married cousins must appear as secure as earthly happiness can be."[21] As soon as they want more space, Dr. Grant conveniently dies, and the two are able to return to the neighborhood of Mansfield Park, and "the parsonage soon grew as dear to her heart, and as thoroughly *perfect* in her eyes, as every thing else, within the view and patronage of Mansfield Park, had long been."[22] The final lines invoke perfection and solidify the stability of the romantic resolution, despite the breakneck narrative speed at which it was achieved. The contrast between the strong assertions of perfect happiness and the ironic, anti-romantic context are what fueled my own teenage fury: they beg for explanation (since no apology is forthcoming).

There are additional anti-romantic techniques that Austen exploits in this ending, namely the intrusive first-person narrative voice (as in the passage above) and references to the narrator *as author*. In general, these first-person intrusions cluster only at the end of Austen's novels, as Austen lowers the curtain on suspension of disbelief and jerks the reader back into the harsh light of reality. In the case of *Mansfield Park*, the narrator intrudes with comments like "My Fanny indeed at this very time, I have the satisfaction of knowing, must have been happy in spite of everything."[23] The use of the first-person possessive pronoun "my" suggests the narrator's proprietary ownership and knowledge of Fanny that only an author could have. At the same time, she claims to have intimate information about historical fact: "I have the satisfaction of knowing" suggests that Fanny either has an independent will or is a live human being rather than a fictional character. Together, the effect is an ironic conflation of fact and fiction, historian and novelist, that makes us readers conscious of our subservient role as readers of a fictional novel and our dependence upon the author's choices.

Austen again exhibits narrative reticence in summarizing the final romantic resolution rather than giving dialogue. In this case, Austen not only uses apophasis but also returns repeatedly to the notion that extreme feeling exceeds the power of words, a basic tenet of the cult of sensibility.

> His [Edmund's] happiness in knowing himself to have been so long the beloved of such a heart, must have been great enough to warrant any strength of language in which he could clothe it to her or to himself; it must have been a delightful happiness! But there was happiness elsewhere which no description can reach. Let no one presume to give the feelings of a young woman [Fanny] on receiving the assurance of that affection of which she has scarcely allowed herself to entertain a hope.[24]

If the narrator of *Northanger Abbey* were describing this scene, she would remark that it is a slight to a heroine's dignity that her own happiness exceeds that of her suitor. Here the tone is less ironic and more peremptory. Edmund's sincerity and Fanny's deep feeling are not put into question. It is almost as though the narrator is fending off any others who would intrude upon the scene with their own offensively inadequate narration. There is a parental, protective feel to the narrator's descriptions of Fanny, especially when coupled with the use of the phrase "my Fanny" in the final chapters. While rushed, this ending is not insincere. Austen may have openly spoken of *Pride and Prejudice* as her "darling child," but her feelings of maternal attachment were certainly as strong in relation to *Mansfield Park* and its heroine as they were to their predecessors. In the ending especially, Austen's narrator models the attachment that she believes Fanny deserves.

Born to Be a Heroine

Mansfield Park is the only novel that vies with *Sense and Sensibility* for readers dissatisfied with its ending. One of the reasons, as in the earlier novel, is the rankling question as to whether Austen paired the "correct" people in the end. Any pain or dissatisfaction inspired by the curtailed romantic conclusion of *Mansfield Park* is compounded by the fact that the Crawford siblings—the ones ultimately rejected by Fanny and Edmund—are so attractive. As we saw above, many early readers felt Fanny should have married Henry Crawford; others had trouble understanding or were unconvinced by Edmund's marrying Fanny after having loved the witty and vivacious Mary Crawford.

Here, Austen allows the false suitor a great deal of space at the ending of the novel, just as she did with Willoughby in *Sense and Sensibility*. Unlike Willoughby, Henry does not arrive for a direct conversation; instead, Austen takes the time to give us an alternative ending for him. In previous chapters, I've demonstrated Austen's use of built-in alternative endings to puncture romance in her early novels; in *Mansfield Park*, the alternate ending is even more explicit, getting the narrator's seal of authenticity.

> Could [Henry Crawford] have been satisfied with the conquest of one amiable woman's affections, could he have found sufficient exultation in overcoming the reluctance, in working himself into the esteem and tenderness of Fanny Price, there would have been

> every probability of success and felicity for him. His affection had already done something. Her influence over him had already given him some influence over her. Would he have deserved more, there can be no doubt that more would have been obtained; especially when that marriage had taken place, which would have given him the assistance of her conscience in subduing her first inclination, and brought them very often together. Would he have persevered, and uprightly, Fanny must have been his reward—and a reward very voluntarily bestowed—within a reasonable period from Edmund's marrying Mary.[25]

This assertion of clear knowledge of an alternative outcome, described at length, is an unusual choice. Having the narrator assert that Henry loved Fanny both passionately and rationally, and that they could have had a happy marriage, works against the dichotomous view of suitors that one would traditionally have in a triangular courtship narrative. It somewhat diminishes the marriage to Edmund to know that a marriage to Henry would not have been disastrous. Once again, Austen surprises the reader out of extravagant expectations of the novel. We get shades of gray where we hope for black and white, realism where we crave romance.

Henry's punishment is also handled with realism. Austen acknowledges both his good qualities and the fact that his weaknesses inadvertently bring about good results for others. In this case, Henry's pride and vanity prevent him from leaving Maria and returning to his own estate. She also comments on the lack of distributive justice in society, where Henry is washed clean of his sins while Maria is never given a second chance:

> That punishment, the public punishment of disgrace, should in a just measure attend *his* share of the offence [*sic*], is, we know, not

> one of the barriers, which society gives to virtue. In this world, the penalty is less equal than could be wished; but without *presuming to look forward to a juster appointment hereafter*, we may fairly consider a man of sense like Henry Crawford, to be providing for himself no small portion of vexation and regret.[26]

The narrator rejects the temptation to claim that an eternal tribunal will compensate for the weaknesses of the earthly one. Again, realism—in this case inequitable social treatment of women—triumphs over the hope for worldly justice.

In *Sense and Sensibility*, Austen explicitly critiqued the selfish excesses of the culture of sensibility and the sentimental novel, yet traces of this quest linger throughout all of her novels. In *Mansfield Park*, where Austen challenges readers to love the less prepossessing characters and see beyond the false power of charm, she similarly challenges us in her ending. Austen challenges readerly expectations of charming endings, which indulge in fantasies of undying and unchanging love—including a sense that second attachments are degrading for romantic heroines in the sentimental tradition. Seen this way, Austen sends a warning in her playful "Let others dwell on guilt and misery" aphorism, where she is "impatient to restore every body, not greatly at fault themselves, to tolerable comfort, and to have done with all the rest." In this understated comment the narrator effectively calls her worthier characters "not greatly at fault" and wishes them neither perfection nor happily ever after, but "tolerable comfort." Are we to read this simply as ironic comedy? Or is there more conveyed by those words, perhaps a warning about overly utopian aspirations for endings—romantic or otherwise? Austen's decisions here mark her transition to more explicit treatment of happiness in the absence of romance and marriage—a theme that features much more strongly in her final novels.[27]

In the endings of both *Sense and Sensibility* and *Pride and Prejudice,* ties between siblings are shown to be at least as important as the romantic alliances. *Mansfield Park* includes some of the most eloquent passages about these "fraternal ties."

> An advantage this, a strengthener of love, in which *even the conjugal tie is beneath the fraternal.* Children of the same family, the same blood, with the same first associations and habits, have some means of enjoyment in their power, which no subsequent connections can supply; and it must be by a long and unnatural estrangement, by a divorce which no subsequent connection can justify, if such precious remains of the earliest attachments are ever entirely outlived.[28]

And indeed, Fanny's deep attachment to her brother William adds spirit and charm to her character, when the reader witnesses the love the siblings share. How does this relationship and the elevation of fraternal ties *over the conjugal* affect Austen's treatment of the marriage plot? My colleague James Thompson, in an excellent article, points out that "the presence of strong sororal bonds is rare to the point of non-existence in previous [English] fiction" before Austen.[29] Clearly Austen valued this important innovation, as she includes it in at least three of her novels. And yet the romantic ending of *Mansfield Park* is *so* fraternal that it is uncomfortable for some readers.

For readers in countries where marriage with first cousins is disallowed by law or custom, Edmund and Fanny's marriage verges on the incestuous. In Austen's time, it was rather common for first cousins to marry. In fact, her brother Henry married their first cousin Eliza, and it doesn't seem to have been viewed amiss. We need to understand how this choice on Austen's part affects her purposes for the ending. In a conventional marriage plot, happy fraternal reunions are not sufficient for an audience's emotional investment or conventional expectation (despite the ending of *Sense and Sensibility*). In *Mansfield Park*, fraternal ties seem to compete with or detract from the romantic happy ending. When Fanny Knight reportedly said that she was "not satisfied with the end [and] wanted more Love between [Fanny] & Edmund," it is of course romantic love that is lacking between the cousins, neither fraternal love nor mutual respect.

There are three primary purposes behind Austen's inclusion of the strong attachment between Fanny and her brother William. One is to show how Fanny craves open affection and recognition, as Austen describes in this complex sentence:

> Fanny had never known so much felicity in her life, as in this unchecked, equal, fearless intercourse with the brother and friend who was opening all his heart to her, telling her all his hopes and fears, plans, and solicitudes respecting that long thought of, dearly earned, and justly valued blessing of promotion; who could give her direct and minute information of the father and mother, brothers and sisters, of whom she very seldom heard; who was interested in all the comforts and all the little hardships of her home at Mansfield; ready to think of every member of that home as she directed, or differing only by a less scrupulous opinion, and more noisy abuse of their aunt Norris, and with whom (perhaps the dearest indulgence of the whole) all the evil and good of their earliest years could be gone over again, and every former united pain and pleasure retraced with the fondest recollection.[30]

By portraying interest in the daily matters of her life as the greatest "felicity" she had ever known and the opportunity to discuss a shared history as "the dearest indulgence," we get a keen sense of Fanny's emotional deprivations. In addition, her animation when William is present is also highly important, because it shows how open and lively Fanny can be when "transplant[ed]" into the right situation: her fraternal ties make it clear, in other words, that Fanny's timidity and awkwardness are largely contextual.[31] (It is also enormously gratifying to hear of someone "noisily" complaining about Mrs. Norris!) Finally, the relationship helps qualify Edmund and Fanny's relationship as *less* fraternal and more conjugal: while she and Edmund also share many years of memories, she already has a brother, and he is not Edmund.

Friendships and familial bonds can in certain circumstances allow a heroine to shape broader social structures, just as marriage can under the best circumstances. As we saw in the ending of *Sense and Sensibility,* the sisters' proximity and the husbands' additional layer of friendship cement the foundation of an expanding community based on shared principles, shared history, and mutual esteem (as well as financial security and social prominence). In *Pride and Prejudice,* Elizabeth at Pemberley and Jane at her neighboring estate also form a community whose joint efforts create a healthier network of friends and family, judiciously co-managing the more difficult members of the extended family. Fanny's influence at Mansfield Park, Thornton Lacey, and ultimately Mansfield Parsonage, creates for William and Susan increased opportunities, eventually undoing much of the damage created by the generational divisions described in the opening of *Mansfield Park.* So, even though the marriage that concludes the novel is unusually endogamic, the emphasis on kinship and fraternal ties enables the restoration of an entire family network and broader community, on an even larger scale than what we saw at the end of *Pride and Prejudice.* The happy ending of *Mansfield Park* is less romantic but extends to the improvement of more individuals than any of Austen's previous endings. Even though it is curtailed, her ending thus fits the epic scale of this novel in its own peculiar way.

Fanny's Conquest

If we reframe our understanding of happy endings, separating the heroine's enlightenment or recognition from the romantic resolution, we must look to another section of the novel. Austen's vivacious heroines (like Catherine, Marianne, Elizabeth, and Emma) tend to have internal obstacles so that their personal rise consists of an enlightenment; Austen's quieter heroines (like Elinor, Fanny, and Anne) tend to gain the *respect or recognition of others*—generally family members—rather than their own enlightenment. These heroines don't need a "till this moment I never knew myself" epiphany. The respect that they lack and are awarded is generally not that of the romantic partner. Thus Elinor's recognition by and renewed confidence with both Marianne and her mother is the first happy ending, and arguably the more important one.

Fanny doesn't need to earn Edmund's respect, as "even in the midst of his late infatuation, [Edmund] acknowledged Fanny's mental superiority."[32] In Fanny's case, her much-needed recognition comes from Sir Thomas, her uncle and adopted father figure, the imposing patriarch of Mansfield Park. After his return from Antigua at the end of volume I, Fanny, formerly the lowest among the household family, rises dramatically to an apex of earned centrality and moral authority in the novel by the end of the novel.

In general, all three of Austen's final novels, composed at the height of the Napoleonic war, are more involved in the nature of political power than her earlier novels—particularly the philosophical problem of the discrepancy between those who merit power and those who wield it. The disjunction between merit and power is more marked in both *Mansfield Park* and *Persuasion* than in any other of Austen's novels. In *Mansfield Park*, Austen draws attention to Sir Thomas's and Mrs. Norris's abuses of power through their mistakes in education. Sir Thomas cows his children into silence and seeming submission, not caring about their internal lives, so long as their manners are correct.[33] For example, after the contraband theatricals, "Sir Thomas was in hopes that another day or two would suffice to wipe away every outward memento of what had been, even to the destruction of every unbound copy of 'Lover's Vows' in the house, for he was burning all that met his eye."[34] Mr. Yates (although not the most reliable witness) characterizes him thus: "never in the whole course of his life, had he seen [a disagreeable father] so unintelligibly moral, so infamously tyrannical as Sir Thomas."[35] The family's evenings after his return from Antigua "passed with external smoothness, though almost every mind was ruffled; and the music which Sir Thomas called for from his daughters helped to conceal the want of real harmony."[36] Sir Thomas eventually realizes that he has "increased the evil [of Mrs. Norris' flattery], by teaching [his children] to repress their spirits in his presence, as to make their real disposition unknown to him."[37] His tyrannical presence and Mrs. Norris's slavish flattery encourage extremes, and leave little room for displaying wise and moderate self-governance.

Fanny's most memorable act of heroism occurs at the second volume break, when she faces Sir Thomas, who comes in great estate to her tiny unheated apartment. Despite the tremendous pressure and guilt he exerts on her, she refuses to marry Henry Crawford, daring to go against the patriarch's wishes. The most painful aspect of the scene is her inability to justify her scruples by revealing her true reasons for distrusting Henry—Henry's immoral behavior with Maria (Sir Thomas's married daughter). Rather than retreating into submission, however, Fanny stands up for her principles. " 'You are mistaken, Sir,'—cried Fanny, forced by the anxiety of the moment even to tell her uncle that he was wrong—'You are quite mistaken.'"[38] Sir Thomas attacks her "in a voice of authority," and Fanny does "almost feel ashamed of herself, after such a picture as her uncle had drawn, for not liking Mr. Crawford."[39] Sir Thomas concludes by accusing her of willfulness, self-conceit, and even ingratitude. The ensuing time is miserable for Fanny, for "her heart was almost broke with by such a picture of what she appeared to him" for her "gross violation of duty and respect."[40] She is effectually banished from the comfort of Mansfield Park to the squalor of her parents' home in Portsmouth. Despite his abuses of power, her ultimate rise in Sir Thomas's esteem several chapters later is a great reward. With his many faults, Sir Thomas is nonetheless the most sensible among the adult inhabitants—worth pleasing and seemingly capable of improvement (unlike the former Ward sisters). Eventually, when Fanny assumes the central moral authority of both novel and estate, merit and authority are united.[41] The happy ending of *Mansfield Park* approaches political allegory. It draws attention to how seldom such unions happen either in society or in romance, and how disparate merit and authority generally are. The ending of this, her most philosophical novel, is equally philosophical in its import.

Marriage plots have traditionally conveyed political meaning: the resolutions of Shakespeare's comedies, for example, always accompany a restoration of political order. Just as nature reflects political disorder in his plays through unseasonable storms or unusual animal behavior, romance outside marriage tends to represent the same thing for both him and Austen. Not only does marriage serve as a microcosm of the state, but it is also profoundly conservative, suggesting an end to individual strife and the birth of community spirit. Since marriage represents the taming or channeling of sexuality for the sanctioned purposes of society, the marriage plot thus traditionally serves as a conservative symbol of national stability and security. Yet here, in *Mansfield Park*, it is also associated with

Fanny's ascension to power, giving a reformative twist to the restoration plot.

The real happy ending of *Mansfield Park* is Fanny's conquest of the esteem of others and ultimately her "conquest" of Mansfield Park itself. Set in contrast to the other imperial connotations within *Mansfield Park,* Fanny's more organic and gradual conquest is qualitatively different. As a wartime novel that is also a state-of-the-nation novel, *Mansfield Park* obliquely defends British forms of government against the French, while commenting on the dangers of empire and tyranny in either governmental or individual hands. The constant references to the author's own absolute power (including what she chooses to "quit" or "dispense") plays into the overall themes of the novel and the references to Sir Thomas's abuses of power at home and likely slaveholding in Antigua. Absolute power is the principal thematic nexus connecting *Mansfield Park* and *Emma,* just as charm connects *Pride and Prejudice* and *Mansfield Park.* In *Emma,* the abuse of power is the heroine's; in *Mansfield Park,* it belongs to Sir Thomas and the novel's peremptory narrator.

Having a weaker husband in Edmund also draws attention to Fanny's growing moral and aesthetic influence. She can control Edmund as she could never control Henry. Fanny married to Edmund has greater agency and importance than she would have had with Henry. Austen thus limits the constricting effects of the mentor-lover convention and instead reverses the hierarchy in this endogamic couple. The Fanny that Edmund finally marries has *already* grown to the highest prominence and authority in the household.

The Improvement of Fanny

From the beginning of the novel, Fanny tends to be viewed by her wealthier relatives in terms of her potential for improvement. The family want her to improve, but not so much as to ever compete with Julia and Maria. "Improvement" becomes such a central theme in relation to the Sotherton estate that it is easy to miss the point that Fanny herself is viewed as an object to be "improved." When Henry decides to make a conquest of Fanny, he announces his intended alteration of her—"I cannot be satisfied . . . without a small hole in Fanny Price's heart."[42] His stated reason is the "wonderful improvement" he sees in Fanny.[43]

The running theme is that Fanny, instead of needing to be improved, is actually a caretaker of nature. Fanny cares about preservation and permanence—whether of avenues of ancient trees or of memory and attachment. I view this as the reason why Austen converts the topaz cross her own brother gave her into an amber cross for the purpose of this novel—amber is a symbol of memory, as it traps its original context in its sap. Rather than ossifying her surroundings, however, Fanny tries to protect the hedgerows and avenues of trees that others will sacrifice to the whims of fashion. In contrast to the "improvers" of the novel, Fanny repeatedly admires permanence (her stargazing) and slow, organic growth. In a key passage, Fanny "rhapsodi[zes]" over a hedgerow's natural metamorphosis, while Mary Crawford makes snide jokes.[44] The direct Burkean suspicion of "improvement" in the novel is what leads critics like Alastair Duckworth and Marilyn Butler to claim the conservative message of the novel, that Austen intends to show it is "impossible" to improve the world directly.[45] Meanwhile, Mary Poovey, Helena Kelly, and others have said that Austen's message is that we all "must" improve the world around us. *Mansfield Park* stands somewhere in between these messages. Fanny's epiphany about the hedgerow is that incremental growth leads to the most lasting change and improvement: "How wonderful, how very wonderful the operations of time."[46]

In Fanny's hands, improvement becomes an altogether different thing. She achieves a milestone in her newfound authority when she takes on the benign "improvement" of her sister Susan by purchasing books for her. "[T]o be a renter, a chuser [*sic*] of books! And to be having any one's improvement in view in her choice! But so it was. Susan had read nothing, and Fanny longed to give her a share in her own first pleasures, and inspire a taste for the biography and poetry which she delighted in herself."[47]

Fanny's accession to authority gives her the means of providing instruction through "pleasure": she buys *poetry*, not conduct books for Susan's benefit; Fanny's authority is wielded through inculcating a moral aesthetic (or "moral taste" as the narrator calls it)[48] with "sympathetic acuteness of feeling" rather than through law and enforcement.[49] She educates from the inside out through sentiment. Generally speaking, both Edmund and Fanny share this mode of teaching, in contrast to other models of education in the novel: they educate sentiments through pleasurable reading.

In returning to Mansfield Park's landscape in the final sentence of the novel, Austen drives this lesson home. The narrator informs us what occurred upon Dr. Grant's death: "On that event [Fanny and Edmund] removed to Mansfield; and the Parsonage there, which, under each of its two former owners, Fanny had never been able to approach but with some painful sensation of restraint or alarm, soon grew as dear to her heart, and as thoroughly perfect in her eyes, as everything else within the view and patronage of Mansfield Park had long been."[50] The view of the parsonage, for the reader, connects most directly to Fanny's debate about the merit of its hedgerow with Mary Crawford. Fanny's approach to authority relies on affection ("growing dear to her heart") and aesthetics ("thoroughly perfect in her eyes"), rather than with illusions of grandeur or control. The last sentence of the novel also transfers the ownership of the parsonage and its hedgerows to Fanny herself. The description of the hedgerow could just as well have been a description of Fanny's own incremental growth; Fanny therefore comes to own herself and her own agency. Rather than her marriage leading to subservience, and rather than her being someone else's project for improvement, Fanny's marriage further consolidates her justified centrality.

Seen in this way, Fanny transforms from creep mouse to matriarch, semi-orphan to central figure, servant to symbol of good governance. The resolution of the marriage plot roots her more firmly in the Mansfield Park arena. It cements her position of authority and engenders hope for the well-being and superior education of future generations. The adoption of her younger sister Susan at Mansfield Park intimates this benevolent future tutelage. The conclusion is therefore perhaps more political and philosophical than romantic.

In this novel more than any other, Austen reveals the subtle distinction between comedy and tragedy, and the thin coating of fortune that separates one from the other. Through the direct interventions of the narrator, the rushed pace of the conclusion, and the elaborate description of alternate (and far inferior) endings, Austen pointedly reminds the reader how easily the ending could have been less "perfect." She gives readers the commodity she trains us to want—a happy ending—and simultaneously leaves the price tag attached in order that we understand its cost not only to probability, but also, as we will see, ultimately to the confidence we have in the individual's direct ability to shape his or her surroundings.

Fanny as Author

Mansfield Park falls short of the utopian ambitions common to Hollywood rom-coms. This may be one of the reasons that the novel has been adapted less than other Austen novels. Patricia Rozema's 1999 filmic adaptation of *Mansfield Park* generated a great deal of attention for its provocative interpretation of the novel.[51] Particularly controversial were its strong allusions to the issues of slavery and race, as interpreted by Edward Said, and its negative interpretation of Sir Thomas's character as plantation owner and cruel abuser (perhaps even rapist) of enslaved people. Rozema breaks other boundaries by introducing homosocial and performative sensuality to Mary's interactions with Fanny. Many of these emendations were made in conversation with postcolonial analyses of the novel as much as with the novel itself. These emendations, however, are not my primary interest here. Not enough attention has been paid to the ways in which the creative *camera work* in the film serves to imitate Austen's anti-romantic narrative techniques. Rozema achieves this partly because of another controversial choice: the Fanny in the film takes on aspects of Austen, particularly as author of her teenage writings. At times, Fanny's self-narration approximates the self-conscious, first-person narrator breaking in upon romantic scenes in *Mansfield Park* and elsewhere. This technique works particularly well in reproducing Austen's trademark ambivalence toward romantic resolution.

In the opening scenes after her childhood arrival, Rozema's Fanny appears at several age points (played by Hannah Taylor Gordon and Amelia Warner) from child to poised young lady, at each stage writing prolifically in her apartment. Fanny narrates aloud as she writes, and the words are—surprisingly—quoted verbatim from Austen's own juvenilia. In an unusual choice, Rozema (both screenwriter and director of this film) attributes Austen's genius for writing comedy to Fanny and converts Fanny into a lively, playful, and rebellious spirit, resembling the snarky implied author of the juvenilia.

Fans of Austen's Fanny might be offended at these changes: Rozema makes Fanny, in effect, more like Mary Crawford. The initial scenes with the adult Fanny feature her running wild with Edmund through the estate—shrieking and laughing, romping and riding—to the annoyance of Sir Thomas, who asks her to "act with some decorum." Fanny calls herself a "wild beast," straddles horses, and gallops in the rain. By making Fanny charming, raucous, and vivacious, Rozema undoes one of Austen's own central goals for the novel: challenging the readers' norms for a heroine. Why must today's heroines be vivacious, charming, and rebellious? Why can't the more introspective and downtrodden woman be an equally good heroine? One of my students called this problem the "Elizabeth Bennetification" of Austen's heroines. Elizabeth's wit and vivacity have become such a feminine ideal that Austen's other heroines—provocatively written to challenge existing examples of feminine heroism in her day—prove too radical for the vast number of directors and screenwriters in ours. Modern audiences have trouble tolerating a heroine who doesn't assert herself. Fanny's original challenge to heroism has not yet been well developed in film.

While many have noted Rozema's radical, provocative interpretations of *Mansfield Park*, few if any have commented on the techniques and choices that make this film—despite its deviations—one of the closest filmic approximations of the narrative techniques in Austen's endings. Rozema's choice to adopt traits that Austen projects in her juvenilia makes it easier for this Fanny to become an ironic narrator for the film. (Her repeated mantra to her sister Susan is "Run mad as much as you choose but do not faint," from "Love and Friendship.") This Fanny inserts anti-romantic elements into the film as an ironic narrator in three principal ways: breaking the "fourth wall," making narrative intrusions, and adding undercutting commentary via camera work.

The film breaks the fourth wall frequently, but only Fanny is allowed this privilege. When Fanny turns to face and address the viewer directly, it forces us momentarily to stop suspending our disbelief and to morph her from the diegetic to the extra-diegetic realms, from fictional character to historical author. Just as Fanny takes on authorlike characteristics in becoming the author of her teenage writings, she also takes on characteristics of the narrator, occasionally narrating her feelings (or comments about a situation) directly to the viewer. This happens mostly near the film's ending. At one point, narrating what happened at Maria's wedding to Mr. Rushworth while holding quill and paper, Fanny appears to be the author of *Mansfield Park* itself! Such metaleptic confusion successfully imitates the narrator's intrusions into the plot of the novel.[52]

The most striking occurrence of this technique happens in the very last shots of the film. Precisely when the viewer (like the reader experiencing narrative lust) most wants the metafictional ironies to cease, the director makes a fascinating choice. Edmund has finally realized that he loves Fanny, and in the middle of their long-awaited embrace, Fanny opens her eyes, looks directly at the camera, and addresses the viewer (figure 18). Her look is happy but also knowing. The effect of this visual strategy nicely replicates Austen's pesky puncturing of our immersion in the ending with her first-person commentary and references to herself as author of the novel. This cheeky frontal address highlights the artifice of the ending, making it feel more orchestrated, less organic, and less romantic. Since Fanny is given authorial powers, it does not so much make us feel as though the plot could have ended otherwise (as in the novel); instead, it makes us feel that *all* was artifice, and the happy ending contrived by one of its participants, perhaps Fanny herself.

The scene creates an uncomfortable trio: with the breaking of the fourth wall, the viewer becomes a bit too involved, and the only one *unaware* of the layers of meaning is Edmund. The romantic resolution thereby loses much of its innocence and immersive romance. While not exactly the same effect as in the novel, this film's

18. The happy trio. *Mansfield Park.*

(Miramax Films & BBC Films, 1999)

use of visual irony at such moments comes closest of any adaptation to re-creating the alienating effects of Austen's interruptions and increased "compression of pages" at the end of *Mansfield Park*.

What Might Have Been

The creative camerawork in Rozema's film comments on the underlying marriage plot itself. For example, at the very end of the film, we see an artificial tableau of the Crawford siblings with two other individuals, the "partners who shared their more . . . modern sensibilities," as Fanny narrates. The four fashionable figures freeze for a few seconds, seemingly posing for the camera (or a portrait). The two in-laws smile slyly at each other, implying they are extramarital lovers as well as partners to the Crawfords. This tableau undercuts the narrative drive for the marriage plot, just as the filming technique of "freezing" the characters without stopping the filming halts

19. Modern Crawfords tableau. *Mansfield Park.*

(Miramax Films & BBC Films, 1999)

the progress of the film. In this portrayal, the Crawfords do not need the marriage plot to satisfy their fashionable and (by Austen's standards) libertine desires. Yet there is also a sadness in the gazes of the Crawfords in this scene that suggests that they too are saddened by the loss of alternative futures (figure 19).

The script adds to the effect of this innovative camera work, while alluding to Austen's narrative techniques. Fanny the narrator repeats the comic refrain: "It could have turned out differently I suppose . . . But it didn't." Fanny as narrator says this three times, in relation to three tableaux: (1) Maria and Mrs. Norris in their isolated misery, (2) the Crawfords in their complicated Westminster domicile in figure 19, and (3) the family remaining at Mansfield Park in figure 20. Each time, the characters freeze for a moment and the music stops between the first and second sentences of this refrain. During this pause the characters assume an artificial pose, each looking out into the distance as though reflecting on other possibilities. Then as

20. Mansfield tableau. *Mansfield Park.*

(Miramax Films & BBC Films, 1999)

the words "But it didn't" are spoken, the characters resume their actions, and the music swells into an unalterable future. Rozema thus amplifies the novel's alternative endings—highlighting the tragic elements and dissatisfaction.

Of the aspects of the plot that might have ended otherwise, Rozema drastically increases the courtship between Henry Crawford and Fanny. In this adaptation, Fanny becomes engaged to Henry Crawford in a sequence of charming and romantic scenes. It is possible that Rozema does this for the sake of adding another biographical similarity between Austen and Fanny. Just as Austen broke off her brief engagement to Harris Bigg-Wither the following morning, Fanny breaks off this engagement the following morning as well. Henry's anger over this betrayal partly impels him to his affair with Maria, making him less culpable in Rozema's film. Additionally, it makes the imbedded alternative ending of Fanny's marriage to Henry Crawford all the stronger. In including the more successful courtship by Henry, Rozema's film adheres more directly to the triangular marriage plot successfully used by Fanny Burney and other novelists, as well as by Austen herself in her first three novels. This change, alongside Fanny's altered character, tends to make the film more conventional than Austen's original novel, despite Rozema's clever techniques.[53] Once again, we are reminded that Austen's and Rozema's audiences are not as dissimilar as we might like to think—particularly in conventional expectations of a heroine's characteristics and dramatic fate.

The Stillness at the Turning of the Wheel, or Halting Narrative Lust

Regarding the psychological dynamic of Austen's endings, Austen finds ways to make her reader self-aware of narrative lust, particularly the impatient desire for a romantic conclusion of the marriage plot. She also teaches readers to become self-aware of many of our suppositions about what it takes to be a heroine. Fanny thus builds on Austen's previous expansions of the concept of heroine: Catherine is rather ordinary; Elinor is overshadowed by her sister; Elizabeth is never cowed by her husband; and Fanny is dominated by the charismatic characters that surround her for most of the novel. Nonetheless, Austen casts these heroines as worthy of centrality and our affection.

In popular reception, as we saw in the previous chapter, an addiction to Austen's happy endings has been compared with poison or even cancer. Austenitis is an illness that causes mature women to waste their lives looking for a Mr. Darcy-type husband. A modern response to this infectious desire to emulate her heroines is to try to counter the desire for romance. Taken one step further, could one inoculate oneself against this overindulgence in hope—perhaps by finding a way to check the narrative drive itself? Some fictional responses to Austen and *Mansfield Park* have converted Austen's warnings about charm into the therapeutic ability to halt longing itself, particularly the longing for (1) one's own happy ending, (2) a starring role as heroine, or (3) the perfect romantic partner. This strand of reception is clearest in Kathryn Duncan's nonfictional *Jane Austen and the Buddha* (2021), as well as in Laurie Viera Rigler's novel *Rude Awakenings of a Jane Austen Addict* (2010).[54]

Kathryn Duncan foregrounds Fanny Price (along with *Persuasion*'s Anne Elliot) as the most enlightened of Austen's heroines in her semiautobiographical comparison of Austen's novels to Buddhist teaching. This ranking runs counter to contemporary tastes, by her own account: "From a Buddhist perspective, what we learn is that Austen's most popular heroine with modern audiences, Elizabeth Bennet, is the least enlightened whereas the less popular and more passive characters, Fanny Price and Anne Elliot, are enlightened."[55] The very traits that give modern Western readers pause, and which Austen purposely chose to test the boundaries for heroines in fiction, are those which also are most valued in Buddhism, according to Duncan.

> Fanny learns to be quiet and observant and, by Western standards, an emotional punching bag. Viewed through Buddhism, though, Fanny becomes a budding bodhisattva, a compassionate being who achieves enlightenment in the service of others. To be a bodhisattva, one must cultivate deep listening, understanding, Right Diligence, and Right Livelihood (helping the unfortunate). Fanny successfully embodies bodhicitta, the awakened mind or the "mind of love."[56]

Duncan does not claim that Austen's works are Buddhist, but she does speculate on the (perhaps coincidental) similarities between certain strains of post-enlightenment stoicism and Buddhism, particularly the recognition of the limits of one's agency and the pervasiveness of selfishness.[57]

In *Mansfield Park*, as in Buddhist thought, Duncan argues, suffering is a means toward enlightenment. She mentions the example of Tom Bertram, who regains his health "without regaining the thoughtlessness and selfishness of his previous habits. He was the better for ever for his illness. He had suffered, and he had learnt to think, two advantages he had never known before."[58] Illness gives him time to stop, think, and reconsider. In a passage from Austen's ending that Duncan does not mention, Sir Thomas reflects about why his nieces and nephews have flourished while his own children floundered:

> In *her* [Susan's] usefulness, in Fanny's excellence, in William's continued good conduct and rising fame, and in the general well-doing and success of the other members of the family, all assisting to advance each other, and doing credit to his countenance and aid, Sir Thomas saw repeated, and for ever repeated, reason to rejoice in what he had done for them all, and acknowledge the advantages of *early hardship and discipline, and the consciousness of being born to struggle and endure.*[59]

Here as elsewhere, Austen intimates that decreased expectations sweeten happy endings.

Other authors also contemplate Fanny's stillness. Anna Keesey describes her movement from dislike of Fanny as "Anglican doormat" to an appreciation of her as "a hero on a winged horse," offering with her "stillness" an antidote for our times where "rough beasts are aslouch on the road to many Bethlehems."[60] Have our modern pieties changed so that Fanny and *Mansfield Park* no longer offend? Duncan cites the place of Robert Wright's *Why Buddhism Is True* on the *New York Times* bestseller list and the appearance of a recent *Time* special issue on mindfulness as evidence that this might be the case.[61]

According to Duncan, "The seeming passivity that makes modern readers fail to appreciate Fanny exemplifies her ability to stop, the first step in achieving enlightenment, and to look deeply. Fanny's narrative of her own life does not require her to be its star."[62] This is particularly important when she is surrounded by "improvers" like the Crawfords and "the spirit of activity" demonstrated so officiously by Mrs. Norris.[63] For Duncan, it is Fanny's ability to wonder at nature that allows her to be in the moment. As she remarks to a perplexed Mary Crawford, "when I am out of doors, especially when I am sitting out of doors, I am very apt to get into this sort of wondering strain." Mary responds, "I see no wonder in this shrubbery equal to seeing myself in it."[64] Similarly, when Fanny is gazing at the stars, she says: "Here's repose! . . . Here's what may tranquillize every care and lift the heart to rapture! . . . There certainly would be less [wickedness and sorrow] if the sublimity of Nature were more attended to, and people were carried more out of themselves by contemplating such a scene."[65] Fanny's approach to nature (theoretically) transcends selfish longing.[66]

Duncan's book relates to Austen's endings because she explicitly ties Fanny's perspective to the act of reading narrative. Duncan describes her own tendency toward narrative lust:

> I can't wait to find out what will happen next, so I zoom hurriedly through books, reading for plot, always dreading the end of a good book because it feels like parting with a friend yet rushing to finish, needing to know what happens next. [. . .] I think this anxious reading style of mine also explains my attraction to Austen. Her work is soothing. [. . .] That amazing, reassuring Austen

> narrative voice makes clear that even if in reality there's no way Elizabeth Bennet gets Darcy, Austen has created a world where she will — and his £10,000.[67]

She describes the narrative drive as a "low-stakes" form of anxiety: "Anxiety comes from a gap between reality and the story we create about our ideal version of our lives. Novels can teach us how to negotiate anxiety by generating low-stakes anxiety. We identify with characters and their plights, causing us some unease, but our own survival is never at stake, allowing us to relax into narrative-induced anxiety."[68] This corresponds exactly with Aristotle's claims about the power of tragedy and the cathartic combination of pity and fear that it awakens. But here, Duncan connects anxiety to the narrative drive per se, even in reading comedies and marriage plots. Duncan also draws an analogy between the way we read and the way we live. Fanny may be a good example of silent meditation and of being "in the moment," yet it is unclear to me that Fanny's character causes readers to slacken their narrative lust for a happy ending.

Rigler's *Rude Awakenings of an Austen Addict* expresses a similar insight about the value of suffering, the consolation of stillness, and the rare ability to be "in the moment" (what T. S. Eliot called "the still point of the turning wheel"). The heroine of this novel, Jane Mansfield, incorporates elements of Austen and Fanny into one hybrid character. Jane Mansfield travels from Regency England to twenty-first-century Los Angeles, magically assisted by a fortune teller whom she meets in both worlds. With her knowledge of both worlds, the fortune teller explains the dangers of high expectations of happy endings.

> Today's women are no less desirous of love, and marrying for love, than they were in your time [Regency England]. But they, like so

> many women before them, simply fear it is an unattainable goal. And thus they settle for what fleeting pleasures they can find, creating an endless cycle of pleasure, despair, pleasure, despair, ad infinitum. Human nature is the same today as it was in your time. The only difference between today's world and your world is that people have more choices now than they did then.[69]

According to the fortune teller (and implicitly Rigler), the modern-day situation for women—including divorce, contraception, safe abortion, and differing societal expectations—has made marriage seem much less permanent, necessary, and significant. Yet modern-day women continue to gauge themselves according to the marriage plot. Whereas the Regency woman might have worried about the possibility of achieving the marital state, the modern woman may fear the impossibility of staying married or staying faithful. The modern woman (and man) has so many choices that it is harder to make a decision that limits one's future opportunities. That doesn't mean, as Jeffrey Eugenides also shows in his 2011 novel *The Marriage Plot*, that we have outgrown either this form of novel or the institution itself. More choices leads to greater expectations of happiness, and therefore also the potential for greater disillusionment.

Jane Mansfield, unable to return to her life in Regency England, finds solace in her new surroundings through an ability to draw, similar to Fanny's mode of contemplating the beauty of stars and hedgerows: "I find drawing a way of revisiting what is beautiful about my past with fond detachment rather than with longing."[70] She eventually learns to apply this same detachment to her own future, which frees her from anxiety: "What is in store for me, I have not the smallest notion, and I glory in that state of not knowing. There is no better place to be. For the past does not exist. There is only the present. Only the eternal beautiful ever-unfolding now."[71] The "beautiful ever-unfolding now" seems a mystical concept and certainly one not incompatible with Buddhist terms of enlightenment.

It is difficult to counter the deeply rooted sense of the narrative ending as a *telos* or ultimate end for us, regardless of whether we mean the stories that we read or the stories we inhabit. Frank Kermode argues that this kind of thinking is deeply rooted in Judeo-Christian eschatology. Duncan and Rigler (among others) find in *Mansfield Park* fodder for an alternative to the marriage plot, or at least to the narrative drive for it that can usurp other aspects of one's life. They find, therefore, in this Austen novel an antidote to Austenitis. I have suggested that Austen herself composed *Mansfield Park* as an antidote to *Pride and Prejudice*; these adaptations go further. Duncan and Rigler suggest that *Mansfield Park* can be an antidote for Austen's novels' effect on audiences and a reliance on happy endings. According to these authors, *Mansfield Park* works against the tyranny of the marriage plot itself.

According to Duncan, "[b]y the end of *Mansfield Park*, it is Fanny who brings healing and compassion to all of the other more active, striving characters who have created the suffering of the novel through focusing only on themselves."[72] This, then, is the culmination of the novel as she sees it, rather than the resolution of the marriage plot. It is possible that Fanny's own lackluster marriage—like Elinor's before her—draws more attention to her own character and how it contrasts with those around her, even her own siblings. Stargazing, plant-admiring, friend to hedgerows and geraniums, protector of discarded treasures, Fanny's unusual heroism involves stasis. Yet this stasis, rather than being stultifying, may well be one secret for learning to live life in the moment and for leaving the rat race called the marriage plot.

CHAPTER 5

The Art of English Happiness

What did she say?—Just what she ought, of course.
A lady always does.—She said enough to shew there need
not be despair—and to invite him to say more himself.

JANE AUSTEN, *Emma*

Charms and Potions

After her philosophical celebration of her least powerful heroine, Austen takes on her most powerful heroine. Emma has the greatest control over her situation of any Austen heroine, born with "very little to distress or vex her," "the power of having rather too much her own way," and "a disposition to think a little too well of herself."[1] Her errors hurt those around her in proportion to her inflated sense of power and entitlement. *A Midsummer Night's Dream* links *Mansfield Park* and *Emma,* and it was apparently on Austen's mind as she composed both novels during 1814. She quotes the play explicitly in *Emma*: "The course of true love never ran smooth— . A Hartfield edition of Shakespeare would have a long note on that passage."[2] I have written elsewhere about how *Mansfield Park* shows the Bertrams succumbing to the Crawfords' charms, just as multiple characters in *A Midsummer Night's Dream* succumb to the "charm" or love potion administered by Puck. The ending of *Mansfield Park* continues in this theme by holding romantic charm at a distance for didactic purposes. In *Emma*, the eponymous heroine, drunk with her own power and imagination, tries to take the place of *Midsummer Night's Dream*'s Titania, Queen of the Fairies, matching (and mismatching) the young people who surround her, ignoring her own life and its disorder. And she embarrasses herself equally, even without kissing Bottom. Emma so eagerly assigns romantic happy endings to others that she forgets to tend to her own plotline.

The main magic potion in *Emma* is the charm of the narrative drive itself, rather than the personal charisma of any character. Emma is an artist, and while Austen shows her drawing and painting, her implicit true vocation may be *novelist* like Austen herself, only without putting pen to paper. Emma stands in front a window in Ford's store and composes a long alternative scene, creating interest where none exists: "A mind lively and at ease, can do with seeing nothing, and can see nothing that does not answer."[3] This impressive coping strategy moves further afield at other times when she creates "interest" in others' lives. Emma sees the characters around her as fodder for her matchmaking schemes—tools in her own plans for speedy plots and happy romantic endings. *Emma* is in many ways Austen's masterpiece, partly because of the way in which it reflects upon the temptations involved with being an author. These temptations include the delectable sense of control over your subject, and the power to create a world to match your own predilections. Emma herself is a wishful author of romances within this novel, and readers (particularly on a second reading) are able to critique her choices of heroine, hero, or plot device on multiple occasions. In this there is analogy between Emma and Austen. *Emma* is a novel only an "imaginist" could write. And its most potent potion is ultimately the imagination itself.

Emma follows *Northanger Abbey* as a tribute to the quixotic tradition, particularly Charlotte Lennox's *Female Quixote*. Here, Emma resembles Lennox's heroine Arabella in many ways, including her situation. Arabella, whose mother has died, lives alone with her father, who inadvertently spoils her education by gratifying all her whims and letting her direct her own reading. Arabella conceives of herself as a heroine in a French chivalric romance, where knights and other courtly princes must risk their lives to prove their worth to an ideal princess. Love is undying yet often results in premature death, and virginity is ubiquitous and sacrosanct. The tales she reads are poisonous to Arabella's ability to exercise her reason and understand her own surroundings. She tortures those around her with unreasonable expectations and far-fetched interpretations of reality. Arabella, like Emma, needs to learn a more quotidian, less precarious, and less stereotypically *French* approach to courtship and happiness.

In order to understand how Austen uses the ending of *Emma* to didactic effect, we first need to understand more of how Austen actively engages the reader's narrative drive and imagination in the novel. Austen's own peculiar "social contract" with the implied reader in *Emma* echoes the political imagery of this novel, written at the height of the Napoleonic wars.[4] This novel also continues the work of *Pride and Prejudice* and *Mansfield Park* in depicting a restoration and reconfiguration of political order at the end of the novel. Comparisons between France and England run through the novel, most obviously in the ongoing contrast of Frank Churchill and Mr. Knightley. In choosing Mr. Knightley at the end, Emma celebrates an English ideal: "the true English style, burying under a calmness that seemed all but indifference, the real attachment which would have led either of them, if requisite, to do every thing for the good of the other."[5] This celebration of poignant, feeling reticence also justifies Austen's own "English" choice of reticence and "calmness" in her endings, in this, her most self-reflective novel.

One of Austen's innovations in this complex novel is to manipulate the reader not only to feel sympathy with Emma but also to see the danger in playing frivolously with others' emotions, particularly as exhibited by Frank's "deeper game."[6] Through her contract with her reader, Austen critiques Frank's frivolous and harmful game, playing against the backdrop of Mr. Knightley's plain, unadorned, direct communication. As we will see, Austen first trains readers to jump to conclusions alongside Emma, and then enables us to be enlightened alongside her as well. One could say that the overall movement of the novel is from a superficial "French" art of play toward a deeper (yet still playful) "English" art of happiness.[7]

The Social Contract between Reader and Author

While the ending of *Emma* doesn't arouse as much ire as many of her other novels' endings, readers may still be frustrated at the elision of details, apophasis, and the omission of key dialogue in favor of summary. Further consideration of the conventional expectations attached to Austen's happy endings can help explain why such endings can make readers feel cheated. The conventions of different genres lend another level of complexity here and can help explain the "letdown" many readers feel with Austen's endings. Most often we are blissfully unaware of such generic conventions until they are broken. My own anger as a teenager at the ending of *Mansfield Park* was based in a sense of betrayal. I felt that Austen had betrayed the expectations that she had set up in the rest of her novel through minute descriptions and analyses, so that their omission at the end was a violation of an unspoken social contract. One of the benefits of this kind of dissonance or shock—whether intended by the author or not—is a new awareness of the terms of the social contract to which we were holding the author and ourselves. Shocks can teach us about what we expect from books and what we expect from society as a whole.

Austen was one of the first authors to write a parodic critique of the tenets of the popular novel of sensibility, even at a young age, and she followed this with an eminently appropriate revision of gothic characteristics in the first novel she completed for publication. This shows that she was unusually observant of literary conventions around her. As we have already seen in previous chapters, when we study Austen's techniques for manipulating her reader, we discover that many of her techniques serve the purpose of shaking the reader out of tacit acceptance of dominant conventions surrounding the novel. Among other things, she challenges us to limit our prejudices and broaden our understanding of what being a heroine entails.

Emma is the novel, among Austen's works, that most abounds in narrative play: it is full of riddles, word games, and double meanings, making the implied reader's interpretive task doubly difficult. The heroine also complicates the narration of *Emma*, for the novel is told primarily from the perspective of a heroine who loves to distort the truth to fit her preconceived opinions and wishes. As a result, we readers are forced to reread Emma's claims in the light of new evidence and revise our interpretations as we go along, whether or not we actually turn back the pages. Here as in both *Northanger Abbey* and *Pride and Prejudice*, Austen provides subtle narrative clues regarding character to encourage the discriminating role of the reader: Austen teaches us carefully to observe words, novels, and even life, by teaching us to become better readers of character. Like the narrator of *Emma*, Austen recognizes that "Seldom, very seldom does complete truth belong to any human disclosure; seldom can it happen that something is not a little disguised, or a little mistaken."[8] In Austen's novels this recognition leads to an enjoyable challenge—the challenge of engaged interpretation and participation in the novel—rather than to a cynical detachment from the attempt to understand others through their words and deeds. Despite the tricks our desires, vanity, and pride can play upon our powers of observation, Austen's novels still give the implied reader hope that we too, like Elizabeth Bennet, can achieve the self-knowledge that will enable us not only to discern the subtleties of the world around us, but also to form friendships and—perhaps—marriages. But Emma does not need marriage to achieve the degree of authority that she wishes. The greatest impediment to her freedom—her father—is someone she loves deeply. She does not wish to be free of her father. So, Austen's ending must also reflect this challenge to the marriage plot. What does the marriage plot offer for a heroine who already has everything?

Emma harkens back to Austen's marvelous comic play called "The Mystery," written in her teens. In "The Mystery," Austen extends incomprehensibility and uncertainty to their logical extremes—the secret discussed in the short play is never revealed, and comprehension of it is thwarted at every turn. *Emma*, sometimes considered the first mystery novel, also engages in purposeful obfuscation. As Peter Knox-Shaw puts it, "In *Emma* the reader is as much in the dark as the characters themselves, and kept guessing about outcomes."[9] As the heroine herself complains, evidence is indeed difficult to interpret when it is as "unmarked, wavering, dubious," as it is in *Emma*.[10] And sifting such evidence is one of the principal challenges both for Emma and the reader of this novel. Miss Bates and her unchecked stream of data bytes provides another source of information that is certainly "unmarked," if not also wavering and dubious. Miss Bates relays tidbits that are important on a second reading of the novel—hints that help unravel the actual relationships that Emma and the first-time reader do not fully understand.

In more ways than one, the ability to observe keenly and judge and translate appearances appropriately is essential for survival. Austen shows in all her novels that those characters who truly love also observe well. (The same could be said of Colonel Brandon and

Elinor of *Sense and Sensibility*, Mr. Knightley of *Emma*, or Anne Elliot and eventually Captain Wentworth of *Persuasion*.) The "true" lovers in all Jane Austen's novels tend to watch their objects from afar rather than hang about them, chattering as the "false" lovers do. Several times during the novel, while Frank is next to Emma, flirting and chatting, Mr. Knightley sits at a distance to observe the interactions not only between Emma and Frank, but also between Frank and Jane. At the letter game, for example, "Frank was next to Emma, Jane opposite to them—and Mr. Knightley so placed as to see them all; and it was his object to see as much as he could, with as little apparent observation."[11] Mr. Knightley's eyes show what his words cannot express—that his love for Emma is neither selfish nor blind.[12] Whereas one of the fundamental ideas of the cult of sensibility was suspicion of rational detachment and objective stances, Austen portrays rational observation in the service of feeling and even of intimacy. Rather than always leading to a loss of objectivity, sympathy can benefit from detachment, through the desire to see one's beloved in context, at a distance. This is another analogy to the movement of narration in Austen's endings. "Zooming out" to enable better observation of individuals in their surroundings, while less romantic in an individualistic sense, nonetheless signifies love—caritas rather than eros. In applying this movement to her endings, and allowing heroes and heroines to "share the limelight" with other, less important characters, Austen challenges our notion of love itself.

Minding the Gap with Emma

In Austen, the reader is involved in the "play" and performative aspects of reading in conversation with the implied author. We "watch" the heroines untangle appearances in a more Platonic sense of uncovering the truth behind the shadows. The heroines are trying to decipher representation of emotions and character, but discovering these is only a small part of the reader's task and joy. We learn, long before our heroines do, who is villainous and who is virtuous, who is in love and who is not, but that is not enough to account for our narrative drive. We have a dance to complete with the implied author as well as truth to uncover.

Purposely crafted, ambiguous situations provide a springboard for Emma's imagination and allow her to indulge her "fancy" by jumping to the wrong conclusions. The ambiguities are not just situational but are also built into the speech of the characters. Consider the following description of Mr. Elton: striving to be simultaneously modest and gallant, "'He was afraid not even Miss Woodhouse'—he stopt a moment—'or Miss Smith could inspire him.'"[13] Does his pause represent a sigh after he utters the name of his beloved Miss Woodhouse? Or does he hesitate out of emotion, anticipating the name of his beloved Miss Smith? The reader must choose—must fill the gap—alongside Emma.

After Mr. Elton proposes to her, Emma reviews the evidence that allowed her to think all along that his attention toward her was on behalf of her friend; she tries to understand her old (mis)interpretation in a long internal monologue which begins: "How she could have been so deceived! [. . .] She looked back as well as she could; but it was all confusion. She had taken up the idea, she supposed, and made everything bend to it. His [Mr. Elton's] manners, however, must have been unmarked, wavering, dubious, or she could not have been so misled."[14] *Were* Mr. Elton's manners "unmarked, wavering, dubious"? Or is this Emma's justification of her own failures of interpretation?

Emma's unreliable decision-making process can be described in three steps: observation, hesitation (accompanied by rationalization), and decision (accompanied by revision of history). First, Emma demonstrates her "quick eye" and her perceptive powers by keenly observing others' behavior. Usually the behavior is in conflict with her preexisting theories. Emma then hesitates a moment to speculate about the significance of this behavior against the backdrop of her preconceptions. This step often includes Emma's most "philosophical" generalizations, as well as downright self-serving rationalization, as she tries to explain away her doubt. Finally, Emma makes a *firm* decision about the behavior, reasserts her former theory, and promptly forgets that there was ever any doubt. She then decides to interpret all future (and past) signs in the light of her decision.

The following excerpt shows her judgment in progress. First, Emma observes Mr. Elton's ambiguous gallantry when he exults over the outing to Randalls:

> [Step 1—Observation] "Well," said Emma to herself. "This is most strange!—After I had got him off so well, to chuse [*sic*] to go into company, and leave Harriet ill behind! Most strange indeed!—[Step 2—Hesitation and Rationalization] But there is, I believe, in many men, especially single men, such an inclination—such a passion for dining out . . . [Step 3—Decision and Revision] and this must be the case with Mr. Elton; a most valuable, amiable man undoubtedly, and very much in love with Harriet; but still, he cannot refuse an invitation . . . What a strange thing love is![15]

Occasionally Emma has more difficulty drawing her preferred conclusions. In these instances, it takes her a little longer to reach Step 3, and we readers have a greater chance of differing in our conclusions:

> [Step 1] This man is almost too gallant to be in love. [Step 2] I should say so, but that I suppose that there may be a hundred different ways of being in love . . . [Step 1] He does sigh and

> languish, and study for compliments rather more than I could endure as a principal. I come in for a pretty good share as a second. [Step 3] But it is his gratitude on Harriet's account.[16]

In each case, Emma observes well initially; however, she proceeds to substitute rationalization for reflection, and a self-willed decision for one based on consideration. She observes the truth, even *thinks* the truth, but then changes her conclusion to fit her fancy.[17]

After she makes her faulty decisions, Emma is exposed to the truth in many small stages until finally she cannot ignore it. Each time Emma receives a hint that her interpretation might be wrong, her word choice and the word choice of the narrative voice (also from Emma's point of view) changes suddenly from certain ("quite sure, very, exceedingly, perfect") to doubtful in Step 2 ("I should say so, but . . ."). Shortly afterward, in Step 3, she once again expresses herself with certainty ("this *must* be the case").

This three-step formulation of Emma's inaccurate judgments serves several purposes simultaneously. It is important for the reader's sympathy with Emma, and may perhaps flatter the reader's self-conceit. Step 1 provides a common point of reference for both reader and Emma, so that Emma's keen observation, which is never placed into doubt by the narrator, can be interpreted by Emma and by the reader. Luckily, Emma's "quick eye" is not *so* rapid that the reader doesn't witness her hesitation in Step 2. This step engages the reader's sympathy, especially because her phrasing reflects hesitation and doubt about her own conclusions. This moment of doubt also creates dramatic irony and encourages the reader's search for alternate interpretations. Although we may not feel superior to Emma on the basis of this second step, the third could arguably have this effect. In Step 3, the two (or more) opposing interpretations have separated completely, forcing the implied reader actively to agree or disagree with Emma's interpretation of events. Her certain wording leaves no room for ambiguity, and the reader rushes to decide. The dynamic thus also encourages the reader's love of foretelling and impatience for resolution.

Another result of this constantly repeated, three-step pattern is that time and time again, Emma *almost* agrees with the reader's (and Mr. Knightley's) interpretation and then rejects it firmly, only to adopt it little by little. The repetition of this pattern may cause the "prodigal child" effect. The reader is made to feel like Emma's guardian, watching her grow up under our eyes and waiting until she finally "sees our light." This may account for paternalistic phrasing among the critics like "our hopes for Emma are fulfilled."[18] Like Mr. Knightley, we can remark that "there is an anxiety, a curiosity in what one feels for Emma [. . .] I wonder what will become of her."[19] We want to see Emma fulfill her potential, and she can do so by seeing what we have already seen. As Emma gradually agrees with us and "returns to the nest," we are increasingly pleased with her and simultaneously reconfirmed in our own perceptive powers. This is one of the ways in which the narrative, like all mystery novels, succeeds by engaging and flattering the implied reader's intellect.

We readers become so accustomed to this three-step pattern, however, that we may also adopt it in our perusal of *Emma*. We come to expect Emma to judge in this fashion, and we learn to try to anticipate it. It seems that Austen was conscious of this effect on the implied reader. At the very end of volume I, for example, Emma wonders why Mr. Knightley appears to detest Frank before having met him, since this seems uncharacteristically prejudiced of Mr. Knightley: "To take a dislike to a young man, only because he appeared to be of a different disposition from himself, was unworthy the real liberality of mind which she was always used to acknowledge in him; [. . .] she had never before for a moment supposed it could make him unjust to the merit of another."[20]

This speculation is strikingly similar in style to Emma's Step 1 observations ("she had never before for a moment supposed"). Occurring as it does at the end of the volume, the speculation is not continued by the narrative voice. Is it not implied—and is it not the case—that the reader takes Steps 2 (hesitation and reflection) and 3 (firm decision) for Emma? This structured judgment-making, especially coming at such an important break, encourages us to fill the gap between volumes with our own speculation and foretelling.

Austen as narrator manipulates and tricks the audience into jumping to conclusions by providing ambiguous evidence (such as Mr. Elton's compliments of Emma's portrait of Harriet). Like her juvenile play "The Mystery," *Emma* is a precursor of the mystery novel. She practices partial revelation in order to cultivate a narrative drive that may be stronger than the care to ensure correct observation. Austen indulges in these seemingly despotic techniques, however, for more social and democratic purposes, even though her tactics and purposes can easily be missed. In making our own errors of judgment, implied readers can feel more forgiving of Emma's errors. In addition, at the very end of the novel, in a touching scene between Emma and Mr. Knightley, we witness an example of social, loving gap-filling.

At the end of the novel, when Frank's letter of explanation has arrived, Emma asks Mr. Knightley to read it. This reading event takes a large portion of the concluding chapters. Up to this point in the novel, there have been other letters, charades, and similar pieces of evidence in the narrative. Until now, these have divided characters from each other in their interpretation of the evidence. In this case, Mr. Knightley makes the reading social, participatory, and consensus-building. He says, "It will be natural for me [. . .] to speak my opinion aloud as I read. By doing it I shall feel like I am near you." When Emma agrees, he gains interest in the project: "he returned to his reading with greater alacrity."[21] Whereas earlier in the novel they read the letters separately and diverge in their responses, by the end of the novel, their reading has become more social and is a good portent of their marriage. They still differ in opinions, but amicably, learning from each other. When he comes to the section of the letter relating to Emma, "he was obliged to read the whole of it aloud—and that related to her, with a smile; a look; a shake of the head; a word or two of assent, or disapprobation; or merely of love, as the subject required . . . ."[22] The list of varied nonverbal responses suggests that Emma and he have mastered a new level of communication. The closing of epistemological gaps here also suggests their growing equality, even though they are bound to continue to err in their judgments from time to time. Austen's despotic manipulations in the end teach a social, participatory good.

The True English Style

Austen wrote during a period of intense national engagement in war with France. All of her books were completed and published during the Regency in England, throughout which Napoleon was never far from the popular consciousness. Writing throughout a period of almost uninterrupted war with France from 1793 to 1815, Austen was not immune to the nationalistic associations of cultural debates over sensibility, artifice, tyranny, and the like. In *Emma* in particular, Austen uses the conflict between Mr. Knightley and Frank Churchill to stand in for the cultural contrast between England and France. The contrast is coded into their names: George is the name of the patron saint of England, and Frank can both refer to a member of the tribe of Franks and the origin of the word "French." Their names thus indicate deeper cultural and moral divides between the two men.

Austen's wartime novels all include patriotic paeans to England. In *Northanger Abbey* it praises English law and order, and in *Emma* it lauds English nature in opposition to tyrannical rule. If the reference in *Northanger Abbey* rails against anarchy, *Emma*'s opposes tyranny. While certainly not devoid of social hierarchies, *Emma* nonetheless celebrates a more natural order. When describing Donwell Abbey, for example, we hear: "It was a sweet view—sweet to the eye and the mind. English verdure, English culture, English comfort, seen under a sun bright, without being oppressive."[23] The word "oppressive" has political overtones. The notion, a carryover from Austen's treatment of the picturesque in *Pride and Prejudice*, is that, if not spontaneous, then order should be marshaled with a light hand to maintain individual freedom.[24]

The light touch is evident as well in the rhetorical comparison at the heart of the novel: the direct speech of the Knightley brothers compared to the elaborate linguistic games of Frank Churchill and Emma. "John Knightley made his appearance, and 'How d'ye do, George?' and 'John, how are you?' succeeded in the true English style, burying under a calmness that seemed all but indifference, the real attachment which would have led either of them, if requisite, to do every thing for the good of the other."[25]

In contrast, the narrator relays Mr. Knightley's perception of Frank's disguised missives, game playing, and social demeanor: "Disingenuousness and double dealing seemed to meet him at every turn. These letters were but the vehicle for gallantry and trick. It was a child's play, chosen to conceal a deeper game on Frank Churchill's part."[26] Jealous of Emma's admiration of Frank, Mr. Knightley explicitly articulates this comparison of French and English manners to Emma: "No, Emma, your amiable young man can be amiable only in French, not in English. He may be very 'aimable,' have very good manners, and be very agreeable; but he can have no English delicacy towards the feelings of other people: nothing really amiable about him."[27] For Mr. Knightley, and the implied author as well, pleasing manners cannot be relied upon to reveal the truth of one's feelings because they are easily assumed for selfish reasons.

Rhetoric is the primary turf on which this proxy war with France is fought. Knightley is direct, plainspoken, and generous, whereas Frank is disingenuous, artful, and selfish. Mr. Knightley communicates directly "in the true English style," while Frank deceives and plays elaborate games.[28] Even at the ending, when Mr. Knightley proposes marriage to Emma, he does not change his fundamental style: "it was in plain, unaffected, gentleman-like English such as Mr. Knightley used even to the woman he was in love with."[29] In contrast, Frank Churchill toys with others' happiness, including the happiness of his fiancée, Jane Fairfax, despite her being in a particularly vulnerable position.

Mr. Knightley prefers the "short, full answer" and consistently admires simple and direct speech, "good sense," "plain" English: "I never hear better sense from any one than Robert Martin. He always speaks to the purpose; open, straightforward, and very well judging."[30] Emma, too, admires this straightforward speech, despite her own linguistic maneuverings, as she shows when (in spite of herself) she is impressed by Robert Martin's letter: "[Emma] read, and was surprized [*sic*]. The style of letter was much above her expectation. There was not merely no grammatical errors, but as a composition it would not have disgraced a gentlemen; the language, though plain, was strong and unaffected, and the sentiments it conveyed very much to the credit of the writer. It was short, but expressed good sense, warm attachment, liberality, propriety, even delicacy of feeling." Not only does he "think[-] strongly and clearly," but the last phrase of her description is telling: that strong, plain, direct speech can be compatible with "even delicacy of feeling" suggests that the language of the heart and the language of reason are not at war.[31]

In Austen's novels, the marriage plot is used for political purposes as well, but with a new edge. In her novels—particularly *Northanger Abbey*, *Pride and Prejudice*, and *Emma*—Austen compares English fiction with the French romances that Lady Arabella reads in the *Female Quixote*. Austen's novels associate French romances with adultery, gothic excess, overindulgence, and frivolity, while English fiction is presented as having greater moral solidity and understatement (with exceptions, such as John Thorpe's favorite novel, *The Monk*). Underpinning Austen's parody of gothic romance in *Northanger Abbey* and supporting the discourse about "Englishness" in *Emma* is an idea that the English specialize in deep feeling accompanied by understated expression. Austen thus communicates her nationalistic preference for England through her endings as well. The lack of elaboration, explicit emotion, and physical detail, just like the conspicuous absence of lace veils and white satin that Mrs. Elton laments in Emma's wedding, demonstrates the solid "Englishness" of which Austen approves.[32]

In *Emma*, Austen ascribes Englishness to a style of plot development in addition to rhetorical style. This can be seen in Mr. Knightley's approach to the marriage plot. Speaking of the marriage between Mr. Weston and Miss Taylor, Mr. Knightley remarks, "A straightforward, open-hearted man like Weston, and a rational, unaffected woman like Miss Taylor, may be safely left to manage their own concerns,"[33] implying that they need no authorial orchestration for their marriage plot to come to fruition. Similarly, when Mr. Knightly recounts Harriet and Robert Martin's reconciliation to a surprised Emma at the end of the novel, he says, "It is a very simple story."[34] This is a humorous comment when one considers how difficult their "simple" story becomes with Emma's interventions and Harriet's folly. Harriet's journey meanders through infatuations with two or three men before it returns to the simple and linear plotline

Mr. Martin has hoped for. Mr. Knightley's comments thus approximate Austen's narrator's rhetorical questions in other novels, such as "Who could be in doubt of what followed?"

The novel itself, full of sections with "wavering, dubious evidence," could not have been written by a Mr. Knightley. Emma, like Frank, is guilty of needlessly engaging in "zigzags" of emotion rather than "straightforward" rational and open attachment.[35] That is also at the crux of Austen's artistry. As a landed and independent gentleman, Mr. Knightley may perhaps overestimate others' agency. While it is easy for him to be direct, it is not the same for women, who only have the power of refusal and are subject to far greater social strictures. This is another version of Austen's double vision. An imaginist herself, Austen must have reveled in the misunderstandings and ambiguity that drive this novel, yet she also valued English directness of communication as an ideal, however untenable in most social situations. Since this novel in particular is about the temptation for an author to overindulge in imagination, it is particularly apt that the marriage plot is resolved in "true English style." His actual proposal of marriage to Emma "was in plain, unaffected, gentleman-like English, such as Mr. Knightley used even to the woman he was in love with."[36] This Englishness shows itself in the understated approach to the marriage plot itself. In sum, what many have seen as embittered reticence in her endings is in this novel literary commentary, political philosophy, and enthusiastic patriotism converted into narrative technique.

Emma, the aspiring novelist or choreographer of people's lives, creates multiple false happy endings for her "characters." She is an unwitting (and somewhat unwilling) subject of her own story. A battle brews inside her between being a heroine and an author. Emma loves to control, and yet it is glamorous, she feels, to be a heroine. Like her sister-in-kind Arabella, she artificially and endlessly postpones the resolution of her own plot. Amusingly, Harriet and Emma have both met their appropriate mates before the novel even begins. Arabella meets the right man early in her novel as well. Both female quixotes are themselves complicit in the endless zigzags of the plot. They make mysteries out of straightforward evidence and confound straightforward courtship.

What Did She Say?

If the movement at the ending of the novel is toward English openness and directness, why does Austen still confound the reader with narrative reticence and rhetorical questions at the end? One of the most famous examples of omitted dialogue in Austen's opus is Emma's response to Mr. Knightley's proposal: "What did she say?—Just what she ought, of course. A lady always does.—She said enough to shew [*sic*] there need not be despair—and to invite him to say more himself."[37] The words not only seem cruelly omitted, but also, since Emma is such a mistress of conversation, it is particularly unusual not to hear her words. This is a moment when we want Emma to drop her artifices and be an authentic "woman" rather than proper "lady" toward Mr. Knightley.

Critics have often misunderstood this silence: Deanna Kreisel, for example, remarks that "Austen seems more interested in characterizing her own novelistic practice than in not reporting Emma's acceptance of Mr. Knightley's offer. Austen's own authorial ladylikeness allows her to say only what she ought—in this case, nothing at all. Austen alerts us here to the parameters of her own narratorial propriety: what she considers worthy and unworthy of narration."[38] While Kreisel is right to draw attention to the connections Austen makes between the two levels of narration—Austen's of Emma and Emma's of herself—it is not propriety that silences Austen. This idea may stem from the Victorian misunderstanding of Austen's primness, which attributed spinster-like prudishness to Austen that is irreconcilable with Austen's juvenilia and letters. The teasing withholding of information at this key moment has nothing to do with propriety, but instead with reader's expectations and involvement.

Austen, like her predecessor Laurence Sterne, tries to involve the reader and especially the reader's imagination through the use of silence. Just as the implied reader of *A Sentimental Journey* must take an active role in filling the gaps within the narrative, so must the implied reader of *Emma*. Just as Sterne trains readers to exercise their imagination (which for him is the only way out of the solipsism of words), Austen also trains and encourages the imagination of the implied reader of *Emma* through omissions and elaborate narrative techniques. Both Emma and the reader must face the difficulties of "translation." James Thompson formulates it thus: "By the end, [Emma] is forced to see that it is difficult to know one's own feelings, more difficult to express those feelings to another, and impossible, finally, to know the other's sensations."[39] Thompson's position is perhaps too extreme, however, for although intimacy is "seldom" possible, Emma and Knightley exemplify that it is *not* impossible: it is this hope of intimacy that alone will ensure our persistent efforts in translation. The result is that *Emma* expresses the same hopeful view of imagination as does Sterne. Austen trains the reader to be an imaginative observer, just as Sterne trains the reader to be an imaginative translator of the world. In both cases, imagination is central to what John Mullan calls "the progress of sociality."[40] In order to comprehend the emotion, one must listen to the *silence* that surrounds the "short, full answers." Mr. Knightley masters a "rhetoric of silence" that does not disrupt the surface order of the community.

Austen instead wields the novel of sensibility's silences and narrative gaps to involve the reader. Austen simultaneously invites the reader (or, in today's context, the screenwriter) to fill in the missing dialogue. She invites the reader to be self-conscious of what the filled gaps reveal about our own assumptions about ideals of the novel and of the characters in them. When we recognize how much we want beauty, or charm, or romantic declarations, we also recognize the injustice of paying more attention—or attention only—to those who are "interesting" in precisely those ways.

Narration in *Emma* differs from *Northanger Abbey*, where the narrator is a self-conscious author for most of the novel, and it differs also from *Sense and Sensibility*, *Mansfield Park*, and *Persuasion*, where the intrusions of the narrator interrupt a relative tendency to want to wallow in the heroine's final victory. In *Emma*, the authorial games are so prominent that we hope to be surprised by something a bit less ambiguous at the end.

As for the final romantic resolution, it is in some ways the most leisurely of the novels. There are no fewer than six chapters from the declaration of mutual love until the end of the novel. This is even more narrative time than Austen gives Elizabeth and Darcy. The question of their gaining permission to marry still haunts them, however, as it does Catherine Morland and Henry Tilney. Like the future Tilneys, the couple here is awarded an "extra chapter" for the resolution of the actual marriage.[41] The delay gives them a chance to compare responses to many of the events around them, as well as to (re)interpret past events. More than three-fourths of the final chapter is dedicated to the conclusion of Robert and Harriet's plot. Mr. Woodhouse's permission is acquired in the penultimate paragraph of the entire novel, and the final paragraph describes their wedding, bringing the traditional marriage plot to a compact end in three sentences.

> The wedding was very much like other weddings, where the parties have no taste for finery or parade; and Mrs. Elton, from the

> particulars detailed by her own husband, thought it all extremely shabby, and very inferior to her own.—"Very little white satin, very few lace veils; a most pitiful business!—Selina would stare when she heard of it."—but, in spite of these deficiencies, the wishes, the hopes, the confidence, the predictions of the small band of true friends who witnessed the ceremony, were fully answered in the perfect happiness of the union.[42]

The sharing of the limelight, so to speak, of the final chapter with Harriet and Robert demonstrates the social restoration that Emma and Knightley's marriage also represents. The free radical is safely bonded; the broader community is served. Unlike Shakespeare's silencing of Beatrice, however, Emma is not silenced at all. The six chapters after their engagement have taught readers to join the "small band of true friends" who have confidence in the happiness of the union. The list in the phrase "the wishes, the hopes, the confidence, the predictions" draws the reader into the active and unabated world of Highbury gossip and curiosity. This is rather the opposite of Anne Elliot's need to understand how *un*interested others are in one's own affairs. Emma is the only heroine who stays home after her marriage; in that sense, her novel is even more endogamous than *Mansfield Park*. Emma is in many ways the antithesis of Anne in Austen's next novel, who leaves her home to no new fixed abode. (In fact, Anne's new husband presents her with a form of *transportation* rather than a home.) In contrast, while Emma's community remains static, it is nonetheless renewed and refreshed through their marriage.

As for other anti-romantic devices, *Emma* shares with *Northanger Abbey* a sudden *deus ex machina* event that enables the final marriage to take place. Rather than a mysterious viscount, Hartfield experiences the (humorously banal) visit of a poultry thief. In this novel, Austen's narrator does not break the fourth wall to apologize for the technique, but it has the important effect of emphasizing how easily the resolution could have been thwarted or at least vastly postponed. In this novel, Austen neither distracts us with metafictional comments nor intrudes with a first-person claim about her heroine. The arrival of turkey thieves in the neighborhood worries Emma's father enough to finally submit to the marriage. Beyond alluding to his own fears of his "prize bird" being taken away, Austen again uses characters' weaknesses to drive a happy ending rather than relying on conversions. The *deus ex machina* here, as with Austen's other farmyard references (consider the cows in *Sense and Sensibility*), humorously deflates a heroine's self-importance. This is important for a heroine who was "never loth to be first."[43] Insofar as Emma shares aspects of Arabella, the heroine of Charlotte Lennox's *Female Quixote,* such a quotidian concern may also puncture French chivalric illusions, while reminding us that England is assuredly not Utopia.

In the end, as Robin Grove humorously puts it, "it is not self-knowledge, or a reformed nature, or a loving heart, but turkeys that make [Emma's] marriage possible—."[44] The comic resolution only makes sense, of course, because of the growth of both hero and heroine; however, Austen stresses in each of her comic endings that the external "reward" for their growth, the consummation in marriage, is anything but automatic. By including the coincidences and relatively trivial occurrences (like turkey thieves) that help bring about the final marriage, she stresses not only the importance of internal growth independent of marriage, but also the rarity of the occasions when the outside world conforms itself to the wishes of the couple in question.

Seldom, Very Seldom

Readers and critics tending toward cultural relativism mention the "seldom, very seldom" passage—occurring as it does immediately after Mr. Knightley's proposal—as an indicator that all will not be well between Emma and Knightley in the future or that Emma has not learned her lesson. Here is the full passage:

> Seldom, very seldom, does complete truth belong to any human disclosure; seldom can it happen that something is not a little disguised, or a little mistaken; but where, as in this case, though the conduct is mistaken, the feelings are not, it may not be very material.—Mr. Knightley could not impute to Emma a more relenting heart than she possessed, or a heart more disposed to accept of his.[45]

These two sentences refer to the fact that Emma suffers under the impression that Mr. Knightley loves Harriet Smith. She decides not to reveal this final folly to him at this key moment. The narrator removes to a distance here and evaluates Emma's behavior explicitly, suggesting both that her "conduct is mistaken" and that this may not much matter since her feelings are genuine. At such a poignant moment, why does the narrator, who has just called Emma "a lady," continue to evaluate her propriety? Is the acknowledgment of imperfect communication at this moment anti-romantic?

Richard Handler and Daniel Segal, in their anthropological account of Austen's narrative authority, make the claim that such intrusions by the narrator mark a relativistic retreat from authority.[46] They claim that Austen exposes the fiction of narrative authority to replace the notion of objective truth with a sense of partial, contextual knowledge. The passage does indeed comment on the impossibility of the complete mutual transparency of souls that one might idealistically wish for in a marriage, but this was not a new idea for Austen and her milieu. Handler and Segal fall into the trap of exaggerating the degree of Austen's skepticism regarding authority and knowledge, or of confusing the kind of Enlightenment skepticism associated with Hume or Smith with its more postmodern kin. As cultural relativists, they tend to see only one half of her dynamic and do not see the didactic meaning that Austen attaches to her epistemological lessons. If "complete truth" could belong "to any human disclosure," without ambiguity or misinterpretation, what would be the use of sympathetic imagination or the art of human interpretation? This fact about human existence means that Emma's quixotic adventures in interpreting the world around her will never cease. She will neither be fully transparent nor subservient to Mr. Knightley. This lack of transparency neither makes her marriage less happy nor truth less objective; it gives opportunities for further adventures of existence and interpretation that we all share, within the novel and beyond its covers.

Titania Restored

Does anything actually change in the course of the novel? The closing resembles the opening, in that the same three people—Mr. Woodhouse, Emma, and Mr. Knightley—are seated together around the fire. And yet this idea is misleading. One could equally say that nothing happens in *A Midsummer Night's Dream,* since we return to the same wedding in Athens between Theseus and Hippolyta, with only a minor amendment or two in the arrangement of the guests. The fact that the intervening scenes in the forest occur at night and resemble a dream does not change the fact that much has occurred. Disorder was intensified and purged out of the system of the four young lovers, for one thing. This seemingly static or cyclical structure may function similarly in *Emma.* Emma and Mr. Knightley loved each other all along; it only took the greater disorder among the pairings for them (especially Emma) to recognize the preexisting fact. The intervening scenes were not a dream, of course, but many of the events were indeed the product of Emma's overactive imagination (as well as meddling).

Emma is a fantasy of Austen's only heroine who feels no financial pressure to marry. It is a fantasy about a woman with an existence more like a Regency man's. Claudia Johnson and others have commented on Emma's masculine performances, including her Pygmalion-like shaping of her Galatea, Harriet. In her happy ending, Emma has the luxury of playing the landed man's traditional role in not having to move his residence. She doesn't move; she remains at the center, and she suffers no loss of independence. The romantic resolution does, however, require a significant act of volition, particularly because of her father and the persistently anti-marriage (if not anti-life) force her father wields. Mr. Woodhouse places himself solidly against the possibility of happy endings by obstructing any change whatsoever.

Marriage in these ways paradoxically involves a greater extent of volition and self-shaping for Emma than for many other heroines. Like Austen's other witty and extroverted heroines, Emma's self-knowledge grows in the course of the novel, with partial epiphanies after Mr. Elton's proposal and (more fully) after the debacle at Box Hill. Her final, deeper self-awareness occurs when she thinks that Mr. Knightley is going to marry Harriet Smith. *Emma* thus follows the pattern of the heroine's achieving enlightenment when she has no hope of marrying the hero. Austen does therefore separate Emma's necessary enlightenment from the icing of her marriage to her old friend, "one of the few people who could see fault" in her.[47] Slippery as Emma's self-awareness is, it may take someone of Mr. Knightley's power to help her continue to hold on to the lessons that she learns, and will continue to learn.

And at the same time, Emma remains in power. One hopes her power ceases to be wanton, uninformed, and tyrannical through the guiding presence of a helpmate; however, the fact that Mr. Knightley moves into her terrain lets Emma still "reign[-] alone" like the "lovely woman" of Mr. Elton's charade.[48] Once again, Austen's ending fits neatly into neither conservative nor liberal molds. While there are certainly strongly conservative elements in the closure, partly by virtue of being a marriage plot, her relationship—partnership—with Mr. Knightley champions a more equal union. Partly because of the novel's involvement with separating English liberty from French repressive rule, the "English" art of happiness resists the female subservience so clearly prescribed in most marriage plots of Austen's time. The partnership modeled in Emma and Mr. Knightley's reading of Frank's letter becomes a model of shared observation and commentary that characterizes this new model of companionate marriage between two flawed individuals. For its time, it is radical indeed.

Clueless but Motivated

Clueless (1995), Amy Heckerling's brilliant adaptation of *Emma*, transposes the novel into 1990s high school life in Los Angeles.[49] In it, Heckerling masterfully plays with Austenian expectations of marriage without ever overtly acknowledging her source material. Jump cuts reveal leaps in interpretation. At the end of the film, when Josh and Cher finally kiss with only minutes left, Cher (the Emma character played by Alicia Silverstone) teases us in her role as narrator. "You can guess what happened next," she quips, just as the scene jump cuts from the kiss to a wedding. Then, as the wedding music starts to surge, she corrects what she just encouraged us to think: "As if! I'm only 16, and this is California, not Kentucky!" We are tempted, in a very Austenian move, to think it is Cher's and Josh's wedding. We instead discover it to be the wedding of two of Cher's teachers—the characters whom she has set up and who resemble the Westons in the plot in being her one successful experience of matchmaking. In this way, cinematic techniques masterfully re-create Austen's innovative literary techniques.

Ending with a wedding is one of the ways in which this film maintains what is expected of an Austen novel, even while having transposed the novel to the teen scene in California. The teasing role of the narrator neatly echoes Austen's own narrative techniques by encouraging us to wish for a romantic marriage, while simultaneously startling us out of our expectations and reminding us that we are watching a fiction. This clever film adeptly copies some of Austen's own devices, turning narrative techniques from *Emma* into cinematic effects in this retelling.

I will mention one other aspect of the film related to its ending. The final scene, the marriage of the Mrs. Weston and Mr. Weston analogues, returns us to the beginning of the novel. During this scene, the three girls—Cher, Dionne, and Tai (the Harriet character)—all make plans for their future weddings. Their three dates make fun of this, but they nonetheless bet on which of "their girls" will catch the bridal bouquet. What follows is a field hockey equivalent of the bridal toss. After a tussle that sends several participants tumbling to the ground, Cher triumphantly catches (or rather snatches) the bouquet (figure 21). This scene evokes for me another of the times that Austen uses characters' weaknesses to bring about positive events, including the final "happy" endings. It has always struck me that (the less appealing) reason that Emma eventually realizes that she wants to marry Mr. Knightley is that she "is never loth to be first."[50] She feels it demeaning when Mrs. Elton takes precedence as a new bride. Emma needs to become a bride and particularly bride to Mr. Knightley to cement her precedence for the future. Thus in this competitive bridal toss and Cher's determination to win, Heckerling

21. Wedding bouquet. *Clueless.*

(Paramount Pictures, 1995)

re-creates this competitive side of Emma, which helps lead to her conjugal conclusion.

Puncturing Perfection

Of the many period-costume adaptations of *Emma*, one stands out for its creativity: the 2020 *Emma*, directed by Autumn de Wilde and written by Eleanor Catton.[51] (The official title includes a period at the end: *Emma.*) This version stands out for its visually striking aesthetic and for the remarkably consistent centrality given to Emma the character, played by Anna Taylor-Joy. Yet the single most unusual directorial choice of the film relates to the happy ending, or more precisely, the proposal scene between Emma and Mr. Knightley.[52]

Emma's supposed superiority in de Wilde's film is conveyed through sumptuous material possessions, domineering attitudes over her staff, and carefully staged mis-en-scènes. Hardly a scene passes where Emma is not framed in perfect symmetry, claiming center stage to the camera. She is generally framed by glittering candelabras or colorfully fringed curtains, if not actually by the halves of her name as in the opening titles. Her perfect mastery echoes through choreographed sitting and standing, as though puppeteer of others' actions. Servants enter and leave in pairs, moving in choreographed synchrony.[53] Emma's invisible hand extends with tyrannical accuracy over the domestic scenes, and there is little relief from the perfection that she craves. Even her matchmaking stems from her own contrivances: "there is such symmetry between us," she remarks about herself and Frank, suggesting that the director's favorite trope has a psychological role for Emma as well. Our relief from the overwhelming tyranny of symmetry occurs only in relation to Mr. Martin and Harriet's subplot. Each time we move from Hartfield to the Martins, the music begins to soar with earthy folk music and the diegetic winds begin to blow. There is freedom in the Martins' world, beyond the reach of Emma's contrivance.

If the casting of Anya Taylor-Joy misses the mark, it is because the Emma of the novel is livelier in imagination, more genuinely sympathetic, and more playful in spirit. We are told on more than one occasion that Emma's temper is "open," and this trait appeals greatly to Mr. Knightley. In a novel where there are so many riddles, charades, mysteries, clues, and obfuscations, open tempers come as a relief. True, the mysteries and complexities are often of Emma's making, but her openness mitigates this flaw in a novel where the character named "Frank" is the least so. In the film, playfulness is sacrificed to the subtle tyranny of conformity and surface order, which Emma uses to her advantage. This lends power to the moments when Emma is suddenly *not* on central stage.

But let us return to de Wilde's creative choices in the proposal scene. Up to this point in the film, Emma has been portrayed as and through a carefully manicured visual perfection. No curl is out of place, no outfit with matching jewelry less than exquisite. Emma is front and center in almost every scene. Not only is she coiffed and spectacularly dressed, but the camera also seems to caress and pamper her. The type of perfection built up to surround Emma in the film is an external sort—the kind of worshipful, spectatorial sense of awe that the Coles might feel in relation to their more genteel neighbor. In that sense, the viewer of *Emma* remains an outsider, a spectator upon the sumptuous visual displays, whereas the reader in *Emma* feeds on the interplay among the different manifestations of Emma—Emma as she thinks of herself, Emma as she reveals herself to be, and Emma as she is seen by others. In the book, readers experience the world from Emma's own perspective enough to make mistakes of interpretation alongside her, yet they also exist outside of Emma enough to criticize her and see her moral failings and intellectual errors. We can love her, err with her, and judge her.[54] There are far fewer chinks in Anya Taylor-Joy's armor, however. We are constantly distracted from any moral lessons or deeper human connections by vividly colored macaroons, glittering hair ornaments, immaculately embroidered dresses, and other tokens of superficial beauty reminiscent of the surface frivolity of Sofia Coppola's *Marie Antoinette*.

As readers, we might feel frustration when we are not allowed to hear Emma's acceptance of Mr. Knightley's proposal. De Wilde humanizes this moment greatly. The viewer well versed in the novel, who is anticipating the momentous revelation of the secret words behind "What did she say? Just what she ought," is instead greeted by an exceedingly ill-timed nosebleed. De Wilde and the screenwriters do indeed add Emma's words to the proposal scene, but they are not what one might expect. The nosebleed that punctures Mr. Knightley's proposal is one of the most unusual ways of distracting

22. Nuptial nosebleed. *Emma.*

(Working Title Films, Blueprint Pictures, Perfect World Pictures, 2020)

the viewer from immersion in the happy ending that I've ever seen (figure 22).

In the film, Emma is disgusted at Jane Fairfax's coldness, calling her a "statue." De Wilde's choice ensures that we do not carry away the same feelings toward Emma herself. In fact, the brilliance of the nosebleed in the proposal scene is that it highlights the relationship between the "lady" and the "woman" who is Emma. The bright red trail of blood stands out in remarkable contrast to the delicate white fabrics and blossoms surrounding her and Mr. Knightley. Emma's humanity bleeds through her perfectly manicured, ironed, and embroidered facade to display her own human frailty at this key moment. (It may also slyly allude to the rupture of her maidenhead.) At the same time, Emma never answers Mr. Knightley's question in the film. Their intimacy does not advance through words but instead through physical contact. A closeup of a sturdily gloved hand gives way in a subsequent scene to a more thinly laced glove

23. Alpha at sunrise. *Emma.*

(Working Title Films, Blueprint Pictures, Perfect World Pictures, 2020)

at the marriage altar. Unusually, the film elides even *more* of Emma's words (and their entire period of engagement) than the novel does. One could say, once again, that despite the intervening two centuries, the film is more conventional than Austen's novel, and that the film's protagonist is not nearly as complex.

So far from "zooming out" to consider Emma's place in her greater society, Emma's central dominance of the screen is so consistent in the film that the viewer is jarred the two or three times she loses her visual centrality. At Donwell Abbey, for example, Emma fades out of focus as it becomes clear that Mr. Knightley intends to converse with Harriet instead of Emma. De Wilde brilliantly uses focus to convey dramatic irony. In another scene, Jane Fairfax and Emma take turns in the field of focus as Frank Churchill skillfully pays attention to both ladies at once. Emma's gradual "mortification" (as modest as it may be overall in this adaptation) is also portrayed through the withdrawal of focus. The moments when her face goes out of focus in

24. Omega at wedding. *Emma.*

(Working Title Films, Blueprint Pictures, Perfect World Pictures, 2020)

favor of others help develop her growing recognition of her jealousy of other women sharing in Mr. Knightley's affections.[55]

Ultimately, though, the most profound modernization of the ending in this film is Emma's awakening to her own class snobbery. Her blubberings in the proposal scene (easily missed, thanks to the spectacular nosebleed) relate to her concern for wounding Harriet. Ironically, here she reveals the very fact to which the "seldom, yet seldom" passage refers (Emma's suspicion that Knightley loves Harriet). The "seldom revealed" truth is precisely what Emma *does* speak when Mr. Knightley proposes in the film. The modern twist makes Harriet more than a plaything. Their friendship continues to the end of this adaptation, and Harriet's previously unknown father, a "galoshes-selling tradesman," is invited to Hartfield.

De Wilde also innovates a cinematic portrayal of Emma's would-be authorship of the stories around her. The film begins as Emma, head lying on a silk-trimmed pillow, just opens her eyes in an early dawn (figure 23); the film ends as her lace-covered eyes close upon the audience at the altar (figure 24). Emma's vision literally brackets the film itself. As the title's period suggests, Emma is a sentence unto herself. She is alpha and omega to this film adaptation. None may question her absolute dominion. This cinematic trick makes Emma the author of the film's action, in a sense. And yet, perhaps, perfection should not have come quite so soon or quite as completely. With such perfections, only a nosebleed can bring her down to human proportions.[56]

Emma the novel is colored and shaped by the rich, lively, unruly, and unreliable tapestry of Emma's mind. No cinematic adaptation has succeeded in capturing her rich and imaginative engagement with the world. The adaptations tend to whittle her down to a spoiled rich girl, as mischievous, selfish, or in need of mortification. In this way, the films are often less progressive than Austen's original. De Wilde's film is no exception: fetishizing her wealth diminishes her to the love of finery, or worse—as a plaything for viewers who are fascinated by Regency culture. In addition, no adaptation completely captures her generous patience toward her father. It seems that De Wilde and some other filmmakers think this attribute would make her seem weak.[57]

Emma, like Shakespeare's Titania, has made love to an ass, paired people wrongly, and had to give up her little pet creature. In the end of both novel and play, order is restored through her (re)-union with her more rational husband. Despite these superficial plot similarities to *A Midsummer Night's Dream*, Emma is more Amazonian—more like Hippolyta—than like Titania. Like Emma and Mr. Knightley, Hippolyta and Theseus comment amicably on the play performed by Bottom and his Mechanicals, as Emma and Mr. Knightley comment on Frank's letter and review the events of the novel. Yet the comparison with Shakespeare's *A Midsummer*

Night's Dream really does not do the novel justice. Emma is more powerful and independent than either of the play's heroines; Austen is more radical in her subversion of the mentor-suitor plot than Shakespeare; and the novel is much more progressive in its creation of a new model of companionate marriage of equals. Rather than silencing Emma, Austen gives her word new weight. Emma *as* author is somewhat chastened, but Austen is not. Empowered by this masterpiece about the beauties and temptations of authorship, Austen must have felt at the height of her powers.

CHAPTER 6

Resources for Solitude

Who can be in doubt of what followed? When any two young people take it into their heads to marry, they are pretty sure by perseverance to carry their point, be they ever so poor, or ever so imprudent, or ever so little likely to be necessary to each other's ultimate comfort.

JANE AUSTEN, *Persuasion*

Persuasion, Austen's final complete novel, potently engages with near misses and second chances. In fact, *Persuasion* begins where Austen threatens to go in her other novels—with the *failure* of a marriage plot. Anne Elliot found a true and requited love eight years before the novel's action, yet this courtship did not end in marriage. The novel's very premise thus invites contemplation of the many ways in which the romantic happy ending can be foiled. As such, many of the lessons that Austen has implanted into the endings of her other novels are conveyed more indirectly, more organically in this novel. Having witnessed Anne's suffering from the first chapter of the novel untempered by competing demands for our sympathy,[1] the implied reader longs for a second chance and Anne's final marriage. Because of this context, Austen gives us a narrator with less reticence at the conclusion and spares the reader from a jarringly rapid change in pace. Yet Austen still includes several of her anti-romantic flourishes in this novel, including rhetorical questions, a reference to narrator as author, and ironic hyperbole. Why does Austen include such distancing techniques in *Persuasion*, making us aware of its fictionality? This seems a cruel blow to a heroine like Anne, who "had been forced into prudence in her youth, [and . . .] learned romance as she grew older."[2] If ever an Austen heroine deserved a romantic happy ending, it is Anne.

In this novel, Austen also invites comparison with Shakespeare's *King Lear*, another work with a complex interweaving of comedy and tragedy, especially as rewritten by Nahum Tate in the late seventeenth century. Tate's was the version performed most during Austen's lifetime. The original Shakespeare play opens with a father ignominiously and foolishly dividing up his land and evaluating the love of his three daughters. In the end, most of the main characters die, including Cordelia, the wisest of the daughters. Part of the rationale for Tate's revision was that Shakespeare's original was too cruel to Cordelia, too unjust overall. The revised version, while still called a "tragedy," saves her life and centers more on a romance between Edgar and Cordelia, who end up happily married and as sole rulers of Lear's kingdom, despite the fact that the two characters never speak to each other in the original version. In Tate's version, the only two major characters to die are the two unworthy sisters.

Anne, like Cordelia, is the sole daughter who refuses to flatter her father, and she suffers because of his disdain.[3] Miss Clay is preferred over Anne because, like the sisters in *Lear*, she knows how to flatter. Like Cordelia, "Anne's word had no weight" in her immediate family,[4] and she is only appreciated by outsiders after the expulsion from her home (Kent and Lady Russell, respectively). The profound sense of solitude within a family setting—exemplified by both Cordelia and Anne—colors the meaning of the happy ending in this novel. Like Cordelia, Anne's life has tragic overtones of loss. The world of both these heroines is full of injustice: the wrong people inherit, the wrong people control public opinion, the wrong people wield authority. A restoration, with Anne in her mother's place as Lady Elliot, appears only as an alternative ending; it is considered—even offered—but never fulfilled. As with Cordelia, Anne could have been elevated to a high social position with considerable power, but only at the cost of her conscience. Yet, as in Shakespeare's tragedy—and alone in Austen's opus—this novel ends *without* a restoration of order.

Solutions to some of these social and political problems are simpler at sea than on land. Austen ameliorates Anne's world through her treatment of the navy. With the shadow of the Napoleonic wars in mind, the navy offers an alternative, meritocratic style of authority that Austen portrays idealistically. Nonetheless, the novel invites new considerations with regard to Austen's happy endings. Tate's *Lear* hovers over the novel, offering an alternative ending much more satisfying for distributive justice than Austen's own ending. Ironically, there is more justice distributed at the end of Tate's "tragedy" than at the end of Austen's comic "happy ending."

Persuasion affords the rare opportunity for understanding the craft of Austen's endings. All other manuscripts were apparently destroyed once the books were published, but the "cancelled chapters" of *Persuasion*'s ending can help reveal Austen's thought process and goals. In the revised, published chapters, Austen still includes several of her characteristic anti-romantic flourishes; however, they have a new poignancy in this novel, where romance has been willfully stifled within the plot. In addition to the anti-romantic techniques mentioned in previous chapters, the canceled chapters reveal that Austen attempts but fails multiple times in her drafts to attribute "perfection" to the ultimate romantic union. Also, darkness clouds the horizon: "the dread of a future war all that could dim her sunshine."[5] Only a few pages from the end, Anne's resolution still feels remote: she "was deep in the happiness of such misery, or the misery of such happiness"—grief, loss, happiness, and relief are tightly intertwined in the novel.[6] Austen achieves *Persuasion*'s vaunted "autumnal" flavor by mixing elements of death and rebirth, loss and hope, grief and happiness.

Persuasion is undoubtedly Austen's most romantic "happy ending," greatly colored by loss. For this reason, the strongest moral lessons included in this novel have more to do with how to live one's life in the *absence* of happy endings. The loss suffered here is more than just individual. Anne is the only Austen heroine who does not end with a landed estate. Anne's temptation to marry Mr. Elliot stems from her desire to follow her mother as Lady Elliot of Kellynch Hall, redeem her family estate from its current dissolution, and generally exercise the power of doing good. In marrying Wentworth and Anne, Austen depicts a societal shift away from the landed gentry toward a more democratic distribution of wealth, as well as a greater meritocracy modeled by naval reward system. Austen's final heroine may be more directly applicable to our contemporary experience for this reason. As we will see, Anne is a master in "the art of knowing our own nothingness,"[7] which helps her accept human subjectivity and limit any utopian ambitions. She also has "resources for solitude" that lend her composure in the face of disappointment.[8] Imbedded in this, the last of Austen's lessons in happy endings, are the most explicit tools for facing their absence. Whereas in both *Sense and Sensibility* and *Mansfield Park* Austen established familial restoration at the expense of the romantic resolution, here we see the reverse: Anne's personal happy ending occurs at the cost of her ability to rectify her family's estate and fortune.

Austen's Revised Ending

The differences between Austen's original and revised endings are profound. The contrast gives us an insight into not only how she edited her novels generally, but also and especially her ideas of what would constitute better and worse conclusions.

Several of Austen's changes increase agency on the part of Anne and especially Wentworth. In the first, canceled version, the final romantic resolution between Anne and Wentworth comes about largely at the instigation of Admiral Croft. Admiral Croft sends Wentworth to Anne to deliver a message regarding Kellynch Hall. Wentworth must deliver the awkward message that the Crofts want to offer Anne the return of Kellynch Hall upon her marriage to Mr. Elliot. It's unclear why Wentworth is the one who must relay this message, but the mission conveniently enables them to clear up the impression that Anne is going to marry Mr. Elliot. In the canceled chapters, others' decisions and chance dominate the resolution, including the good fortune of a "gentle, steady rain"[9] to keep them inside the same house for long enough to reach an understanding. Austen's first version includes neither the famous scene of the overheard conversation between Anne and Captain Harville nor Wentworth's written response to it. *Persuasion* without Wentworth's letter seems unthinkable!

Austen's first version shows greater narratorial reticence and a desire to summarize romantic conversations, as so often in past novels. In the revised version, Austen rewards the reader with a more direct expression of Anne's thoughts about love and loyalty, while also hearing a complete and romantic declaration in the letter from Wentworth. In the face of the rumors and shifting misunderstandings that permeate this novel, a tangible written declaration is particularly gratifying to both Anne and the reader. Austen's revisions to the ending also increase the sense of equality between Anne and Wentworth: this includes Anne's speech on the gendering of attachment, her attack on the skewed portrayal of women in literature, Austen's own portrayal of Anne's heroism, and a transfer of authority from Wentworth to Anne.

Austen's earlier ending for *Persuasion* includes more of the kinds of anti-romantic intrusions that we have been considering in this book. The narrator is far more involved as an author and intrudes with multiple rhetorical questions that are excised from the final ending, such as "[I]f she did not return to the charge with unconquerable Perseverance, or did not with a more passive Determination walk quietly out of the room—(as she certainly might have done) may she not be pardoned?" and "If she *had* no horror of a few minutes Tête-à-Tête with Capt. W—, may she not be pardoned for not wishing to give him the idea that she *had*?"[10] Austen first defaults to familiar disruptive techniques but decides in favor of more organic choices.

Persuasion differs from the novels that precede it in that Anne never receives the familial recognition that Elinor and Fanny receive in their respective novels. Ultimately, *Persuasion* refuses the restoration generally associated with comedies and the marriage plot. It is the only one of her novels where the ending is really a *break* from the past, *separating* the heroine further from her family. It is the only novel that ends without the heroine's becoming mistress of an estate or fixed residence: "Anne had no Uppercross Hall before her, no landed estate, no headship of a family." Instead, Anne becomes "the mistress of a very pretty landaulette."[11] Rather than becoming the mistress of an estate, Anne becomes the mistress of a vehicle. She is Austen's only traveling heroine, and the mobility alone marks this novel as a departure from the more traditional marriage plot's restoration of order and stable community.

The Allure of Perfection

As we have seen, Austen thrives in portraying subtle combinations of comedy and tragedy as well as the thin coating of fortune that separates one from the other. This is true particularly of the novels whose heroines are quieter and more introspective. *Sense and Sensibility*, *Mansfield Park*, and *Persuasion* might have been labeled "problem novels," if we could transfer the term used for the Shakespeare's tragicomic plays. In *Persuasion*, the narrator pointedly reminds the reader, again and again, how easily her endings could have been less "perfect." Near the end of *Persuasion*, for example, the narrator poignantly asks: "Who can be in doubt of what followed? When any two young people take it into their heads to marry, they are pretty sure by perseverance to carry their point, be they ever so poor, or ever so imprudent, or ever so little likely to be necessary to each other's ultimate comfort."[12]

But it is actually quite easy to imagine the story ending otherwise, especially since it did so eight years earlier, when these same two young people did not "carry their point." The question and rejoinder open the final chapter at a moment of uncertainty before receiving Wentworth's letter. Even *after* receiving the letter from Wentworth in the final chapter, Anne's "heart prophesied some mischance, to damp the perfection of her felicity."[13] Anne knows from experience that one cannot rely on fortune, and the rhetorical question mocks the reader's sense of the "tell-tale compression of the pages." This disjunction points to the highly contingent nature of marriage as a resolution, even when the love is mutual.

Austen's hyperbolic use of the word "perfect" helps demonstrate her explicit insistence on the comic harmony established by her novels. The word "perfect," generally a rare word for the understated Austen, appears prominently at the end of most of the novels. The word both asserts the happiness of the ending and simultaneously punctures it through ironic hyperbole. The word "perfect" appears twice at the last paragraphs of *Northanger Abbey*, as well as in the final lines of both *Emma* and *Mansfield Park*. She uses this word to expose readers' expectations of happy endings.

At the end of *Emma*, for example, even after warning us that "perfect happiness is not common, even in memory," we hear successively that Emma and Mr. Knightley undergo "Such a change! . . . From perfect misery to perfect happiness!"; that "Within an hour [Mr. Knightley] had passed from a thoroughly distressed state of mind to . . . perfect happiness"[14]; and in the final words of the novel, that "the wishes, the hopes, the confidence, the predictions of the small band of true friends who witnessed the ceremony, were fully answered in the perfect happiness of the[ir] union."[15] In *Northanger Abbey*, we learn that the reader and characters are "hastening together to perfect felicity," and by the end of the novel, that "to begin perfect happiness at the respective ages of twenty-six and eighteen, is to do pretty well."[16] Even by the end of *Mansfield Park*, arguably the darkest of the novels, Fanny Price finds Mansfield Parsonage "as thoroughly perfect in her eyes, as every thing else, within the view and patronage of Mansfield Park, had long been."[17]

The manuscript chapters of *Persuasion* tellingly reveal how stubbornly Austen tries to assert this perfection. In her revisions of the final chapters, she tries three successive times to attribute perfection to Captain Wentworth. Attempt 1: "Captain Wentworth's aid in recovering Mrs. Smith's property convinced her of his being [. . .] nearer Perfection, than her intercourse with the World had . . ."; Attempt 2: "And having done so much for her[,] scarcely could his wife [. . .] think him nearer perfection"; Attempt 3: "Mrs. Smith's estimate of his Perfections could be surpassed only by [that of his] Wife[—]."[18] Yet none of these options satisfied Austen. Nonetheless, her line about Anne's perfection in the penultimate chapter remains unchanged from early draft to final copy: "Her character was now fixed on [Wentworth's] mind as perfection itself." Significantly, the locus of "perfection" near the end of *Persuasion* remains Anne rather than Wentworth.

It seems odd, even allowing for the more ironic passages, that one who wrote in a letter to her niece Fanny Knight that "pictures of perfection as you know make me sick & wicked" (Letter to Fanny, Mar. 23–25, 1817), and who criticized novelists' attempts to draw overly virtuous characters in favor of "mixed" or probable characters, should in her own endings seem to contradict this principle. The reader is likely to feel, along with Mr. Knightley at Box Hill, that "perfection should not have come so soon."[19] Again, why would Austen advise and uphold realism in regard to character but not in regard to plot? What is the function of her insistence upon comic resolution, amounting most often to ironic hyperbole? She certainly was painfully aware, as she writes in her juvenilia, that "Perfect Felicity is not the property of Mortals, and no one has a right to expect uninterrupted Happiness."[20]

Part of her inspiration for her invective against "pictures of perfection" is most likely the "perfect heroine" convention that Austen loved to mock. Austen most likely disapproves for didactic reasons: overly "perfect" heroines either decrease emotional involvement on the reader's part or lead to slavish imitation, as Richardson promoted through his published volumes collecting moral sayings from his heroines. Such unrealistically exemplary heroines include not only Richardson's heroines but also Charlotte Smith's heroines, Louisa in Jane West's *A Gossip's Story,* and Laura, the heroine of Mary Brunton's *Self-Control,* though most are less extraordinary than Radcliffe's Emily St. Aubert of *Udolpho*. To some extent, these heroines vie with one another for perfection. Laura of *Self-Control* judges Miss Julia Dawkins on her simplistic caricature of another fictional paragon, Louisa: "Having no character of her own, Julia was always, as nearly as she was able, the heroine whom the last read novel inclined her to personate. But [. . .] her copies were always caricatures. [. . .] After perusing the Gossip's story, she, in imitation of the rational Louisa, suddenly waxed very wise—spoke in sentences—despised romances—sewed shifts—and read sermons."[21] The Austen family's own copy of *Self-Control* from Godmersham still exists and is now owned by Chawton House, where I examined its marginalia. While it is impossible to be certain that any marginalia is in Austen's own hand, there is a placement of exclamation marks at several points (and even the word "stupid") where the heroine is being particularly sanctimonious.

Even in *Persuasion*, Austen cannot resist puncturing her heroine's romantic aspirations. After the concert, where Anne is buoyed by detecting Wentworth's jealousy, Anne walks to see her friend Mrs. Smith. The narrator describes that "prettier musings of high-wrought love and eternal constancy, could never have passed along the streets of Bath, than Anne was sporting with from Camden-place to Westgate-buildings. It was almost enough to spread purification and perfume all the way." To anyone familiar with Bath, however, this final "almost" is significant, as purification was greatly needed, particularly near Westgate Buildings, where there were "great Hot Beds of Dung."[22] Even in this most flowery narration of Anne's happiness, therefore, her joy is checked by horrid pollution and muck. Austen, unlike Anne, is unwilling to ignore the decay around her. Rather than Elinor's demeaning cow pasturage or Emma's helpful poultry thieves, the final deflating image here is decidedly more urban in nature.

A final example from *Persuasion* can help elucidate Austen's dogged pursuit of perfection a little further. After trying three times to attribute "perfection" to Wentworth in her ending, Austen's final published novel uses the word very differently in its final paragraph. It is used in a subjunctive description of an alternate reality for Mrs. Smith: "She might have been absolutely rich and perfectly healthy, and yet be happy."[23] Austen pulls the rug out from under the attractions of perfection here by suggesting that good fortune can paradoxically *diminish* one's ability to be happy. She underscores what has been implicit in all her mature novels—that suffering enhances one's appreciation of, and perhaps even chances of, eventual happiness.[24]

Luxurious Indulgence of Hope

As we have seen, Austen's endings mediate between comedy and tragedy, between romance and anti-romance, between hope and despair. Austen clearly learned from her mentor Dr. Johnson about the dangers of hope, that the "understanding of man, naturally sanguine, may, indeed, be easily vitiated by the luxurious indulgence of hope," and yet that hope is also, in his words again, "necessary to the production of every thing great or excellent."[25] Hope for a happy ending motivates us to try to shape our lives to the best of our abilities; however, excessive reliance on future outcomes will generally lead to disappointment and cynical detachment, as we saw beginning to happen with Elizabeth Bennet. Like Dr. Johnson, Austen teaches her reader to hope to learn to be a hero(ine), but also to tolerate their fate in the absence of a happy ending.

In one of our first encounters with Anne in the novel, the narrator reveals her sentiments regarding hope and happy endings. "How eloquent could Anne Elliot have been! how eloquent, at least, were her wishes on the side of early warm attachment, and a cheerful confidence in futurity, against that over-anxious caution which seems to insult exertion and distrust Providence! She had been forced into prudence in her youth, she learned romance as she grew older: the natural sequel of an unnatural beginning."[26]

This "unnatural beginning" was her thwarted happy ending over eight years earlier, when Lady Russell convinced her to give up her engagement to Wentworth in favor of prudence. The action of the novel itself is thus the "natural sequel" of "learning romance." Learning romance is here associated with "a cheerful confidence in futurity"—both in what we can control (achieve through our own "exertion") and what is outside our control (in the divine hands of "Providence").

This sheds light on another aspect of Austen's strange endings: after trying to insert a form of the word "perfect" into the ending at least three different ways, Austen gives marked prominence to Mrs. Smith in *Persuasion*'s last lines. This choice seems a bit odd for a minor character and could be seen as detracting from a reader's desire to hear more of the newly engaged Anne and Wentworth. Austen uses strong language to describe Mrs. Smith's cheerful disposition in the face of disappointment, calling it "the choicest gift of heaven."[27] While recounting the material improvements in Mrs. Smith's life at the end of the novel, the narrator surprisingly states that

> Mrs. Smith's enjoyments were *not* spoiled by this improvement of income, . . . improvement of health, and the acquisition of such friends . . ., for her cheerfulness and mental alacrity did not fail her; and while these prime supplies of good remained, she might have bid defiance even to greater accessions of worldly prosperity. She might have been absolutely rich and perfectly healthy, and yet be happy. Her spring of felicity was in the glow of her spirits, as her friend Anne's was in the warmth of her heart.[28]

Despite her many innovative strategies and structural precautions, Austen's narrator nonetheless needs to inform us that the happy ending does not corrupt even those who, luckily and fictitiously, experience it within the life of the novel itself. Austen includes a similar line about Wentworth himself, in the last words he speaks in the novel: "I must endeavor to subdue my mind to my fortune. I must learn to brook being happier than I deserve."[29] A similar line is ventured for Anne: "An interval of meditation, serious and grateful, was the best corrective of everything dangerous in such high-wrought felicity, and she went to her room and grew steadfast and fearless in the thankfulness of her enjoyment."[30] Rather than the perspective of an embittered spinster refusing enjoyment to those who have suffered, and rather than the techniques of an author who has caved in to convention and its obligatory happy endings, such flourishes instead belong to an author who, although she probably knows she is dying at an early age, refuses to succumb to despair.

Knowing Our Own Nothingness

Shakespeare, of course, allows the saintly Cordelia to die at the end of his play. Audiences from the Restoration up through Jane Austen's lifetime felt this was too cruel, and used the revised ending that Tate wrote rather than enact such an unjust end. The overtones from *King Lear*'s plot might evoke in the reader (both of Austen's time and today) a familiar sense of doom that contrasts with the expectations of the marriage plot. The novel, like the play, also dramatizes the gap between those who know how to shape the world and those who have the power to do so. In *Persuasion* as in *Lear*, those most worthy to rule seldom have the power to do so. Austen determines to reward her most mature heroine; however, the degree of suffering that she has experienced makes for an ending that differs in tone from all her other novels.

As in Shakespeare's play, negations and the word "nothing" do outsized work to set the heroine apart from the other characters. Our first introduction to Anne is through the eyes of Sir Walter, and in contrast to his eldest daughter Elizabeth: "Anne, with an elegance of mind and sweetness of character, which must have placed her high with any people of real understanding, was *nobody* with either father or sister; *her word had no weight*, her convenience was always to give way—*she was only Anne.*"[31] Those who are nothing to us cannot persuade us, because we are not creatures moved by reason alone. Anne's words have no weight *because* she is "nothing" to Sir Walter and Elizabeth. The willingness to be persuaded is also an act of love.

In *Persuasion*, the use of the words "nothing" and "nobody" underscores the degree to which our subjectivity and prejudices can blind us to others. Austen frequently contrasts Elizabeth's affection for Mrs. Clay with her indifference to Anne in these terms. Lady Russell feels that "never had [Elizabeth] pursued [her own will] in more decided opposition [. . .] than in this selection of Mrs Clay; turning from the society of so deserving a sister, to bestow her affection and confidence on one who ought to have been *nothing* to her but the object of distant civility."[32] Elizabeth uses the same word to Mrs. Clay about Anne: "[Anne] is *nothing* to me, compared with you."[33] Similarly, in recounting the distant past, when Elizabeth and Sir Walter thought that even for Anne a marriage to Wentworth was degrading, they refer to him as "nothing"; however, his wealth ultimately gives him existence in their sight. Eight and a half years later, therefore, "Captain Wentworth, with five-and-twenty thousand pounds, and as high in his profession as merit and activity could place him, was *no longer nobody.*"[34] Being "nothing" or "nobody" to someone thus reveals the prejudices of the evaluator: Lady Russell values Anne, Elizabeth dislikes her, and Sir Walter cares only about wealth, rank, appearance, and himself.

Anne is not innocent of using this kind of evaluation and negation in relation to Lady Dalrymple and Miss Carteret, her distant relations. Anne is disgusted by her family's fawning attentions to these repellant individuals: "Anne was ashamed. Had Lady Dalrymple and her daughter even been very agreeable, she would still have been ashamed of the agitation they created, but they were *nothing*. There was no superiority of manner, accomplishment, or understanding."[35]

Anne defines being *something* as having "superiority of manner, accomplishment, or understanding." Anne clarifies her ideas further in a conversation with Mr. William Elliot: "the company of clever, well-informed people, who have a great deal of conversation; that is what I call good company." In general, Austen and Anne use this phrase to distinguish superficial concerns for status from deeper individual connections.[36]

Deeply imbedded in *Persuasion*, from the early chapters, are tools for self-improvement in the absence of happy endings. This leads us to the most important use of this concept of nothingness—"the art of knowing our own nothingness":

> Anne had not wanted this visit to Uppercross, to learn that a removal from one set of people to another, though at a distance of only three miles, will often include a total change of conversation, opinion, and idea. She had never been staying there before, without being struck by it, or without wishing that other Elliots could have her advantage in seeing how unknown, or unconsidered there, were the affairs which at Kellynch Hall were treated as of such general publicity and pervading interest; yet, with all this experience, she believed she must now submit to feel that another lesson, in *the art of knowing our own nothingness* beyond our own circle, was become necessary for her.[37]

Physical distance is helpful to Anne in approximating an impartial spectator's view. It is easy to assume that others care about what is of most central importance to ourselves. This quiet selfishness and egocentrism can be mitigated by "the art of knowing our own nothingness." But the mock-heroic scale of this passage makes an additional point. Austen describes Anne's travel of only three miles between households as being from "commonwealth" to commonwealth with "a total change of conversation, opinion, and idea," as though she were a naval hero crossing oceans.[38] The fact that the lesson in "nothingness" applies at such a tiny distance underscores the separation within her family and her isolation from all. Anne has known little of the playful camaraderie she witnesses among both the Musgroves and the sailors: "that seemingly perfect good understanding and agreement together, that good-humoured mutual affection, of which she had known so little herself with either of her sisters."[39] Such affection by definition lessens the effect of distance upon the tendency to forget others' perspectives. The great contrast here is the love between Anne and Wentworth, which survives separation from the other side of the world.

Most likely, the author herself, traveling from her cottage in Chawton to the Chawton Great House or to Edward's Godmersham Park estate and back to Chawton again—as well as to the many households in Southampton, Bath, and elsewhere that she visited in her itinerant years—learned the "art of knowing our own nothingness" through similar means. The gendering is reversed here to disguise the connections between Austen and her heroine: Austen visited her brothers' homes rather than her sisters', and she also disliked Bath, not as Anne does for associations with the death of her mother, but instead for associations with the death of her father and the ensuing years without a fixed home. Austen also had to "plead" with her brother Edward, among others, for transportation to visit her friends in a neighboring town, not having a carriage at her own disposal. "It had not crossed anyone's mind that she might have plans of her own," and she could not come and go as she pleased.[40] The thought of having a landaulette at her own disposal must have been the stuff of fantasy indeed.

Stuart Tave and Mary De Forest, among others, have written about the similarity between *Persuasion* and Homer's *Odyssey*, largely because of the strong role of travel and the homelessness of the heroine. Some readings figure Anne as Penelope waiting for the return of her love, Captain Wentworth, who most literally is sailing around the sea, unable to return (he thinks) to his love. There are also reasons for seeing Anne as the heroic traveler in this novel: Anne, not Wentworth, is described as the person traveling to "every little social commonwealth" in the novel, and when there is an emergency, Anne is the one that the world-traveling, hardy—yet oddly dependent—sailors look to for guidance. In the mock-heroic tradition that Austen gently uses to stretch the definitions of female heroism, she challenges the gendering of courage to put Anne at the same level as the naval captains. In a real sense, Anne is *both* Penelope and Odysseus. It takes her understanding of travel, regardless of actual distances, to learn the "art of knowing our own nothingness."[41] While she does not have the freedom for actual travel, she has the mental capacity that may be even rarer than the opportunity. Others, like her father and sisters, could travel the world without ever seeing beyond their own myopic horizons.

Nonetheless, Austen allows such selfish meanness into the final pages of the novel. We learn that Mary, while happy that Anne was marrying someone richer than the Musgrove sisters' husbands, "had something to suffer perhaps when [she and Anne] came into contact again, in seeing Anne restored to the rights of seniority, and the mistress of a very pretty landaulette; but she had a future to look forward to of powerful consolation. Anne had no Uppercross-hall before her, no landed estate, no headship of a family; and if they could but keep Captain Wentworth from being made a baronet, she would not change situations with Anne."[42] It is tempting on first reading this passage to think that the "powerful consolations" of a future with Wentworth, and so on, are Anne's. But the passage and the sentiment are much meaner: the "powerful consolations" are *Mary's* in recognizing the limitations of Anne's good fortune compared to her own. The final line almost suggests that Mary will actively work to ensure that Wentworth rises no further. Austen's decision to include this pettiness in the ending of the novel is similar to her allowing Mrs. Elton to narrate Emma's wedding. It shows that one of the ways Austen tempers her happy endings is refusing to silence her selfish characters unrealistically.

Resources for Solitude

While at the Musgroves', we learn that Anne's younger sister Mary cannot tolerate solitude:

> [B]eing alone, [Mary's] being unwell and out of spirits was almost a matter of course. Though better endowed than the elder sister, Mary had not Anne's understanding nor temper. While well, and happy, and properly attended to, she had great good humour and excellent spirits; but any indisposition sunk her completely. She had no *resources for solitude*; and inheriting a considerable share of the Elliot self-importance, was very prone to add to every other distress that of fancying herself neglected and ill-used.[43]

Whenever Mary is alone, she is also "unwell and out of spirits." What is it about Anne's "understanding or temper" that gives her such resilience and "resources for solitude"?

In a recent article, Janice Hadlow writes that resilience is what Austen prizes most in her heroines. It is also key, Hadlow says, for understanding the harsh treatment that Austen gives to some of her characters, particularly Mrs. Musgrove: "In *Persuasion,* [Austen] has no patience with Mrs. Musgrove's rose-tinted recollections of her dead sailor son, tartly reminding us that the 'poor Richard' for whom everyone is now lamenting, was when alive merely 'thick-headed, unprofitable Dick Musgrove' whom nobody much cared for. His mother's 'fat sighings' are, she suggests, really nothing more than self-indulgence. What Austen really prizes is resilience. All her favorite characters display it."[44] If Anne Elliot is the best example of these "resources," the young Marianne Dashwood is one of the least: "*Sense and Sensibility*'s Marianne comes closest to giving into despair, but even she finds the courage to claw her way back to a chastened resignation of her lot. We cannot afford, Austen suggests, to allow ourselves the bitter pleasure of surrendering to terrible events. We need to find a little iron in our souls if we're not to be crushed by the horrors the world throws at us."[45] As we saw, ironic detachment can easily become excessive and devolve into "spleen" in the case of the wittier Bennets. Despair is of course an alternative response to disappointment, one to which Marianne Dashwood nearly succumbs.

Austen's message here, as so often in her works, responds to the novel of sensibility, in which so many protagonists die, often by their own hands. Marianne herself, as I have written elsewhere, is modeled on one such character, the eponymous hero of Goethe's *The Sorrows of Young Werther*. Resilience curtails these alternative responses to inevitable disappointment: detachment, despair, and self-destruction. One could in fact say that resources for solitude are also resources for disappointment. As Janice Hadlow writes, "Austen's coolly pragmatic attitude to the management of despondency doesn't make me love her any less. I can rejoice in the escape she offers from the pressures of a hostile world; but I can also be fortified by the self-discipline she insists upon as a means to survive them. The tough love she advocates can be just as consoling in its way as the light, bright and sparkling comfort that's so easy to enjoy."[46] Hadlow sees self-discipline as a key factor in this successful response.

This interpretation would also accord with Anne's comments to Captain Benwick about his reading choices: "he repeated, with such tremulous feeling, the various lines which imaged a broken heart, or a mind destroyed by wretchedness, [. . .] that she ventured to hope he did not always read only poetry."[47] Instead, she prescribes for him "memoirs of characters of worth and suffering, [. . .] as calculated to rouse and fortify the mind by the highest precepts, and the strongest examples of moral and religious endurance."[48] Self-discipline is not, however, the only ingredient in resources for solitude.

Austen's idea of "resources for solitude" seems to involve a good deal of service to others. In Anne's case, "the art of knowing our own nothingness" is another component of her resources for solitude. Activity spent in the service of others seems equally important for both Elinor Dashwood and Anne Elliot. Both heroines help a number of different families, who tend to show little interest in the heroines' own lives. While seemingly thankless, it appears that this help is far from purposeless. The service helps give them purpose for living, even in the absence of thanks and intimacy. By the end of *Sense and Sensibility*, Marianne joins Elinor in recognizing and acknowledging her own individual and civic responsibilities. If nothing else, heroines like Anne and Elinor can enjoy being of service to others and being *needed* if not loved.

Resources for solitude might be related to the need for civility that we noted in the ending of *Pride and Prejudice*. Recall that Elizabeth comments on how she and Darcy grow in "civility." In *Persuasion*, as in all her novels, Austen zooms outward in her romantic happy endings. Sharing the spotlight with other characters in the final paragraphs of her novels is important to Austen's intended message. Harriet absorbs a large section of Emma's final ending, just as Mrs. Smith takes a good portion of Anne's in their respective novels. Austen trains her readers to be heroes and heroines by observing and giving to the world around them, even in the absence of a conjugal resolution.

Perfume and Carnivals

Roger Michell's film *Persuasion* (with screenplay by Nick Dear) was created during the 1995 blossoming of Jane Austen films.[49] Michell's film created a strong contrast with the style of Merchant Ivory productions, predominant in historical films of classic novels. Whereas Merchant Ivory romanticized the past and made all aspects bright and beautiful, the 1995 *Persuasion* reacted against this romantic idealization. This film showed the darkness of the rooms, the dirt on the clothes, the perspiration and unshaven messiness of most Regency society—it tried to be grittier and seamier. Streets were muddy and without sanitation, teeth were cleaned with birch twigs, and warm immersion baths were an unheard-of luxury. Because of this overall purpose, one might expect the ending of this adaptation to maintain the grittier side as well.

The demand for a traditional, conjugal happy ending, however, proves even stronger than the desire to challenge Merchant Ivory aesthetics. This version departs from the novel suddenly at the end in order to reward Anne and Wentworth with particular romance. The filmmakers decided to create a hyperbolic expression of the joy of their belated reconciliation. As soon as Wentworth and Anne kiss, a carnival suddenly appears behind them and fills the screen, complete with clowns, acrobats, stilt walkers, and fire breathers who materialize precisely at that moment (figures 25 and 26). The kiss itself, on a public street, was a subject of much conversation at the time of the release of the film, and I remember some starched purists from the Jane Austen Society of North America (JASNA) complaining that such a display of public affection was historically inappropriate. These fans were reluctant to allow the novel to be

25. Engagement carnival begins. *Persuasion.*

(Sony Pictures Classics / BBC Films, WGBH / Mobil Masterpiece Theater, Millesime Productions, 1995)

romanticized; the magical realist carnival, in contrast, drew perplexed shrugs rather than ire.

The carnival scene resembles Colonel Brandon's ejaculatory gold coins in Ang Lee's 1995 *Sense and Sensibility:* it uses grand spectacle to convey the release of pent-up tension. The Regency society that Austen portrays sharply limits public displays of private feelings, and her novels frequently portray the difficulty of relaying private feeling within public settings. Courting couples generally did not have access to private tête-à-têtes. Austen herself comments on this difficulty in the very same scene in *Persuasion.* In the novel, as in the film, Anne and Wentworth are oblivious of their surroundings, finally achieving a private moment of paradoxical intimacy in the anonymity of their public surroundings: "there, as they slowly paced the gradual ascent, heedless of every group around them, seeing

26. Engagement carnival continues. *Persuasion.*

(Sony Pictures Classics / BBC Films, WGBH / Mobil Masterpiece Theater, Millesime Productions, 1995)

neither sauntering politicians, bustling housekeepers, flirting girls, nor nursery-maids and children, they could indulge in those retrospections and acknowledgements."[50] The narrator itemizes spectacles that Anne and Wentworth do not see. The film's hyperbolic action seems more fitting when one considers this sense of being alone in a bustling crowd.

The film may also be attempting to capture Austen's hyperbole at the ending of *Persuasion*. When Charles asks Wentworth to walk Anne home and leaves them gloriously alone together, "[t]here could be only a most proper alacrity, a most obliging compliance for public view; and smiles reined in and spirits dancing in private rapture."[51] *Rapture* is a strong word for Austen. She was determined to include the word in this ending, however, even in her earlier drafts. There she wrote that "Bath could scarcely contain any other two

Beings at once so rationally & so rapturously happy."[52] The narrator also uses strong language to express Anne's feelings on reading the letter from Wentworth—"a revolution . . . almost beyond expression."[53] The filmmakers, rather than try to exhibit this tension and hyperbole, use a passing carnival to channel all the pent-up passion into a vigorous display of "rapture" and "revolution." The carnival, including its "wild beasts," passes as quickly as it disappears, and the two lovers are once again alone on the street. The carnival thus provides both a shield to their intimacy and also an indirect expression of it. Perhaps this scheme would have been more effective in the film if the attraction between the two main characters were portrayed more strongly, and one could sense the passion under the surface.

Anne's Bloom

In casting Amanda Root as the oldest of Austen's heroines, the filmmakers used makeup to portray her as pale and wan, looking older and sadder early in the film, and gradually changing her makeup and adding rosy cheeks as she grows happier. Root's lips remain pale and colorless throughout. Around the turn of the millennium, I told my classes that I thought this was a brave choice to make Anne unglamorous and that the film thus made an important point about what audiences expect from films. Like Austen, the filmmakers were willing to challenge audiences' expectations of conventional, statuesque beauty. Or so I thought.

I received a shock when I purchased a VHS copy of the film. Instead of Amanda Root, an entirely different, buxom and conventionally beautiful woman was posing as Anne Elliot on the cover in a much more revealing gown than Anne ever wears in the film (figure 27a). This has since been corrected in new covers, but only by hiding Amanda Root's face altogether in the current cover of

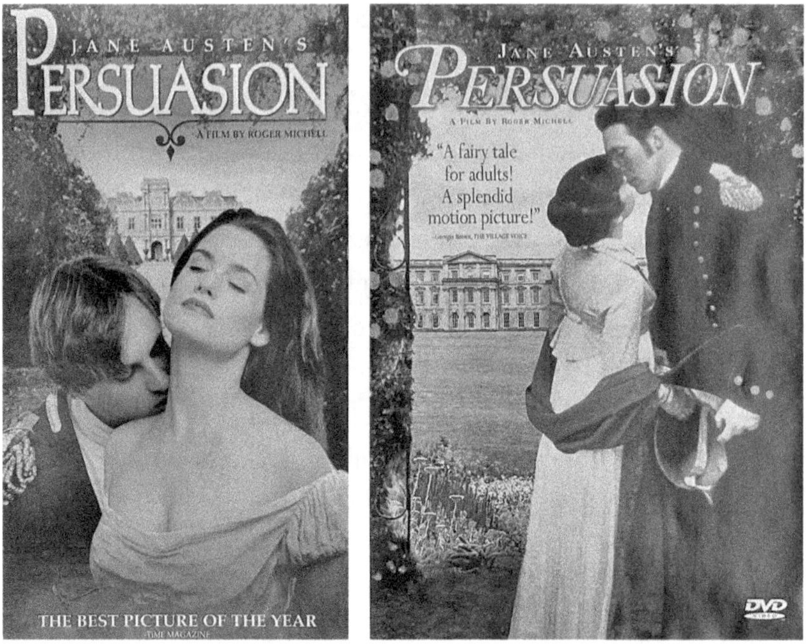

27. Buxom Anne and hidden Anne. *Persuasion.*

(VHS and DVD from the author's collection; Sony Pictures Classics / BBC Films, WGBH / Mobil Masterpiece Theater, Millesime Productions, 1995)

the DVD (figure 27b). So even though the filmmakers apparently tried to achieve a more feminist treatment or expansive definition of beauty, the publicity team or creators of the VHS cover felt that in order to sell enough copies of the film, a more traditionally sexy actress was required.

Even more insidious may be what does *not* change in the remaking of the cover.[54] Both covers include a stately home in the background. This is particularly ironic, when one of Austen's innovations in *Persuasion* was to make the couple *not* inherit an estate. Despite successive feminist revolutions, readers and audiences still want stereotypical beauty and eroticism, and despite the lessons of

28. Castle Wentworth. *Persuasion.*

(ITV / Grenada Television Ltd. co-production with WGBH Boston, 2007)

Northanger Abbey, they resist commonness in their heroines. The same goes for other conventions of the marriage plot, such as the desire for wealth and stability for the couple at the end. Austen's faith in her early nineteenth-century audiences ironically seems to exceed filmmakers' faith in late twentieth-century audiences nearly 200 years later.

Prince Charming's Castle

Film adaptations have had difficulty accepting Austen's final deviations from the marriage plot regarding the lack of an estate.[55] The 2007 iTV adaptation directed by Adrian Shergold and written by Simon Burke remedies Austen's departure from happy ending conventions by going so far as to have Wentworth (Rupert Penry-Jones) *buy* Kellynch Hall as a wedding present for Anne (Sally Hawkins). He blindfolds her while taking her there for the grand surprise, and

29. Sailing into the sunset. *Persuasion.*

(Sony Pictures Classics / BBC Films, WGBH / Mobil Masterpiece Theater, Millesime Productions, 1995)

they dance in front of their new home, celebrating (figure 28). "I thought you might like to see your wedding present," Wentworth says while removing her blindfold. These are the final words of the film; only springlike birdsong follows during the credits afterward. The 2007 version thus makes the ending conform to the Cinderella-type happy ending, where the beautiful and virtuous but undertrodden girl marries a prince charming who provides for her. The irony is that in this revision, while Wentworth does provide her a home, he dramatically gives her her *own* home back. The 1995 *Persuasion* takes a different tack (literally): the final scene shows Anne on a large naval ship sailing off into the sunset with Wentworth in command (figure 29). While stereotypically romantic, this ending also misses the point of Austen's ending.

By making these substitutions, both films erase some of the loss and pathos that make the ending of the novel *Persuasion* so moving and Austen's choices so radical. The films elevate the romantic resolution to the point that the external obstacles to their happiness are either entirely removed or erased, rather than momentarily held at bay. The filmmakers in 1995 may have tried to temper euphoria by having Admiral Croft announce that Napoleon has just escaped Elba, making the "alarm" of the final sentence very real. And while this would account for Wentworth's setting out so soon to sea again, it doesn't harmonize with Anne's happy presence on a ship heading for a naval battle. The result is confusion rather than irony. It seems that audiences' desire for a final estate, such as Price Charming's castle, or if that fails, riding—or sailing—off together into the sunset, has not dissipated much in our society during the past 200 years. The lust for the romantic happy ending is unabated and has changed its terms very little despite the intervening time and social movements.

Another made-for-TV adaptation also emphasizes wealth, but in the form of software start-ups. *Modern Persuasion* (2020) transposes Anne Elliott to a marketing firm in New York, and Wentworth a millionaire tech CEO in Silicon Valley.[56] Alex Appel and Jonathan Lisecki's film was not highly reviewed; however, the screenplay by Jonathan Lisecki and Barbara Radecki was surprisingly and delightfully true to the plot (if not the emotions) of Austen's novel. Even small details and most characters, even minor ones, are carefully translated into a modern setting. The film has a metafictional level, in that the Anne character (Wren) and Wentworth (Shane) fell in love in college, where they read *Persuasion* together. She refuses to move with him to San Francisco, where he goes to create a tech start-up. In honor of their relationship, he names his business Laconia (after Wentworth's first ship), and she names her cat and constant companion Wentworth. Their final reconciliation occurs in two stages: first, Shane sends her a text translating Wentworth's letter into modern words, acknowledging his love for her. She receives this text in the crowded room of a conference, not dissimilar to the novel's attempts to communicate private feelings in an oppressively public setting. The effect is not instantaneous, however. Wren goes to his house, and in this final reconciliation, they recite together the lines of Wentworth's letter, alternating sentences, building on the successful use of the letter in previous adaptations. Here the effect is appropriately bittersweet. Overall, the screenplay is excellent, while the acting and tone unfortunately do not capture the deep emotions of *Persuasion*, even beyond its materialistic undertone.[57]

The Pen Was in Her Hands

If I haven't yet made it sufficiently clear, Austen's revised final chapters are incomparably better than the canceled drafts; they provide some of the important factors that set *Persuasion* apart from her other novels and have made it Austen's second-most beloved novel. *Persuasion* represents a culmination of Austen's redefinition of heroines and their happiness. Without the revisions, we would not have the brilliant window conversation with Captain Harville, where Anne defends her sex against the descriptions written by men, saying that "Men have had every advantage of us in telling their own story. [. . .] The pen has been in their hands."[58] Nor would we have had Wentworth's telling response.

As Wentworth overhears this conversation, he also drops his pen.[59] Subconsciously, he relinquishes both his pen and his false descriptions of Anne. He has not actually written them, like the authors Anne and Harville are alluding to; however, he has cherished false notions of her in his angry bosom. Like Emma, Wentworth has contorted reality to fit his preconception of Anne's weakness. The 1995 film misses the brilliance of this Freudian slip by substituting a shaker for the pen. When Wentworth relinquishes his pen, he also abdicates a certain male privilege, and it serves as a fitting precursor to his letter.

The makers of the 2007 *Persuasion* unaccountably chose to perform Austen's canceled chapters rather than her final version of the ending. As mentioned above, the final reconciliation of Anne and Wentworth is brought about mostly by Admiral Croft, rather than through the agency of the principals. But the most interesting choice made by Shergold and Burke in this adaptation is to represent Anne's travels through her running. Anne is Austen's traveling heroine, foreshadowing her role as a naval wife, and demonstrating the way in which she makes the most of her movement from one "social commonwealth" to another. In the 2007 film, however, there is a long set of shots with Anne running to find Wentworth after receiving his letter. She runs left, she runs right; she runs toward the camera, she runs away from the camera; she runs from high angle, she runs from a low angle; she bumps into people; she elicits stares (figure 30). Perhaps the idea was to reclaim Anne's agency in these final (exhausting) scenes, but the effect is a bit ridiculous. The public display of desperation also runs counter to the beautiful way Austen's novel displays private affection within a public scene.

Wentworth's letter is popularly beloved and widely available on all sorts of merchandise. I once witnessed a touching scene in a ballroom of an annual JASNA meeting. A young man dressed in Regency garb dropped to one knee and (loudly enough for much of the room to hear) recited Wentworth's letter to his beloved. The room burst into applause, and I am pretty confident that she accepted him. The most successful aspects of *Persuasion*'s filmic adaptations also surround Wentworth's famous letter. On the surface, one might think that a letter would be difficult to represent in a film, but filmmakers have been ingenious. Even in the 2007 version, despite largely basing the film's ending on the canceled chapters, the filmmakers nonetheless include Wentworth's letter (it is the letter that inspires such an acrobatic response from Anne).

30. Running mad. *Persuasion.*

(ITV / Grenada Television Ltd. co-production with WGBH Boston, 2007)

The 1995 film version dramatizes Anne's reading of the letter most beautifully, having Anne and Wentworth's voices alternate in its reading. First the voice is predominantly (an off-stage) Wentworth's, but gradually there is more overlap in the voices, and a greater share of the words are read by Anne as she internalizes the letter. This is a lovely cinematic translation of the transfer of authority and locus

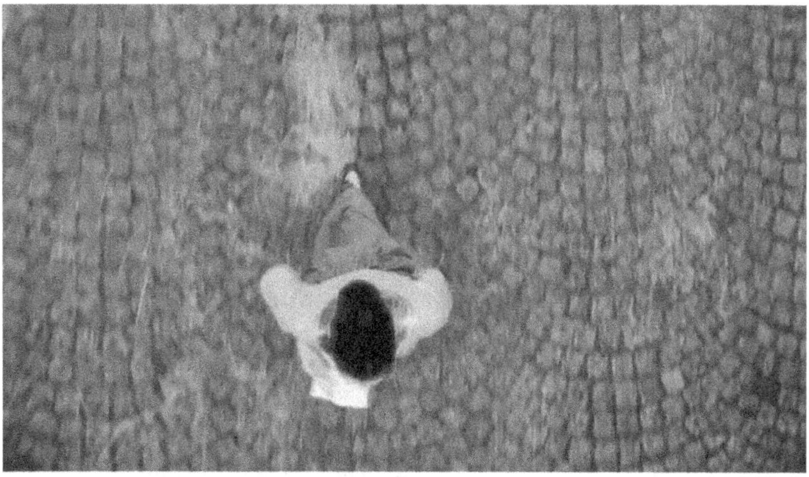

of power from Wentworth to Anne at the end. Anne, who has only had the power of refusal, now regains a degree of authorship and a voice. This technique takes Emma and Mr. Knightley's shared reading of Frank's letter in *Emma* one step further: here the reading of the letter is portrayed as a kind of coauthorship. The 1995 film, like the novel, thus offers an even greater example of the companionate marriage between equals. There is plenty of romance in this, the last of Austen's completed novels, and it is heightened rather than punctured by the sorrow that precedes it.

CONCLUSION

Coauthoring Happiness

Writing . . . is but a different name for conversation. . . .
The truest respect which you can pay to the reader's
understanding is to halve this matter amicably, and leave
him something to imagine, in his turn, as well as yourself.

LAURENCE STERNE, *Tristram Shandy*

I do not write for such dull Elves
As have not a great deal of Ingenuity themselves.

JANE AUSTEN, letter to Cassandra, January 29, 1813

In a letter to her niece Fanny Knight, Austen once wrote about the likelihood of romantic happy endings. "There are such beings in the World perhaps, one in a Thousand, as the Creature you & I should think perfection, where Grace & Spirit are united to Worth, where the Manners are equal to the Heart and Understanding, but such a person may not come in your way, or if he does, he may not be the eldest son of a Man of Fortune, the Brother of your particular friend, & belonging to your own County" (Letter to Fanny, Nov. 18–20, 1814).[1] The odds don't look good for finding and marrying your true love.

Austen's more realistic description here contrasts strongly with her reputation as reliable purveyor of happy endings.

Austen's romantic happy endings come at a price to realism. Austen stresses in each of her comic endings that the external "reward" for the characters' growth, the consummation in marriage, is anything but automatic. By including the coincidences and relatively trivial occurrences (like turkey thieves) that help bring about the final marriage, she stresses the rarity of the occasions when the outside world conforms itself to the wishes of the couple in question. This loss of inevitability also serves as a cost to the reader—particularly a reader interested primarily in the romantic conclusion.

The cost to realism and loss of inevitability are only two forms of the "price of happiness" that I refer to in the title of this book. I do not mean that one can "put a price" on happiness, nor do I mean that happiness can be bought. Nor do I mean—as some have argued— that an embittered Austen passive-aggressively exacts a toll or penalty on her readers out of disappointment at her own lack of a romantic happy ending. Instead, I use this phrase as a metaphor to explain hidden economies in Austen's endings. Austen does exact a price for the happy romantic endings that she provides, but not out of bitterness. She reveals cost at two levels—for characters within her novels and for her readers.

Pursuit of Happiness

For Austen, all forms of happiness require some degree of effort. Individual happiness cannot be solid or lasting without discipline, effort, self-awareness, and goodness. And many of her characters struggle to achieve those things. There are those who need to "*brook* their good fortune" (such as Captain Wentworth) or learn to be a little more natural (such as Marianne Dashwood and Emma Woodhouse), but these insights nonetheless do not arrive without effort. Moral growth is costly in terms of labor and sacrifice, difficult decisions, and precious time. Even romantic happiness is not a passive gift one simply receives.

Similarly, there is effort involved for her readers encountering her endings. When Austen makes the successful romantic resolution in all her novels overtly *fictional,* she reveals that these happy romantic endings are the necessary boon of the traditional marriage plot, to which her novels generically adhere. The price she exacts is a jarring shock out of complacence. The very gratuitous, accidental, and fictional nature of these romantic resolutions makes us delve deeper. The abrupt changes in pace and the overt fictionality force us out of our anticipated romantic stupor. Much as the spectator in Plato's allegory of the cave is yanked forcibly out of the cave to see the sun, Austen forces us out of our comfortable chairs in the darkness of the theater, and into the light that exposes makeup, trapdoors, and scripts usually only seen by those behind the curtain. She exposes the novel as theater—puppetry and shadows—and herself as author of those visions. Unlike the easy endings of many rom-coms, her happy endings come with a dose of pain and recognition.

Austen's endings force reflection *about* the longing for happy endings. She forces us to acknowledge our complicity in establishing and reinforcing certain conventional standards of happiness, such as the traditional elevation of marriage as cure-all or the prejudicial selection of heroes and heroines who deserve "happy endings" because they happen to be youthful, beautiful, or vivacious. Austen exposes the arbitrary and biased nature of these expectations. These lessons are just as relevant today as they were 200 years ago, as I've shown via adaptations of *Northanger Abbey*, *Mansfield Park*, and *Persuasion*. In her novels, we are suddenly placed in the position of a decision maker, a coauthor of the novels, an adjudicator of conventional ideas. We must evaluate the prerequisites of happiness—if not of the characters' happiness, then certainly of our own.

Austen's lifetime witnessed a huge body of work on the nature of individual happiness.[2] Austen's manipulation of expectations of happiness reveals similar ideas to those prominent in eighteenth-century discourses. Austen was a toddler when Thomas Jefferson, in writing the Declaration of Independence, memorably changed Locke's triumvirate of "life, liberty, and property" to "life, liberty, and the pursuit of happiness." She was writing "Love and Friendship" when the US Constitution was ratified. Debates flourished as to whether happiness depends on others or needs to be achieved independently, whether it is primarily a rational or an emotional state, whether stoicism or sentimentalism most contributes to it, whether it can be felt immediately or has to be assessed in retrospect, to what extent freedom is its prerequisite, and how it relates to moral concepts such as duty and virtue.[3] These were and still are important questions.

John Locke suggested that *pursuing* "real" happiness is more important for our human liberty, moral development—and even happiness—than *having* it, as paradoxical as that may sound.[4] A solid sense of what would give us lasting happiness becomes our key to judgments throughout our life. It may be similar to the guide Fanny alludes to in *Mansfield Park*: "We have all a better guide in ourselves, if we would attend to it, than any other person can be."[5] The "pursuit of happiness" demands considerations and judgments similar to the demands of "conscience," and its success requires wisdom.

Austen creates gaps at the cusp of her endings that force us to consider what is within a character's control. Her radical breaks—in tone, style, level of detail, and pacing—between the action of her novels and the final romantic resolution separate the types of resolution that fall within our control and the aspects of our future that we cannot control. Real happiness is never fixed or finalized, but it remains something that can be glimpsed, shared, and felt by those who have gained a modicum of self-knowledge. Self-improvement and managing disappointment are within our power, but romantic success in marriage depends greatly upon luck (even more so perhaps than economic success). Her characters must always grow intellectually and ethically *before* any romantic resolutions take place. The individual growth is essential but not sufficient for romantic resolution. This distinction reveals the huge degree of grace, providence, or sheer good luck required to find and marry one's true love.

Ultimately, Austen cares much more about educating her audience than reforming her heroines and heroes. Like many of the Scottish moral philosophers, Austen attempts to educate her reader through sympathy, developing her own economics of emotion, manipulating the degree of sympathy that readers can feel with her fictional characters. She carefully titrates these emotional responses in order to achieve particular effects that accord with her political and moral philosophy. She wields charm, romantic attraction, tantalizing dialogues, and degrees of resolution—withholding or providing them teasingly—in service of her larger purposes: teaching the reader about the nature of happiness.

Reclaiming Fiction

Austen's fiction manages to work on multiple levels in the reader's psyche, particularly because of the ways in which she manipulates our sympathies, expectations, suspense, and disappointments. Psychoanalyst Elisa Galgut explains how Austen makes her fictional worlds matter to our real-life worlds by contrasting her against Agatha Christie and J. K. Rowling: "Once we enter into the fictional world of Hercule Poirot or Harry Potter, we may [. . .] become so absorbed in the fictional world that we may forget, albeit temporarily, that it is a fictional world—the pretend mode becomes the dominant mode of relating, and connection with the real world (temporarily) forgotten."[6] Galgut claims that Austen, in contrast, does not allow us to immerse ourselves so fully in an alternate reality. This is key to the price that Austen exacts on her reader. We are not invited to question the reality of Ann Radcliffe's elaborate gothic settings; to do so would detract from one's reading: suspension of disbelief is never put into doubt in *The Mysteries of Udolpho*.[7] Austen constructs reality differently from these authors and more ironically: "What happens within [Austen's fictional world] is relieved of the consequences inherent in the real world referred to. [Her novels are] to be taken—in other words—as play."[8] Radcliffe's works do not share the metafictional "doubleness" of Austen's works, and thus do not bear equal significance for "the real world." In other words, her many techniques for highlighting the artificiality of her happy endings provides a kind of irony or doubling that engages readers more deeply in a contemplation of their own lives.

Austen's overt fictionality in her endings limits suspension of disbelief, and encourages readers to evaluate events and characters according to their own beliefs, experience, and standards. In Galgut's words, novels like Austen's "ask[-] us to hold on to *both* the fictional and real worlds, and not to collapse them."[9] Austen's novels "encourage the reader not to forget that she is engaging in a particular kind of literary make-believe, which requires, in addition to an engagement with the world of the novel, a kind of *self* consciousness."[10] It is this doubleness that Austen's endings conspicuously achieve. Austen also depicts sample readers who are and are not capable of double reading and self-reflection. Emma, like Lady Arabella the female Quixote, lacks this capacity—even more so perhaps than Catherine Morland. But perhaps the best example of a reader blind to the larger relevance of his book is Sir Walter reading the Elliot entry in his copy of the *Baronetage*. His book is a mirror (reflection only in the shallowest sense), rather than a window to a larger world.

Shakespeare's Bottom and his players mimic a different failure in such "doubleness" when they are so insistent on both pleasing the audience and anticipating the audience's suspension of disbelief. Bottom and company refer to the *fictionality* of their play so much that they lose sight of the play itself.[11] With the exception of *Northanger Abbey*, Austen waits to play with doubleness until the beginning of her final romantic resolution. It is thus partly timing that distinguishes Austen's techniques: she defers the doubleness so that the reader has time to suspend disbelief and develop sympathy, entering fully into the novel. She then jars us into doubleness to encourage reflection at the end.

Coauthoring Marriage

Let's conclude where we started, with the marriage plot. If one looks closely at Austen's endings, one can see that each of her endings champions something new and radical about an ideal of marriage. For example, in *Pride and Prejudice*, Elizabeth dares to tease and deny her social superiors and gets to marry her intellectual equal; in *Emma*, our heroine has the freedom to live more like a wealthy man, yet she decides to marry someone who will read life alongside her; and in *Persuasion*, it is the man who must recognize his failures and wait for reconciliation—a role usually assigned to the woman in the courtship novel. Austen both satisfies and challenges our expectations of charming endings, where we indulge our fantasies of undying and unchanging love. Her anti-romantic details puncture but do not ruin the romance. Austen teaches her reader to hope to learn to be a hero(ine), but also to tolerate their fate in the absence of a happy ending. Her later novels, in particular, place more emphasis on tools for living without the romantic happy ending. These tools include Fanny's resilience and constancy in the face of external pressures, Emma's imagination that can lend color to a monotonous life, and Anne's "resources for solitude."

Austen challenges us to rethink the protagonists of the marriage plot as well, rebelling against the "perfect" and unrealistic heroines of Richardson, Radcliffe, or Burney. She redefines the prerequisites of happy endings, as well as what qualifies as heroic action, particularly by women. In turning to the heroism of common things, as she does most explicitly with Catherine Morland of *Northanger Abbey*, Austen makes heroism available to all. This is not to say that all are heroes and heroines. She shows that spectacular and rare situations are not requisite for demonstrating courage or for making substantial decisions. *Sense and Sensibility*'s Elinor wields words and exertion in her neighbors' parlors with a courage equal to that of many a soldier, showing that daily life is just as valuable fodder for heroic action as the battlefield or the podium. Fanny transitions from a "creep mouse" in the house of her relatives to the moral center of the estate and the novel, showing that happy endings need not necessarily fall to the most charming or beautiful characters. Austen's revision of female heroism is perhaps most pronounced in Anne Elliot, who travels among "commonwealths" at a distance of only three miles and shows greater fortitude in a crisis than the battle-trained naval officers around her. Choosing to speak or hold silence, choosing to walk or take a carriage, choosing to make or break an appointment—small decisions can require courage and indicate character, virtue, worldview, even heroism. These choices are all extremely relevant to the daily life of her readers.

Each of her novels asserts the importance not only of companionate marriage but also of the marriage of equals, with a foundation of friendship and mutual respect. That may sound commonsensical today, but her models were as new for the novel as were her complex means of portraying them. Austen does indeed provide excellent advice on healthy relationships and successful marriages. Even though her characters are entirely fictional, they are also based on a rock-solid observation and understanding of human nature. Her genius was in creating realistic characters that simultaneously provide us with fantasy outlets for the lives we would wish to lead, remind us that real life usually does not live up to our ambitions, *and* teach us how we as readers perpetuate unhealthy expectations. Austen is not an embittered spinster who kills hope in the bosom of her reader. Like her admired Samuel Johnson, she understood both that great things cannot be achieved without hope and that few things can destroy us more fully than disappointment, in the absence of resources for solitude. Her novels educate her readers' sentiments, preparing us—if we read them carefully—for all sorts of real-life endings.

Austen weans readers from the charm and power of the drive for fictional, fantasy happiness, and eases us back into reality, achieving greater didactic effect. The dangers of novel reading that Austen playfully enumerates in *Northanger Abbey* are, in other words, real: Austen's elaborate rhetorical and narrative devices in her endings are intended to protect readers from and to teach them about the dangers of happy endings. Just as she consistently criticizes popular notions of the way readers respond to fiction, she attempts to chasten their lust for the happy ending by making readers essentially coauthors of the heroine's fate. Austen surprises us readers out of extravagant expectations: we get shades of gray where we hope for black and white, realism where we crave romance. Austen succeeds in maintaining her "double vision," or her ability to be simultaneously romantic and anti-romantic.

Many tend to look at her novels nostalgically, as pretty dreams of order and harmony that contrast with our own world of chaos and loneliness; however, it's worth considering that they may have served the same psychological function for the author herself. There is an immense distance between the world she inhabited and the world she portrays. Her heroines' happy endings are far from any reality that she herself ever witnessed. The power of Austen's endings comes from her unusual juxtaposition of seeming opposites: romantic happiness and individual fulfillment, tradition and innovation, comedy and tragedy, fantasy and realism, desire for happy endings and the suspicion of happy endings, hope and contentment. She manages to provide both while showing the benefits and weaknesses of each solution without the other. Any attempt to limit her novels to a singular unironic vision inevitably diminishes their wisdom and value.

Austen both spoofs and honors the traditional marriage plot. In her endings, we witness her efforts to balance her seemingly contradictory goals for her comedies of marriage: she requires the sentimental investment of the reader, yet checks it through metafictional ploys and ironic social commentary; she promotes a belief in the power of love, yet tempers it with knowledge of the realities of economic exigencies; she perpetuates a hope for happiness in marriage, while recognizing the hazards and limits for women in this state; and finally, she encourages the desire for distributive justice at the end, making it clear that she only awards it partially and fictitiously. The ubiquity of vice and folly also helps create the odd mixture of happiness and sadness, celebration and restraint, romance and cold showers of reason, that characterize Austen's endings. In her single-minded dedication to the novel as an art form, she assembles narrative techniques that manipulate the reader's mind and heart, not only to learn the intended lessons of each novel alone, but also to understand ourselves and our assumptions about happiness much more deeply.

Austen pointedly reminds the reader how easily the ending could have been less "perfect." Where one's individual power is not strong enough to overcome external and corruptive forces, the heroines in her novels learn tolerance for their inability to get what they want. Austen does not conceive of a name for this ability until she writes *Persuasion*: "resources for solitude." A similar dynamic is true for the reader as well. Where aspects of the endings remain unjust or tragic, Austen indirectly counters them through the currency of sympathy. Because of her ability to involve her reader in both the fictional and real worlds simultaneously, she can reveal the separation of fiction and real life, while drawing a real life moral. She shows, in other words, that the reader shares responsibility with the author for a just outcome of the story. What the author omits in distributive justice, readers must dispense in sympathy.

For better or worse, Austen never allows us to lose our own hope for "perfect felicity." Yet in a world where cinematic and social media expectations often flee the hard realities behind their screens, Austen's nuanced art teaches readers that cultivating one's own sympathy and sense of responsibility for others' welfare might itself—whatever else may happen—be a source of happiness.

Acknowledgments

My own Austen years are filled with important mentors.

My brother Hans Bjarne Thomsen introduced me to Jane Austen. His passionate nocturnal recitals of Chaucer—easily discernible from my bedroom—provided early lessons in the power of literature.

My teachers through the years—notably, the late Wayne Booth, George Butte, Timothy Fuller, the late Gwin Kolb, and Stuart Tave—revealed aspects of Austen that I likely would not have discovered on my own. They also showed me that an avocation can become a vocation.

My self-proclaimed "patroness," the late Joän Pawelski, sent me as a young graduate student to a wide range of Chicago-area high schools to talk about Jane Austen—an (occasionally hair-raising) adventure I will never forget.

Colleagues from the Jane Austen Society of North America (JASNA) and the American Society for Eighteenth-Century Studies (ASECS) are too many to list, but I thank them all for enduring friendships and shared knowledge.

I am grateful to the librarians and volunteers at Chawton House, Jane Austen's House Museum, the Hampshire Archives, King's College Library at Cambridge University, the British Museum, and the British Library for their assistance in this research.

It was under the auspices of international Austen societies that I first developed this work. I presented a keynote lecture to the Jane Austen Society of Australia in 1996 and developed it further for a speech to the JASNA Victoria Region chapter as a JASNA traveling lecturer in 2000. I particularly thank Susannah Fullerton and Joan Austen-Leigh for these opportunities. I have also presented portions of this work to the North Carolina region of JASNA at events organized by the tireless Sue Scott, Karin Wiberg, and Sara Tavola.

I am so grateful to the lovely community of individuals who have helped make the Jane Austen Summer Program an important part of the past decade, particularly my cofounder James Thompson. The Jane Austen & Co. Zoom series took events online at a time when such communities became particularly precious. These groups of scholars, authors, and general readers have cheered me, inspired me, challenged me, and deepened my understanding of Austen. My particular thanks to Jenny Abella, Danielle Christmas, Tristanne Connolly, Anne Fertig, Mary Floyd-Wilson, Suzanna Geiser, Laurie Langbauer, Kimiyo Ogawa, Jared Powell, Gisele Rankin, Emily Sferra, Beverly Taylor, and Sarah Schaefer Walton, for your help in building these communities.

At the University of North Carolina at Chapel Hill, I am grateful for the yearlong leave and senior faculty fellowship that allowed me to write this volume. My students have enriched and enlivened my readings of Austen through more than 25 years of vigorous interrogations, interpretations, comparisons, adaptations, and term papers. I treasure these memories.

I'm grateful to Catherine Goldstead and Matt McAdam at Johns Hopkins University Press and their excellent team, as well as anonymous reviewers for encouragement and useful criticism.

As always, I've benefitted from the excellent writing advice of my friends Susan Allen Ford and Debra Romanick Baldwin. Susan, in particular, read and commented on a full draft of the manuscript.

Finally, I express my gratitude to my children—Emma, Thomas, Clara, and Henry—for warming my heart by randomly quoting Austen at the dinner table, and to Benjamin, for proving that happy marriages are not only the stuff of fiction.

Further Reading and Viewing

These lists are not meant to be exhaustive by any means. They are a small sampling. I've grouped them thematically, so that readers can read or watch a series of adaptations for a book group, class, or other event. I have marked my favorites in each group with an asterisk.

ACTION-PACKED AND PARANORMAL

Grace, Maria. *Pemberley: Mr. Darcy's Dragon: A Pride and Prejudice Variation.* White Soup Press, 2016.

Grahame-Smith, Seth. *Pride and Prejudice and Zombies.* Quirk Books, 2009.

*Kowal, Mary Robinette. *Shades of Milk and Honey* (Glamourist Histories Series). Tom Dougherty, 2011.

Meyer, Stephenie. *Twilight.* Little, Brown, 2005.

Mullany, Janet. *Jane and the Damned.* HarperCollins, 2010.

Winters, Ben H., and Jane Austen. *Sense, Sensibility, and Sea Monsters.* Quick Books, 2009.

ADAPTATIONS ABOUT AUSTEN ADDICTS

*Cohen, Paula Marantz. *Suzanne Davis Gets a Life.* Paul Dry, 2014.

*Hale, Shannon. *Austenland.* Bloomsbury, 2010.

Hale, Shannon. *Midnight in Austenland.* Bloomsbury, 2012.

*Hess, Jerusha, director. *Austenland.* Sony Pictures Classics, 2013.

*Pattillo, Beth. *Jane Austen Ruined My Life*. Guideposts, 2009.
*Rigler, Laurie Viera. *Confessions of a Jane Austen Addict*. Penguin, 2008.
*Rigler, Laurie Viera. *Rude Awakenings of a Jane Austen Addict*. Penguin, 2010.
*Zeff, Dan, director. *Lost in Austen* (TV miniseries). Mammoth Screen, 2008.

AUTOBIOGRAPHIES WITH AUSTEN

Cohen, Rachel. *Austen Years: A Memoir in Five Novels*. Farrar, Straus, Giroux, 2020.
*Deresiewicz, William. *A Jane Austen Education: How Six Novels Taught Me about Love, Friendship, and the Things That Really Matter*. Penguin, 2011.
*Duncan, Kathryn. *Jane Austen and the Buddha*. McFarland & Company, 2021.
Smith, Amy Elizabeth. *All Roads Lead to Austen: A Year-Long Journey with Jane*. Sourcebooks, 2011.

BEST HISTORICAL ROM-COM ADAPTATIONS

Coke, Cyril, director. *Pride and Prejudice* (TV miniseries). BBC, 1980.
De Wilde, Autumn, director. *Emma*. Working Title Films, 2020.
Langton, Simon, director. *Pride and Prejudice* (TV miniseries). BBC, 1995.
Lee, Ang, director. *Sense and Sensibility*. Columbia Pictures, 1995.
McGrath, Douglas, director. *Emma*. Miramax, 1996.
Michell, Roger, director. *Persuasion* (TV miniseries). BBC, 1995.
Wright, Joe. director. *Pride and Prejudice*. Focus Features, 2005.

CHRISTIAN-THEMED ADAPTATIONS

Arthur, Sarah. *Dating Mr. Darcy: A Smart Girl's Guide to Sensible Romance*. Tyndale House, 2005.
Smith, Debra White. *First Impressions* (The Austen Series). Harvest House, 2018.
Smith, Debra White. *What Jane Austen Taught Me about Love and Romance*. Harvest House, 2007.
Stewart, Haley. *Jane Austen's Genius Guide to Life: On Love, Friendship, and Becoming the Person God Created You to Be*. Ave Maria Press, 2022.

Ward, Eucharista. *A Match for Mary Bennet: Can a Serious Young Lady Ever Find Her Way to Love?* Sourcebooks Landmark, 2009.

CONSUMERIST AUSTEN ADAPTATIONS

Coolidge, Martha, director. *Material Girls*. Metro-Goldwyn-Mayer, 2006.

Garcia, Angel, director. *Prada to Nada*. MWM Studios, 2011.

*Heckerling, Amy, director. *Clueless*. Paramount Pictures, 1995.

Ojha, Rajshree, director. *Aisha*. Anil Kapoor Films, 2010.

CONSUMERIST CRITIQUES IN AUSTEN ADAPTATIONS

*Baraka, Rhonda F., director. *Pride and Prejudice: Atlanta* (TV movie). A&E Network, 2019.

Chadha, Gurinder, director. *Bride and Prejudice*. Pathé Pictures International, 2004.

*Ephron, Nora, director. *Sleepless in Seattle*. TriStar Pictures, 1993. (An adaptation of Austen and *The Shop around the Corner*.)

Jalaluddin, Uzma. *Hana Khan Carries On*. Penguin Random House, 2021. (An adaptation of Austen, *The Shop around the Corner*, and *Sleepless in Seattle*.)

Lubitsch, Ernst, director. *The Shop around the Corner*. MGM, 1940.

GREATEST LIBERTIES TAKEN WITH THE NOVELS

Cracknell, Carrie, director. *Persuasion*. Mad Chance Productions, 2022.

Garcia, Angel, director. *Prada to Nada*. MWM Studios, 2011.

Jarrold, Julian, director. *Becoming Jane*. HanWay Films, 2007.

Leonard, Robert Z., director. *Pride and Prejudice*. Metro-Goldwyn-Mayer, 1940.

*Rozema, Patricia, director. *Mansfield Park*. Miramax Productions, 1995.

GUIDES TO CAREER AND ACHIEVEMENT

Andrews, Sophie. *Be More Jane: Bring Out Your Inner Austen to Meet Life's Challenges*. Cico Books, 2019.

*Deresiewicz, William. *A Jane Austen Education: How Six Novels Taught Me about Love, Friendship, and the Things That Really Matter*. Penguin, 2011.

Kayne, Andrea. *Kicking Ass in a Corset: Jane Austen's Six Principles for Living and Leading from the Inside Out*. University of Iowa Press, 2021.

GUIDES TO DATING AND FRIENDSHIP

Arthur, Sarah. *Dating Mr. Darcy: A Smart Girl's Guide to Sensible Romance*. Tyndale House, 2005.

Kantor, Elizabeth. *The Jane Austen Guide to Happily Ever After*. Regency, 2012.

Ross, Josephine. *Jane Austen's Guide to Good Manners: Compliments, Charades, and Horrible Blunders*. Bloomsbury, 2006.

Smith, Debra White. *What Jane Austen Taught Me about Love and Romance*. Harvest House, 2007.

Stewart, Haley. *Jane Austen's Genius Guide to Life: On Love, Friendship, and Becoming the Person God Created You to Be*. Ave Maria Press, 2022.

LGBTQ ADAPTATIONS

Ahn, Andrew, director. *Fire Island*. Jax Media and Searchlight Pictures, 2022.

Hercs, Kelsey, playwright. *Threadbare Morality: The Queer Musings of Miss Mary Bennet*. Dixon Place Theater. http://dixonplace.org/performances/threadbare-morality/.

*Kessel, John. *Pride and Prometheus*. Saga Press, 2008

Wood, Margot. *Fresh*. Amulet, 2021.

MARY BENNET LORE

Aitken, Virginia. *Mary Bennet's Chance*. Pen Press, 2011.

Cowley, Katherine. *The Secret Life of Miss Mary Bennet*. Tule, 2021.

Cowley, Katherine. *True Confessions of a London Spy*. Tule, 2022.

*Gunderson, Lauren, and Margot Melco. *Miss Bennet: Christmas at Pemberley*. https://www.dramatists.com/cgi-bin/db/single.asp?key=5611.

*Hadlow, Janice. *The Other Bennet Sister: A Novel*. Henry Holt, 2020.

*Kessel, John. *Pride and Prometheus.* Saga Press, 2008

McCullough, Colleen. *The Independence of Miss Mary Bennet.* Pocket Books, 2008.

Mingle, Pamela. *The Pursuit of Mary Bennet: A Pride and Prejudice Novel.* Harper Collins, 2013.

Paynter, Jennifer. *The Forgotten Sister: Mary Bennet's* Pride and Prejudice. Lake Union, 2014.

Peterson, J. C. *Being Mary Bennet.* HarperTeen, 2022.

Sarath, Patrice. *The Unexpected Miss Bennet.* Berkley, 2011.

Street, Amy. *Becoming Mary: A Pride and Prejudice Sequel.* Kindle, 2015.

Ward, Eucharista. *A Match for Mary Bennet: Can a Serious Young Lady Ever Find Her Way to Love?* Sourcebooks Landmark, 2009.

MOST CREATIVE CINEMA

*Black, Andrew, director. *Pride and Prejudice* [*Pride and Prejudice: A Latter-Day Comedy*]. Bestboy Pictures, 2003.

Diarmuid, Lawrence, director. *Emma* (TV movie). A&E Network, 1996.

*Heckerling, Amy, director. *Clueless.* Paramount Pictures, 1995.

*Rozema, Patricia, director. *Mansfield Park.* Miramax Productions, 1995.

*Su, Bernie. *Lizzie Bennet Diaries* (YouTube series). Pemberley Digital, 2012.

*Wright, Joe, director. *Pride and Prejudice.* Focus Features, 2005.

OFF-THE-WALL FILM ADAPTATIONS

Buck, Chris, and Jennifer Lee, directors. *Frozen.* Walt Disney Pictures, 2013.

*Chadha, Gurinder, director. *Bride and Prejudice.* Pathé Pictures International, 2004.

Coolidge, Martha, director. *Material Girls.* Metro-Goldwyn-Mayer, 2006.

*Ephron, Nora, director. *Sleepless in Seattle.* TriStar Pictures, 1993.

Garcia, Angel, director. *Prada to Nada.* MWM Studios, 2011.

Maguire, Sharon, director. *Bridget Jones's Diary.* Miramax Productions, 2001.

*Menon, Rajiv, director. *Priyuralu Pilichindi* [original title: *Kandukondain, Kandukondain*]. Zee Tamil / Sri Surya Films, 2000.

*Nunez, Victor, director. *Ruby in Paradise*. Full Crew / Say Yea, 1993.
*Steers, Burr, director. *Pride and Prejudice and Zombies*. Cross Creek Pictures, 2009.
*Su, Bernie. *Lizzie Bennet Diaries* (YouTube series). Pemberley Digital, 2012.
Winning, David, director. *Sense, Sensibility, and Snowmen* (TV movie). Hallmark Movies and Mysteries, 2019.
*Wright, Joe, director. *Atonement*. Universal Pictures, 2007.

SOUTH ASIAN AND EAST ASIAN AUSTEN

*Chadha, Gurinder, director. *Bride and Prejudice*. Pathé Pictures International, 2004.
*Dev, Sonali. *The Emma Project*. HarperCollins, 2022.
*Dev, Sonali. *Incense and Sensibility*. HarperCollins, 2020.
*Dev, Sonali. *Pride, Prejudice, and Other Flavors*. HarperCollins, 2019.
*Dev, Sonali. *Recipe for Persuasion*. HarperCollins, 2021.
*Jalaluddin, Uzma. *Ayesha at Last*. Penguin Random House, 2019.
*Kamal, Soniah. *Unmarriageable*. Ballantine Books, 2019.
*Menon, Rajiv, director. *Priyuralu Pilichindi* [original title: *Kandukondain, Kandukondain*]. Zee Tamil / Sri Surya Films, 2000.
*Yamashita, Karen Tei. *Sansei and Sensibility*. Coffee House Press, 2020.

STEAMY ADAPTATIONS (JUST A FEW OF THE MANY)

*Dev, Sonali. *Pride, Prejudice, and Other Flavors*. HarperCollins, 2019.
Fielding, Helen. *Bridget Jones's Diary: A Novel*. Penguin, 1996.
Fielding, Helen. *Bridget Jones's Diary: The Edge of Reason*. Penguin, 2001.
Hale, Shannon. *Midnight in Austenland*. Bloomsbury, 2012.

THEATER ADAPTATIONS

*Gunderson, Lauren, and Margot Melco, playwrights. *Miss Bennet: Christmas at Pemberley*. https://www.dramatists.com/cgi-bin/db/single.asp?key=5611.
Gunderson, Lauren, and Margot Melco, playwrights. *The Wickhams: Christmas at Pemberley*. https://www.dramatists.com/cgi-bin/db/single.asp?key=5984.

Hamill, Kate, playwright. *Pride and Prejudice*. https://www.dramatists.com/cgi-bin/db/single.asp?key=5789.

Hamill, Kate, playwright. *Sense and Sensibility*. https://www.dramatists.com/cgi-bin/db/single.asp?key=5174.

*Hamill, Kate, playwright. *Emma*. https://www.dramatists.com/cgi-bin/db/single.asp?key=5174.

Hercs, Kelsey, playwright. *Threadbare Morality: The Queer Musings of Miss Mary Bennet*. Dixon Place Theater. http://dixonplace.org/performances/threadbare-morality/.

TIME TRAVEL WITH AUSTEN

Bennett, Stuart. *The Perfect Visit*. Longbourne Press, 2011.

Flynn, Kathleen A. *The Jane Austen Project: A Novel*. HarperColllins, 2017.

Rigler, Laurie Viera. *Confessions of a Jane Austen Addict*. Penguin, 2008.

*Rigler, Laurie Viera. *Rude Awakenings of a Jane Austen Addict*. Penguin, 2010.

*Zeff, Dan, director. *Lost in Austen* (TV miniseries). Mammoth Screen, 2008.

WORLD RELIGIONS SURVEY OF AUSTEN ADAPTATIONS

*Cohen, Paula Marantz, *Jane Austen in Boca: A Novel*. St. Martin's Press, 2002.

*Duncan, Kathryn. *Jane Austen and the Buddha*. McFarland & Company, 2021.

*Jalaluddin, Uzma. *Ayesha at Last*. Penguin Random House, 2019.

*Kamal, Soniah. *Unmarriageable*. Ballantine Books, 2019.

Stewart, Haley. *Jane Austen's Genius Guide to Life: On Love, Friendship, and Becoming the Person God Created You to Be*. Ave Maria Press, 2022.

*Yamashita, Karen Tei. *Sansei and Sensibility*. Coffee House Press, 2020.

YOUNG ADULT ADAPTATIONS

DasGupta, Sayantani. *Debating Darcy*. Scholastic, 2022.

Dass, Sarah. *Where the Rhythm Takes You*. HarperCollins / Balzer + Bray, 2021.

Cantor, Jillian. *The Code for Love and Heartbreak*. Inkyard, 2020.

*Grace, Maria. *Pemberley: Mr. Darcy's Dragon: A Pride and Prejudice Variation.* White Soup Press, 2016.

*Kowal, Mary Robinette. *Shades of Milk and Honey* (Glamourist Histories Series). Tom Dougherty, 2011.

Peterson, J. C. *Being Mary Bennet.* HarperTeen, 2022.

Price, Tirzah. *Pride and Premeditation.* HarperTeen, 2021.

*Zoboi, Ibi. *Pride: A Pride and Prejudice Remix.* HarperCollins, 2018.

Notes

INTRODUCTION
"Perfect Felicity"

1. See Cynthia Whissell, "According to Their Plots, Jane Austen's Novels Are Not Comic Romances with Happy Endings," *English Language and Literature Studies* 8.2 (2018): https://www.ccsenet.org/journal/index.php/ells/article/view/75381.
2. Lloyd Brown, an early scholar of Austen's rhetorical style, remarks that Austen's artifices contribute to "the transparent *inevitability* of her happy endings." *Bits of Ivory: Narrative Techniques in Jane Austen's Fiction* (Baton Rouge: Louisiana State University Press, 1973), 222–23; my emphasis. I would like to suggest that Austen's deliberate artifices and heightened fictionality actually work *against* such a sense of inevitability.
3. This metafictional dynamic owes something to the quixotic tradition of authors such as Miguel de Cervantes, Henry Fielding, Charlotte Lennox, Samuel Richardson, Laurence Sterne, and J. W. von Goethe, but Austen develops these flourishes into a more subtle and organic aspect of her narratives.
4. Deanna K. Kreisel, "Where Does the Pleasure Come From? The Marriage Plot and Its Discontents in Jane Austen's *Emma*," *Persuasions: The Jane Austen Journal* 29 (2007): 217–26, 222.
5. Anna Quindlen in Susannah Carson, ed., *A Truth Universally Acknowledged: 33 Great Writers on Why We Read Jane Austen* (New York: Random House, 2009), 102.
6. Sonia Rao, "Jane Austen Fans Expect a Happy Ending. Masterpiece's 'Sanditon' Tested Their Limits," *Washington Post* (Feb. 27, 2020): https://

www.washingtonpost.com/arts-entertainment/2020/02/27/jane-austen-fans-expect-happy-ending-masterpieces-sanditon-tested-their-limits/.

7. Edward Rothstein, "Ideas and Trends: Jane Austen Meets Mr. Right," *New York Times* (Dec. 10, 1995): section 4, page 1. Merchant Ivory productions are directed by James Ivory and include *Room with a View* (1985), *Howard's End* (1992), and *Remains of the Day* (1993)—two novels by E. M. Forster and one by Kazuo Ishiguro. Perhaps because these movies are based on works by Forster and Ishiguro, they tend to focus on colonialist narratives and a nostalgic aesthetic.

8. In contrast, the Napoleonic inheritance laws introduced during Austen's lifetime ensured that Europe's estates would be broken up. British primogeniture laws and entailments preserve centralized wealth and property; Napoleonic inheritance laws disperse wealth and property, weakening the landed gentry as a class yet providing more equal inheritances among siblings.

9. See Jocelyn Harris, *A Revolution Almost beyond Expression: Jane Austen's* Persuasion (Newark: University of Delaware Press, 2007), 171.

10. Jane's brother Frank was also a partner in Henry's bank. When the bank failed, the brothers stopped sending monthly support to their mother and sisters. See Claire Tomalin, *Jane Austen: A Life* (New York: Vintage Books, 1999), 255–56.

11. The exception here may be *Pride and Prejudice*. Chapter 3 suggests another possible interpretation of Austen's own response to this novel as "rather too light and bright and sparkling."

12. SS, 409. All quotations from Austen's six major novels are taken from the Cambridge editions, abbreviated as NA (*Northanger Abbey*), SS (*Sense and Sensibility*), PP (*Pride and Prejudice*), MP (*Mansfield Park*), E (*Emma*), and P (*Persuasion*). The volumes dedicated to juvenilia and later manuscripts will be referred to as J and LM, respectively. Quotes from the letters are taken from Deirdre Le Faye, ed., *Jane Austen's Letters*, 4th ed. (London: Oxford University Press, 2011). References to the manuscript pages of *Persuasion* are from *Manuscript Chapters of* Persuasion (London: Athlone Press, 1985).

13. E, 470.

14. When I say "the reader" in this way, I do not assume that all readers have identical reactions. We all react differently, and each successive reading can differ too, even for the same individual. Throughout this book, I build my

argument on reader-response theory as laid out by Wolfgang Iser and Wayne Booth. Their theory posits that texts can, by their structure and rhetoric, create an "implied reader"—an ideal reader that the text creates and invites. I would say that the implied reader, when encountering Austen's omissions of key details in her romantic endings, feels annoyed, or at least surprised. But actual readers' responses may differ widely and change over time. At some level, though, if we do not react to these purposeful gaps Austen has created, it is because we have chosen not to—we have chosen to differentiate ourselves from an implied reader's response. See Wolfgang Iser, *The Act of Reading: A Theory of Aesthetic Response* (London and Henley: Routledge and Kegan Paul, 1978; *Art des Lesens*, 1976); Wayne C. Booth, *The Rhetoric of Fiction* (Chicago: University of Chicago Press, 1983).

15. When I use phrases like "Austen wants her reader to . . ." or "Austen expects her reader to . . .," I am not claiming knowledge of Austen's private thoughts. This is shorthand for the reader-response theory described in note 14 above. Just as the text creates an implied reader through its structure, it also creates an implied author. Also, as a rule of thumb, if I discover a clever pattern in Austen's novels, I will always give her the benefit of the doubt and assume that she put it there on purpose.

16. John Halperin, for example, writes that "[i]f she has one overriding fault as a writer, it is her obvious and over-hasty desire, near the ends of her novels, to . . . get the thing over with," resulting in what he calls her "botched ending[s]" (*The Life of Jane Austen* [Baltimore: Johns Hopkins University Press, 1984], 78, 249). R. F. Brissenden, although generally less hostile, still notes the "formulaic patness with which everything is wound up" in "*Mansfield Park*: Freedom and the Family," in *Jane Austen: Bicentenary Essays*, ed. John Halperin (Cambridge: Cambridge University Press, 1975), 156–71.

17. MP, 533; my emphasis.

18. Halperin, *Life*, 249.

19. Halperin, *Life*, 250. Critics Marvin Mudrick and John Halperin popularized one psychoanalytic/biographical explanation in particular: they attribute a general psychological detachment, weakness, or coldness to Austen—an inability to enjoy or describe happiness at close hand.

20. D. A. Miller continues in the psychoanalytic strain, but muses more on the topic of closure itself. He claims that Austen's endings reveal her discomfort

with the ambiguity and disorder inherent to novels: according to Miller, Austen secretly harbors a "fascinated delight with unsettled states of deferral and ambiguity," yet her "rigorous ideal of a wholly and properly intelligible world" causes her to wield her narrative authority with a heavy hand, eliminating all ambiguity, silencing all discontent, and censoring all difficulties in the conclusions of her novels, just as she effectively polices her own desires. *Jane Austen, or the Secret of Style* (Princeton, NJ: Princeton University Press, 2003), 64–66. Nonetheless, I would argue that the ironic devices in her endings inherently invoke a degree of double meaning.

21. Beth Pattillo, *Jane Austen Ruined My Life* (New York: Guideposts, 2009), 233–34.
22. Marvin Mudrick, *Jane Austen: Irony as Defense and Discovery* (Princeton, NJ: Princeton University Press, 1952); Miller, *Secret of Style*.
23. Tony Tanner represents this approach when he complains of Marianne Dashwood's cursory disposal: "She is married off to Brandon to complete a pattern, to satisfy that instinct for harmonious arranging which is a part of the structure both of that society and the book itself. Her energy is sacrificed to the overriding geometry." "Introduction," in *Sense and Sensibility* (Harmondsworth, Middlesex: Penguin, 1969), 7–34, 31.
24. Mary Poovey claims that Austen turns away from "social realism and criticism" and "escape[s] into romance" in her endings, with the unfortunate result that "those fairy-tale endings [. . .] stop realism dead in its tracks." *The Proper Lady and the Woman Writer* (Chicago: University of Chicago Press, 1984), 206, 238.
25. *Miss Austen Regrets*, directed by Jeremy Lovering (London: BBC, 2007).
26. *Becoming Jane*, directed by Julian Jarrold (London: HanWay Films, 2007).
27. P, 270.
28. *The Princess Diaries*, directed by Garry Marshall (Burbank, CA: Walt Disney Pictures, 2001); *The Princess Diaries 2: Royal Engagement*, directed by Garry Marshall (Burbank, CA: Walt Disney Pictures, 2004); *Ella Enchanted*, directed by Tommy O'Haver (Los Angeles: Miramax Productions, 2004).
29. See, e.g., Andrew Black's film *Pride and Prejudice: A Latter-Day Comedy* (Provo, UT: Bestboy Pictures, 2003) and Beth Pattillo's *Jane Austen Ruined My Life*.
30. BBC productions are much like those from Hollywood. Andrew Davies is said to have felt guilt over the ending that he wrote for season one of

Sanditon (Caroline Halleman, "Andrew Davies Says He Feels a Bit Guilty About Sanditon's Shocking Ending," *Town and Country Magazine* (Feb. 24, 2020): https://www.townandcountrymag.com/leisure/arts-and-culture/a31079438/sanditon-shocking-ending-andrew-davies-season-2-interview/). When asked about his choice to end *Sanditon* with Charlotte's marital expectations thwarted, he said, "audiences, I think, are perhaps too used to having all their expectations fulfilled. I did feel sorry—a lot a lot of people were posting on Twitter in the UK, 'How could you, how could you?'. . . I did feel a bit guilty." In the same interview, however, Davies also reveals that he banked on the audience's demand for a happy ending in order to get the producers to agree to a second season: "if we get a second series, we're certainly going to eventually give Charlotte an ending that she would like," he taunted.

In another article, Alison Flood writes, "The ending [of *Sanditon*] has enraged and upset viewers, but most of all, I think, surprised them. This is Austen, and we know what we're entitled to." So, even though the content bears little resemblance to anything Austen wrote, the attachment of her name made viewers feel entitled to one of her endings. Davies calculated that this entitlement would lead to demand for a second season for 2022 and—since season two also ended with Charlotte's desires thwarted—it seems that he is fond of this ploy. By the end of the third and final series in 2023 (equivalent to the third volume of a novel), viewers eventually get what they feel entitled to: a happy ending. See Allison Flood, "*Sanditon*: Why Are Austen Fans So Enraged by Andrew Davies' Ending?" *The Guardian* (Oct. 14, 2019): https://www.theguardian.com/books/booksblog/2019/oct/14/sanditon-jane-austen-fans-itv-andrew-davies-ending.

31. Sophie Gilbert sums up the predicament nicely. All who love Austen, she says, must come to terms with the essential paradox of her writing: "No one did more to challenge the conventions and strictures of marriage for women in the 19th century, while simultaneously enshrining it as the ultimate happy ending." "Making Peace with Jane Austen's Marriage Plots," *The Atlantic* (July 20, 2017): https://www.theatlantic.com/entertainment/archive/2017/07/making-peace-with-jane-austens-marriage-plots/534051/.

32. Katie Roiphe, "The Ambiguities of Austen: Why Did the Novelist of Happy Endings Die Alone?" *The Weekly Standard* (June 9, 1997): 34–36.

33. Jeffrey Eugenides, *The Marriage Plot* (New York: Farrar, Straus, Giroux, 2011). See also "Eugenides Spins a Modern Kind of 'Marriage Plot,'" interview

by Melissa Block and Guy Raz, *All Things Considered*, NPR (Oct. 5, 2011): https://www.npr.org/transcripts/141080967.

34. *Fire Island*, directed by Andrew Ahn (New York: Jax Media / Searchlight Pictures, 2022). After reciting the opening line of *Pride and Prejudice*, Noah says: "You know who said that? Jane Austen, the queen. Fucking shit. Pretty dope way to start a story, right? Well no offense to my girl, Jane, but that sounds like some hetero nonsense. Listen, I don't know much about a good fortune, but not every single man is looking for a wife."

35. Rachel Cohen, *Austen Years: A Memoir in Five Novels* (New York: Farrar, Straus, Giroux, 2020); Tessa Carman, "*The Austen Years*: A Review in Six Movements," *Mere Orthodoxy* (May 5, 2021): https://mereorthodoxy.com/book-review-austen-years-rachel-cohen/.

36. Roiphe, "Ambiguities of Austen," 34–36.

37. "Sarah Arthur's *Dating Mr. Darcy: A Smart Girl's Guide to Sensible Romance* (2005), published by Tyndale, a Christian press, coaches young evangelical readers through reflections on themselves and their potential marriage partners, using *Pride and Prejudice* as a touchstone. Debra White Smith's "Austen Series," published from 2004 to 2006 by the Christian press Harvest House, recasts each of Austen's novels as a present-day romance starring characters of faith." Juliette Wells, "True Love Waits: Austen and the Christian Romance in the Contemporary U.S.," *Persuasions: The Jane Austen Journal On-Line* 28.2 (Spring 2008): https://jasna.org/persuasions/on-line/vol28no2/wells.htm.

38. Devoney Looser, *Making Jane Austen* (Baltimore: Johns Hopkins University Press, 2017); Juliet Wells, *Everybody's Jane: Austen in the Popular Imagination* (London: Continuum, 2012); and Janine Barchas, *Matters of Fact in Jane Austen: History, Location, and Celebrity* (Baltimore: John Hopkins University Press, 2013).

39. There are exceptions to this rule. In *Ruby in Paradise*, the Catherine Morland figure chooses a career over romance; in *Lost in Austen*, the two heroines split—Elizabeth Bennet prefers computer science over Darcy, and Amanda Price prefers Mr. Darcy over twentieth-century conveniences; in *Fire Island*, the gay male lovers distinctly question monogamy while nonetheless falling in love. *Ruby in Paradise*, directed by Victor Nunez (Full Crew / Say Yea, 1993); *Lost in Austen*, directed by Dan Zeff, TV miniseries (London: Mammoth Screen, 2008).

40. See Laura Mooneyham White, *Jane Austen's Anglicanism* (New York: Routledge, 2016), and Alastair Macintyre, *Ethics in the Conflicts of Modernity: An Essay on Desire, Practical Reasoning, and Narrative* (Cambridge: Cambridge University Press, 2016).
41. While events in the plot leading to the happy endings *could* be attributed to Providence, that is not how Austen uses them. In order to give small actions and decisions sufficient moral significance, Austen needs to deemphasize divine intervention. Yet at the same time, Austen includes a healthy dose of skepticism about the degree to which a given individual can truly reform herself or transform the world around her.
42. The Steventon novels—NA, SS, and PP—were revised over a long period and rewritten to overlap with one another. The three Chawton novels—MP, E, and P—were written in a shorter time and clearer sequence.

CHAPTER 1
Commonplace Happiness

1. NA, 259.
2. This first possibility is a commonplace of novels of sensibility, which tend to divide readers into two groups—those who care for their readers with appropriate sensibility and those who do not, inviting readers to join the elite club of those who "feel" strongly.
3. C. S. Lewis, *On Stories: And Other Essays on Literature* (New York: Harvest Books, 2002), 17.
4. See Christopher Miller, *Surprise: The Poetics of the Unexpected from Milton to Austen* (Ithaca, NY: Cornell University Press, 2015).
5. Anonymous, *Evils of Adultery and Prostitution; With an Inquiry into the Causes of Their Alarming Increase, and Some Means Recommended for Checking Their Progress* (London: printed for T. Vernor, 1792). Quoted in Katherine Binhammer, "The Persistence of Reading: Governing Female Novel-Reading in *Memoirs of Emma Courtney* and *Memoirs of Modern Philosophers*," *Eighteenth-Century Life* 27.2 (2003): 1–22, muse.jhu.edu/article/44395.
6. NA, 164.
7. There is also a scrawled "Jack Smith" that she entered for contrast—a different spouse for a rebellious mood.

8. MP, 544.
9. NA, 31.
10. See Claudia Johnson, "The Novel Jane Austen Wrote When She Was Twelve," *Paris Review* (Sep. 14, 2018): https://www.scribd.com/article/388641862/The-Novel-Jane-Austen-Wrote-When-She-Was-Twelve.
11. As listed on the British Library website. Incidentally, the only novel listed in the British Library catalogue that was published by or for Crosby in 1803 is *The Pretty Pilgrim; Or the Marvelous Journey of Evelina Evans*, a much more elaborate title than Austen's.
12. Anthony Mandal gives a lovely, thorough account of the publishing context in *Jane Austen and the Popular Novel: The Determined Author* (New York: Palgrave MacMillan, 2007).
13. NA, 30.
14. The only other lengthy treatment of Austen's endings is Ashley Tauchert's *Romancing Jane: Narrative, Realism and the Possibility of a Happy Ending* (New York: Palgrave, 2005).
15. Rachel Blau DuPlessis, *Writing beyond the Ending: Narrative Strategies of Twentieth-Century Women Writers* (Bloomington: Indiana University Press, 1985), 3–4.
16. Claudia Johnson, *Equivocal Beings: Politics, Gender, and Sentimentality in the 1790s—Wollstonecraft, Radcliffe, Burney, Austen* (Chicago: University of Chicago Press, 1995), 18.
17. Penny Gay, *Jane Austen and the Theater* (Cambridge: Cambridge University Press, 2002); Paula Byrne, *Jane Austen and the Theater* (London: Bloomsbury Academic, 2007).
18. C. L. Barber, *Shakespeare's Festive Comedy: A Study of Dramatic Form and Its Relation to Social Custom* (Princeton, NJ: Princeton University Press, 1972, 2012).
19. Samuel Richardson, *A Collection of the Moral and Instructive Sentiments, Maxims, Cautions, and Reflexions Contained in the Histories of Pamela, Clarissa, and Sir Charles Grandison* (London: printed for S. Richardson; and sold by C. Hitch and L. Hawes; J. and J. Rivington; Andrew Millar; R. and J. Dodsley; and J. Leake, at Bath, 1755), Early English Books Online Text Creation Partnership, 2011, https://quod.lib.umich.edu/e/ecco/004835423.0001.000/1:2?rgn=div1;view=fulltext.
20. Richardson, *Collection*, vi.

21. Samuel Richardson, *The History of Sir Charles Grandison* (New York: Cross-cut & Sterling, 1902), VII:295 (hathitrust.org).
22. This famous aphorism was first spoken by Vindice in *The Revenger's Tragedy,* attributed to Thomas Middleton and first performed in 1606. See Brian Walsh, ed., *The Revenger's Tragedy: A Critical Reader* (London: Bloomsbury Arden Shakespeare, 2016).
23. NA, 31.
24. Ann Radcliffe, *The Mysteries of Udolpho; A Romance, Interspersed with Some Pieces of Poetry* (London: G. G. and J. Robinson, 1794).
25. NA, 6–7.
26. NA, 5–9.
27. NA, 30.
28. Mary Brunton, *Self-Control* (Project Gutenberg), https://www.gutenberg.org/files/41196/41196-h/41196-h.htm.
29. C. S. Lewis, *The Horse and His Boy* (New York: Macmillan, 1988), 17.
30. NA, 7.
31. NA, 261.
32. NA, 6.
33. Actually, it appears eighteen times, if you include the twice-used, ungrammatical "amazing" as an adverb.
34. NA, 135.
35. NA, 11.
36. NA, 256; my emphasis.
37. NA, 261; my emphasis.
38. NA, 259.
39. NA, 240–41; my emphasis.
40. We have no direct knowledge of the form in which Austen left her *Northanger Abbey* manuscript at her death, yet it is extremely unlikely that she would not have marked both chapter numbers and volume break in its 31 chapters. The structural symmetry that I point out is additional evidence that she intended two volumes.
41. NA, 259.
42. NA, 260; my emphasis.
43. NA, 241. Austen attributes glory to the alternate ending she describes for Catherine.
44. NA, 260.

45. NA, 261.
46. NA, 252.
47. NA, 252–53.
48. NA, 261.
49. NA, 261.
50. NA, 258.
51. NA, 5.
52. NA, 261.
53. For more on the "interesting," see Inger Sigrun Brodey, "Making Sense of Sensibility," *Persuasions: The Jane Austen Journal* 39 (2015): 62–80.
54. *Northanger Abbey*, directed by Giles Foster (London: BBC/A&E, 1987).
55. *Ruby in Paradise*, directed by Victor Nunez (Full Crew / Say Yea, 1993); *Atonement*, directed by Joe Wright (Universal City, CA: Universal Pictures, 2007).
56. Roger Ebert, "Review of *Ruby in Paradise*," RogerEbert.com (Nov. 26, 1993).
57. NA, 203.
58. Charlotte Lennox, *Female Quixote, Or the Adventures of Arabella* (London: A. Millar, 1752).
59. Peter Brooks, *Reading for the Plot: Design and Intention in Narrative* (New York: Vintage, 1984), 95.
60. Brooks, *Reading for the Plot*, 22.

CHAPTER 2
Expecting Literary Justice

1. Susan Allen Ford, "The Immortality of *Sense and Sensibility*: Margaret's Tree House, Edward's Handkerchief, Marianne's Rescue," *Persuasions: The Jane Austen Journal On-Line* 38.1 (Winter 2017): https://jasna.org/publications-2/persuasions-online/vol38no1/ford/.
2. SS, 409.
3. SS, 427.
4. I will take an untraditional approach to the spelling of Austen's juvenilia. It is customary to maintain her misspellings in "Love and Freindship" and "the Beautifull Cassandra" [*sic*], but I prefer not to patronize her in that way.
5. SS, 411.
6. SS, 415.

7. NA, 253.
8. See Barbara M. Benedict's excellent essay on this novel: "Jane Austen's *Sense and Sensibility*: The Politics of Point of View," *Philological Quarterly* 69.4 (1990): 453–70.
9. SS, 418.
10. SS, 430.
11. LM, 78.
12. SS, 428.
13. Tony Tanner and Mary Poovey, although with different approaches, both critique Austen's endings for this uncomfortable disjunction between the ideals of equality and justice that the novels elicit on the one hand, and the ugly social facts that persist at the end of the novels (such as the success of many unjust characters and institutions) on the other. These critics claim that Austen compromises her principles through such endings.
14. William Shakespeare and Henry Cunningham, *A Midsummer Night's Dream* (London: Metheun, 1905), act II, scene 2, ll. 453–63.
15. Tony Tanner, "Introduction," in *Austen, Sense and Sensibility* (New York: Penguin, 1988), 31.
16. SS, 429.
17. SS, 430.
18. SS, 382.
19. SS, 379.
20. SS, 429.
21. SS, 429.
22. SS, 430. This is perhaps why one of the original readers that Austen records called it a "stupid ending"; quoted in William Galperin, "'Describing What Never Happened': Jane Austen and the History of Missed Opportunities," *ELH*, 73.2 (Summer 2006): 355–82.
23. Richard Simpson (attr.), *North British Review* 52 (April 1870): 129–52, in B. C. Southam, ed., *Jane Austen: The Critical Heritage* (London: Routledge; New York: Barnes and Nobel, 1968), 241–65; 133.
24. Southam, *Jane Austen*, 133–34.
25. Sayre N. Greenfield and Linda V. Troost, "Before It Was All about Mr. Darcy: Nineteenth-Century Views of Austen's Characters," *Persuasions: The Jane Austen Journal On-Line* 38.1 (2017), 134.

26. I pursue this in greater detail in both "Making Sense of Sensibility," *Persuasions: The Jane Austen Journal* 39 (2015): 62–80, and *Ruined by Design: Shaping Novels and Gardens in the Culture of Sensibility* (New York: Routledge, 2008, 2012).
27. Ang Lee and Emma Thompson's film version casts Alan Rickman, whose brooding softness and intensity reveal the depth of his feeling. Rather than making up for an absence in Austen, however, I argue that Lee and Thompson are in fact diminishing one of Austen's purposeful choices, and emphasizing conventional romance instead of irony.
28. SS, 361.
29. SS, 375.
30. SS, 430; my emphasis.
31. SS, 425.
32. One reason Gustave Flaubert's indebtedness to Austen in English is that the key characteristics do not appear in the French translations. I have argued elsewhere that Flaubert's use of Free Indirect Discourse stems from Austen's and that the sense of male canonicity among French authors alone has prevented this acknowledgment. In any case, Austen subtly shows an antecedent to this technique as well.
33. Gustave Flaubert, *Madame Bovary* (Part II, Chapter 8), trans. Eleanor Marx-Aveling, Project Gutenberg, https://www.gutenberg.org/files/2413/2413-h/2413-h.htm.
34. SS, 332.
35. SS, 101.
36. SS, 403.
37. SS, 431. See James Thompson, "Sororadelphia, or 'Even the Conjugal Tie Is beneath the Fraternal,'" *Persuasions: The Jane Austen Journal On-Line* 30.1 (Winter 2009): https://jasna.org/persuasions/on-line/vol30no1/thompson.html.
38. Bernard Mandeville, *The Fable of the Bees or Private Vices, Publick Benefits*, 2 vols. (Liberty Fund, 1732).
39. SS, 428; my emphasis.
40. SS, 428; my emphasis. This humorous logic is strikingly similar to Hobbes's imaginative account of human intellectual equality: "I find yet a greater equality amongst men, than that of strength. [. . .] For such is the nature of

men, that howsoever they may acknowledge many others to be more witty, or more eloquent, or more learned; Yet they will hardly believe there be many so wise as themselves: For they see their own wit at hand, and other mens at a distance. But this proveth rather that men are in that point equall, than unequall. *For there is not ordinarily a greater signe of the equall distribution of any thing, than that every man is contented with his share.*" Thomas Hobbes, *Leviathan, or The Matter, Forme, & Power of a Common-Wealth Ecclesiastical and Civill* (London: Printed for Andrew Crooke, at the Green Dragon in St. Paul's Churchyard, 1651), part I, chap. 13.

41. Alistair M. Duckworth, *The Improvement of the Estate: A Study of Jane Austen's Novels* (Baltimore: Johns Hopkins University Press, 1994); Marilyn Butler, *Jane Austen and the War of Ideas* (Cambridge: Clarendon Press, 1988); Mary Poovey, *The Proper Lady and the Woman Writer* (Chicago: University of Chicago Press, 1984); Helena Kelly, *Jane Austen, the Secret Radical* (New York: Alfred A. Knopf, 2017).

42. *Priyuralu Pilichindi* [original title: *Kandukondain, Kandukondain*], directed by Rajiv Menon (Zee Tamil: Sri Surya Films, 2000); *Prada to Nada*, directed by Angel Garcia (Los Angeles: MWM Studios, 2011); *Material Girls*, directed by Martha Coolidge (Beverly Hills, CA: Metro Goldwyn Mayer, 2006); and *Frozen*, directed by Chris Buck and Jennifer Lee (Burbank, CA: Walt Disney Animation Studios, 2013).

43. Even worse, *Sense, Sensibility, and Snowmen* turns Elinor into the spontaneous and irresponsible sister, altogether erasing the less immediately attractive aspects of her character. *Sense, Sensibility, and Snowmen*, directed by David Winning (Kansas City, MO: Hallmark Movies and Mysteries, 2019).

44. *Sense and Sensibility*, directed by Ang Lee (Culver City, CA: Columbia Pictures, 1995).

45. Susan Allen Ford notes that the script calls for Brandon's throwing sixpences to the crowd. Ford interprets this gesture more charitably: "this symbol—the concluding image of the film though not of the screenplay—might have underscored Austen's representation of the financial realities for women and the way those realities underline the courtship plot. Instead, those coins are transformed into something beautiful, a shower of silver. Romance is validated, and the harsh economic underpinnings of marriage elided, as the screenplay makes clear: 'The coins spin and bounce, catching the sun

like jewels' while 'the wedding procession makes its glorious way from the church'" (202). Ford, "The Immortality of *Sense and Sensibility*."

46. One might also say that he loses connection with his former community and relatives, none of whom seem to attend their wedding.

CHAPTER 3

The Limits of Romance

1. Sayre N. Greenfield and Linda V. Troost, "Before It Was All about Mr. Darcy: Nineteenth-Century Views of Austen's Characters," *Persuasions: The Jane Austen Journal On-Line* 38.1 (2017).
2. PP, 384.
3. PP, 422.
4. PP, 414.
5. PP, 49.
6. PP, 418; my emphasis.
7. In a conduct book Austen likely read, John Gregory explains it thus: "Wit is the most dangerous talent you can possess . . . Wit is so flattering to vanity, that they who possess it become intoxicated, and lose all self-command." *A Father's Legacy to His Daughters* (London: T. Cadell and W. Davies, 1808), 35.
8. PP, 174.
9. PP, 25.
10. Leta Sundet wrote an alternative, provocative description of cynicism in Austen: "Austen understands cynicism to be primarily an attempt to protect oneself from *un*pleasant surprise by ensuring that one is never surprised at all—a kind of aping of control; she also understands that it is an incredibly *attractive* vision, compelling to observe, compelling to emulate: cynicism not only provides a sense of security but it also exudes sophistication" (unpublished dissertation).
11. Samuel Johnson, *The Yale Digital Edition of the Works of Samuel Johnson* (New Canaan, CT: Yale University Press, 2014), http://www.yalejohnson.com/, III.11–12.
12. According to Samuel Johnson, "an attempt to preserve life in a state of neutrality and indifference, is unreasonable and vain" (*Works of Samuel Johnson*, III.256).

13. PP, 160.
14. PP, 408; my emphasis.
15. PP, 412.
16. Susannah Carson, ed., *A Truth Universally Acknowledged: 33 Great Writers on Why We Read Jane Austen* (New York: Random House, 2009), 89; original emphasis.
17. *Pride and Prejudice*, directed by Cyril Coke (TV miniseries) (London: BBC, 1980); *Pride and Prejudice*, directed by Simon Langton (TV miniseries) (London: BBC, 1995); *Pride and Prejudice*, directed by Joe Wright (Universal City, CA: Focus Features, 2005).
18. PP, 406.
19. PP, 406–7.
20. The ending was later added back into the British version. It turned out that British audiences also wanted the "sugar in their champagne," as Joe Wright put it. Mark Harrison, "2005's *Pride and Prejudice* and the Fuss Over Its Bonus Ending," *Film Stories* (Jan. 25, 2022).
21. *Pride and Prejudice* [*Pride and Prejudice: A Latter-Day Comedy*], directed by Andrew Black (Provo, UT: Bestboy Pictures, 2003).
22. Ellen Fein and Sherrie Schneider, *The Rules: Time-Tested Secrets for Capturing the Heart of Mr. Right* (New York: Grand Central Publishing, 2001).
23. Books centering on Mary Bennet include Patrice Sarath's *The Unexpected Miss Bennet* (New York: Berkley, 2011), Virginia Aitken's *Mary Bennet's Chance* (Brighton, UK: Indepenpress, 2011), Shanon Winslow's *Return to Longbourn* (Heather Ridge Arts, 2013), Pamela Mingle's *The Pursuit of Mary Bennet: A Pride and Prejudice Novel* (New York: William Morrow, 2013), Jennifer Paynter's *The Forgotten Sister: Mary Bennet's Pride and Prejudice* (Seattle: Lake Union, 2014), and Amy Street's *Becoming Mary: A Pride and Prejudice Sequel* (2015). One of the earliest Mary-centered adaptations is Colleen McCullough's *The Independence of Miss Mary Bennet* (New York: Pocket Books, 2008). This novel seems motivated less in revisiting Mary than in overturning Austen's plot and characters in general. The novel tends to raise Mary and demonize Elizabeth in turn. The object of parody in this fictional rewriting of *Pride and Prejudice* is not so much the novel as the fan who loves the novel obsessively.
24. Eucharista Ward, *A Match for Mary Bennet: Can a Serious Young Lady Ever Find Her Way to Love?* (Naperville, IL: Sourcebooks Landmark, 2009).

25. Janice Hadlow, *The Other Bennet Sister: A Novel* (New York: Henry Holt, 2020).
26. Lauren Gunderson and Margot Melco, *Miss Bennet: Christmas at Pemberley*, Dramatists Play Service (accessed Mar. 2, 2023), https://www.dramatists.com/cgi-bin/db/single.asp?key=5611.
27. John Kessel, *Pride and Prometheus* (New York: Saga Press, 2008).
28. Kelsey Hercs's play *Threadbare Morality: The Queer Musings of Miss Mary Bennet* has not been published, but it has been performed. You can read about its performance at Dixon Place (http://dixonplace.org/performances/threadbare-morality/) or a review by Tara Isabella Burton, "Kelsey Hercs Puts a Queer Spin on *Pride and Prejudice*," *Village Voice* (Aug. 30, 2017), https://www.villagevoice.com/2017/08/30/kelsey-hercs-puts-a-queer-spin-on-pride-and-prejudice/.
29. Beth Pattillo's *Jane Austen Ruined My Life* (Harlan, IA: Guideposts Books, 2009); Shannon Hale's *Austenland* novel (New York: Bloomsbury, 2007) and film (Culver City, CA: Sony Pictures, 2013), and its sequel *Midnight in Austenland* (New York: Bloomsbury, 2013); Dan Zeff's *Lost in Austen* (TV miniseries) (London: Mammoth Screen, 2008); Rigler's *Confessions of an Austen Addict* (Boston, MA: Dutton, 2007) and *Rude Awakenings of an Austen Addict* (Boston, MA: Dutton, 2010); and Paula Marantz Cohen's *Suzanne Davis Gets a Life* (Philadelphia: Paul Dry, 2014).
30. Helen Fielding's blockbuster novel *Bridget Jones's Diary: A Novel* (London: Penguin, 1996) has had a vigorous afterlife. The first film adaptation was directed by Sharon Maguire: *Bridget Jones's Diary* (Buffalo, NY: Miramax Productions, 2001).
31. Pattillo, *Jane Austen Ruined My Life*, 1–2.
32. Pattillo, *Jane Austen Ruined My Life*, 194.
33. Pattillo, *Jane Austen Ruined My Life*, 191.
34. Pattillo, *Jane Austen Ruined My Life*, 94, 147.
35. Pattillo, *Jane Austen Ruined My Life*, 3.
36. Pattillo, *Jane Austen Ruined My Life*, 214.
37. Pattillo, *Jane Austen Ruined My Life*, 260–61.
38. Pattillo, *Jane Austen Ruined My Life*, 214–15.
39. Zeff, *Lost in Austen*.
40. Laurie Viera Rigler achieves the same double effect in her two Austen novels, *Confessions of a Jane Austen Addict* (London: Penguin, 2008) and *Rude Awakenings of a Jane Austen Addict* (London: Penguin, 2010).

41. Shannon Hale's *Austenland* (New York: Bloomsbury, 2010) was made into a film by the same name, directed by Jerusha Hess (Culver City, CA: Sony Pictures Classics, 2013).
42. *Northanger Abbey*, directed by Jon Jones (TV movie) (Isle of Man, UK: Granada Television, 2007).
43. Cohen, *Suzanne Davis Gets a Life*, 8.
44. Cohen, *Suzanne Davis Gets a Life*, 183.
45. Cohen, *Suzanne Davis Gets a Life*, 187.
46. Cohen, *Suzanne Davis Gets a Life*, 187–88.
47. Cohen, *Suzanne Davis Gets a Life*, 195.
48. *Pride and Prejudice and Zombies*, directed by Burr Steers (Culver City, CA: Cross Creek Pictures, 2009); Janet Mullany, *Jane and the Damned* (New York: HarperCollins, 2010). The subgenre of Mary novels also includes examples of the political plot. Katherine Cowley's *True Confessions of a London Spy* (San Clemente, CA: Tule Publishing, 2022) follows the first novel in the series, *The Secret Life of Miss Mary Bennet* (San Clemente, CA: Tule Publishing, 2021), in showing Mary Bennet's undercover work to find a murderer and uncover a plot to overthrow the British government.
49. Uzma Jalaluddin, *Ayesha at Last* (New York: Penguin Random House, 2019); Ibi Zoboi, *Pride: A Pride and Prejudice Remix* (New York: Harper Collins, 2018); Soniah Kamal, *Unmarriageable* (New York: Ballantine Books, 2019); Sonali Dev, *Pride, Prejudice, and Other Flavors* (New York: HarperCollins, 2019); Karen Tei Yamashita, *Sansei and Sensibility* (Minneapolis: Coffee House Press, 2020); *Pride and Prejudice: Atlanta*, directed by Rhonda F. Baraka (TV movie) (New York: A&E Networks, 2019).
50. *Bride and Prejudice*, directed by Gurinder Chadha (Paris: Pathé Pictures International, 2004).
51. Maria Clara Pivato Biajoli, "*Pride and Prejudice and Zombies*: Jane Austen Consumed by Her Popularity," *Éspectro da Crítica* 1.1 (2016).

CHAPTER 4
The Thin Veil of Comedy

1. I pursue Austen's critique of charm in *Mansfield Park* at much greater length in "Tyrants, Lovers, and Comedy in the Green Worlds of *Mansfield Park* and

A Midsummer Night's Dream," in *Shakespeare and Austen*, ed. Marina Cano and Rosa Maria Garcia Periago (New York: Palgrave Macmillan, 2019).

2. Alasdair MacIntyre also notes this focus in his study of the history of virtue theory: "Fanny is charmless; she has only the virtues, the genuine virtues, to protect her," whereas, for characters like Mary Crawford, "charm is the characteristically modern quality which those who lack or simulate the virtues use to get by." *After Virtue: A Study in Moral Theory* (Notre Dame, IN: University of Notre Dame Press, 2007), 242. Citing Albert Camus, MacIntyre describes charm as the quality "that procures a 'Yes' before a question has even been asked."
3. LM, 230–34. For an account of the long history of readers who dislike Fanny, see the excellent essay by Linda Troost and Sayre Greenfield, "A History of the Fanny Wars," *Persuasions: The Jane Austen Journal* 36 (2014): 5–33.
4. MP, 3.
5. MP, 326.
6. This sentence, like several others in *Mansfield Park* and *Emma*, is a clear forerunner of Virginia Woolf's modernist techniques. The long sentence allows a view of thoughts and an interior world shifting, rather than just getting a snapshot of individual ideas at a time.
7. MP, 515.
8. MP, 524.
9. MP, 524.
10. MP, 526, 527.
11. MP, 532.
12. MP, 326.
13. MP, 533.
14. MP, 533.
15. MP, 535.
16. MP, 543.
17. MP, 544.
18. MP, 533.
19. MP, 544.
20. MP, 544.
21. MP, 547.
22. MP, 548; my emphasis.

23. MP, 533.
24. MP, 545.
25. MP, 540.
26. MP, 542; my emphasis.
27. MP, 533.
28. MP, 273–74; my emphasis.
29. James Thompson, "Sororadelphia, or 'Even the Conjugal Tie Is Beneath the Fraternal,'" *Persuasions: The Jane Austen Journal On-Line* 30.1 (2009).
30. MP, 273.
31. MP, 321.
32. MP, 545.
33. For much more on this topic, see my "Papas and Ha-has: Authority, Rebellion, and Landscape Gardening in *Mansfield Park*," *Persuasions: The Jane Austen Journal* 17 (December 1995): 90–96. And for a broader treatment of the same topic, Inger Sigrun Brodey, "Avenues, Parks, Wilderness, and Ha-has: The Use and Abuse of Landscape in *Mansfield Park*," in *Approaches to Teaching* Mansfield Park, eds. Marcia McClintock Folsom and John Wiltshire (New York: Modern Language Association, 2014), 175–89.
34. MP, 223.
35. MP, 244.
36. MP, 224.
37. MP, 535.
38. MP, 363.
39. MP, 365.
40. MP, 368–69.
41. "Susan, she found, looked up to her and wished for her good opinion; and new as anything like an office of authority was to Fanny, new as it was to imagine herself capable of guiding or informing any one, she did resolve to give occasional hints to Susan, and endeavor to exercise for her advantage the juster notions of what was due to every body, and what would be wisest for herself, which her own more favored education had fixed in her" (MP, 459).
42. MP, 267.
43. MP, 267.
44. MP, 244.

45. According to Alistair M. Duckworth, we live in "a world incapable of being redeemed through individual moral agency, or of being improved through fictional means." *The Improvement of the Estate: A Study of Jane Austen's Novels* (Baltimore: Johns Hopkins University Press, 1994), 229.

46. MP, 244.

47. MP, 461.

48. MP, 274.

49. MP, 460.

50. MP, 548.

51. *Mansfield Park*, directed by Patricia Rozema (Los Angeles, CA: Miramax Productions, 1995).

52. Such authorlike double roles might be more appropriate to Emma Woodhouse than to Austen's Fanny.

53. Finally, in a last nod to Austen's life, Edmund tells Fanny that he has contacted Egerton, Austen's first publisher, about publishing her writing. In this act, Edmund takes on the role of either Austen's father or her brother Henry. The film ends as they walk happily to Mansfield Parsonage, discussing the publication of her novels (Rozema, *Mansfield Park*).

54. As in Kathryn Duncan, *Jane Austen and the Buddha* (Jefferson, NC: Toplight Books, 2021), as well as in Laurie Viera Rigler's novel *Rude Awakenings of a Jane Austen Addict* (New York: Plume, 2009).

55. Duncan, *Jane Austen and the Buddha*, 21.

56. Duncan, *Jane Austen and the Buddha*, 24.

57. Peter Knox-Shaw argues that Austen's novels embody the important ideas of the Enlightenment: science, reason, and social reform as well as "an emphasis on the limits of individual heroism" and distrust of doctrine. *Jane Austen and the Enlightenment* (Cambridge: Cambridge University Press, 2004), 5. Kathryn Duncan cites Alexander Pope on resigned acceptance: "All are but parts of one stupendous whole, / Whose body Nature is, and God the soul" (lines 267–68); he exhorts, "Know thy own point" (line 283) and closes his poem with "Whatever is, is right" (line 294). *Jane Austen and the Buddha*, 15.

58. MP, 534; quoted in Duncan, *Jane Austen and the Buddha*, 25.

59. MP, 547; italics in the last line added.

60. Anna Keesey quoted in Troost and Greenfield, "Fanny Wars," 29.

61. Duncan, *Jane Austen and the Buddha*, 191.

62. Duncan, *Jane Austen and the Buddha*, 24.
63. MP, 284.
64. MP, 244.
65. MP, 132.
66. Austen, wary of "perfection" as always, gives Fanny an ulterior motive in this scene—competing with Mary over Edmund's attentions. Janice Hadlow's *The Other Bennet Sister* echoes Fanny's experiences with nature. Of Mary Bennet's discovery of Wordsworth's poetry and the sublime beauty of the Lake Country, she writes: "Her small human concerns seemed of no account when set against such severe, indifferent splendor; at the same time, there was a kind of joy in allowing its grandeur to overwhelm her, to abandon herself to something she did not fully comprehend." *The Other Bennet Sister: A Novel* (New York: Henry Holt, 2020), 338.
67. Duncan, *Jane Austen and the Buddha*, 9.
68. Duncan, *Jane Austen and the Buddha*, 21.
69. Rigler, *Rude Awakenings*, 265.
70. Rigler, *Rude Awakenings*, 280.
71. Rigler, *Rude Awakenings*, 289.
72. Rigler, *Rude Awakenings*, 25.

CHAPTER 5
The Art of English Happiness

1. E, 3.
2. E, 80.
3. E, 251.
4. According to Peter Knox-Shaw, "Austen began *Emma* shortly before the hiatus in the war with France that followed on Napoleon's abdication in April 1814, and she finished it in March 1815 just at the moment that the deposed Emperor was resuming power." *Jane Austen and the Enlightenment* (Cambridge: Cambridge University Press, 2004), 197.
5. E, 107.
6. E, 377.
7. These old stereotypes of France and England are intensified by war.
8. E, 470.

9. Peter Knox-Shaw, *Enlightenment*, 199.
10. E, 145.
11. E, 377.
12. Austen's philosophy seems close to Adam Smith's on this point: Smith claims that communication is not necessary for sympathy, but rather, imaginative sympathy is necessary for communication. *The Theory of Moral Sentiments and On the Origins of Languages*, Stewart ed. (Henry G. Bohn, 1759), 337.
13. E, 75.
14. E, 145.
15. E, 119.
16. E, 51.
17. Elizabeth Bennet, in *Pride and Prejudice*, also suffers from the same willful misjudging, but Elizabeth shows herself to be more mature than Emma because she expresses and can laugh at Step 2—the step between observation and conclusion, which is based upon a predetermined opinion. Elizabeth says, "Heaven forbid! . . . To find a man agreeable whom one is determined to hate! Do not wish me such an evil" (PP, 79). She can laugh at her own inconsistencies, while Emma does not recognize her own similar ones.
18. Stuart Tave, *Some Words of Jane Austen* (Chicago: University of Chicago Press, 1973, 2019), 242.
19. E, 41.
20. E, 162.
21. E, 485.
22. E, 485.
23. E, 391.
24. The balance between artifice and nature is often overlooked in Austen's description of Pemberley: "It was a large, handsome, stone building, standing well on rising ground, and backed by a ridge of high woody hills;—and in front, a stream of some natural importance was swelled into greater, but without any artificial appearance. Its banks were neither formal, nor falsely adorned." Landscape gardeners have dammed the stream to make it of greater importance in front of the house. The issue is not adornment and artifice per se, but "false adornment."
25. E, 107.
26. E, 377.

27. E, 160–61.
28. E, 107.
29. E, 489.
30. E, 63, 107.
31. E, 53.
32. Melinda Watts writes, "France continued to be the leading source for luxury dress and furnishing silks during the nineteenth century, as it had been throughout the eighteenth century, while England's technical prowess enabled the country to excel at mass production for the middle-market consumer." Fine lace veils, she reports, would also have come from France, or alternatively Flanders. "Nineteenth-Century European Textile Production," Metropolitan Museum, Heilbrunn Timeline of Art History (October 2004): https://www.metmuseum.org/toah/hd/txtn/hd_txtn.htm.
33. E, 12.
34. E, 515.
35. E, 143.
36. E, 489.
37. E, 470.
38. Deanna Kreisel, "Where Does the Pleasure Come From? The Marriage Plot and Its Discontents in Jane Austen's *Emma*," *Persuasions: The Jane Austen Journal* 29 (2007): 218–27.
39. James Thompson, "Intimacy in Emma," in *Casebook: Jane Austen's* Emma, ed. David Monaghan (New York: St Martin's Press, 1992), 120.
40. John Mullan, *Sentiment and Sociability: The Language of Feeling in the Eighteenth Century* (Oxford: Clarendon Press, 1990).
41. Only volume III has 19 chapters. The others have 18 each. The novel also features multiple parallel scenes among the volumes, to heighten the asymmetry of the additional chapter.
42. E, 528.
43. E, 76.
44. Robin Grove, "Jane Austen's Free Enquiry: *Mansfield Park*," *Critical Review* 25 (Jan. 1, 1983): 132–50.
45. E, 470.
46. Richard Handler and Daniel Segal, *Jane Austen and the Fiction of Culture* (Tucson: University of Arizona Press, 1990).

47. E, 9.
48. E, 76.
49. *Clueless*, directed by Amy Heckerling (Los Angeles: Paramount Pictures, 1995).
50. E, 76.
51. *Emma*, directed by Autumn De Wilde (London: Working Title Films, 2020).
52. See also my "Perfection Comes at a Price in Latest Adaptation of Austen's *Emma*," *The Conversation* (March 27, 2020): https://theconversation.com/perfection-comes-at-a-price-in-latest-adaptation-of-austens-emma-134279.
53. Brodey, "Perfection."
54. See Wayne C. Booth's classic chapter, "The Control of Distance in *Emma*," in *The Rhetoric of Fiction* (Chicago: University of Chicago Press, 1983).
55. One could say that a narcissistic film character's idea of "mortification" is the loss of the full focus of the camera. But isn't Mr. Woodhouse the real narcissist, rather than Emma?
56. Partly owing to the visual medium, the film tends to rely on physical rather than emotional vulnerability, e.g., Mr Knightley's naked bottom and Emma's needing to pee in the woods behind a tree.
57. The 2009 *Emma* directed by Jim O'Hanlon and starring Romola Garai as Emma may be the best adaptation in this regard, capturing the caring relationship between Emma and her father. In this version, Emma even calls off the wedding because of her father, before Mr. Knightley comes up with the plan of moving to Hartfield. I also admire this film for the radical step of portraying Harriet's wedding and omitting Emma's altogether. *Emma* (TV miniseries), directed by Jim O'Hanlon (London: BBC Drama, 2009).

CHAPTER 6
Resources for Solitude

1. In reducing the number of protagonists, Austen has solved a problem of sympathy from *Sense and Sensibility*. In the earlier novel, the reader's sympathy tends to be divided between the sisters: a move toward Elinor is often a move away from Marianne, and vice versa. In *Persuasion*, readerly sympathy can be lavished upon Anne.
2. P, 32.

3. Unlike Anne, however, Cordelia was the favorite daughter beforehand.
4. P, 6.
5. P, 275.
6. P, 249–50.
7. P, 45.
8. P, 39.
9. *Manuscript*, 318. Quotations from the canceled chapters are from the facsimile edition *Manuscript Chapters of* Persuasion (London: Athlone Press, 1985).
10. *Manuscript*, 315–16.
11. P, 272.
12. P, 270.
13. P, 260.
14. The expression here is one step intensified from *Sense and Sensibility*, where "[Edmund] was brought . . . from misery to happiness . . ." (SS, 361).
15. E, 231, 432, 484.
16. NA, 250, 252.
17. MP, 473.
18. *Manuscript*, 38. See also Jan Fergus's excellent treatment in *Jane Austen: A Literary Life* (London: Macmillan, 1991), 167.
19. E, 371.
20. JW, 204.
21. Mary Brunton, *Self-Control*, Project Gutenberg, https://www.gutenberg.org/files/41196/41196-h/41196-h.htm.
22. Jocelyn Harris, *A Revolution Almost beyond Expression: Jane Austen's* Persuasion (Newark: University of Delaware, 2008), 166.
23. P, 274.
24. This is Kathryn Duncan's point about *Persuasion* in *Jane Austen and the Buddha: Teachers of Enlightenment* (Jefferson, NC: Toplight, 2021).
25. Samuel Johnson, *Rambler* 2. "The necessity and danger of looking to the future." Quoted by Claudia Johnson in "The 'Twilight of Probability': Uncertainty and Hope in *Sense and Sensibility*," *Philological Quarterly* (Spring 1983): 171–86, 184–85.
26. P, 32.
27. P, 167.
28. P, 274.

29. P, 269.
30. P, 266.
31. P, 6; my emphasis.
32. P, 17–18; my emphasis.
33. P, 157; my emphasis.
34. P, 270; my emphasis.
35. P, 162, my emphasis.
36. Here Austen inverts this usage by converting "nothing" into an expression of love. Subjectivity can erase others, but it can also erase distances. She hopes that she is over her love for Wentworth, but when she encounters him, we read: "Alas! with all her reasoning, she found, that to retentive feelings eight years may be little more than nothing" (P, 65). Rather than being made "nothing" by others, they now seem to have been erased from each other's consciousness: "Once so much to each other! Now nothing!" (P, 68).
37. P, 45; my emphasis.
38. P, 45, 46.
39. P, 43–44.
40. Claire Tomalin, *Jane Austen: A Life* (New York: Vintage Books, 1999), 206.
41. P, 45, 46.
42. P, 272.
43. P, 39; my emphasis.
44. P, 73.
45. Janice Hadlow, "Why We Turn to Austen in Dark Times," *Electric Literature* (April 6, 2020): https://electricliterture.com/why-we-turn-to-jane-austen-in-dark-times/.
46. Hadlow, "Why We Turn to Austen in Dark Times."
47. P, 108.
48. P, 109.
49. *Persuasion* (TV miniseries), directed by Roger Michell (London: BBC Films, 1995).
50. P, 261–62.
51. P, 261.
52. P, 321.
53. P, 257.
54. Many thanks to Susan Allen Ford for pointing this out to me.

55. *Persuasion* (TV movie), directed by Adrian Shergold (London: Clerkenwell Films / WGBH, 2008).
56. *Modern Persuasion* (TV movie), directed by Alex Appel and Jonathan Lisecki (New York: Tangerine Entertainment, 2020).
57. And then there is the Netflix *Persuasion* directed by Carrie Cracknell, of which, perhaps, the less said the better. I will just note that in the desire to update *Persuasion* with modern language, behavior, and sentiments, Cracknell and writer Alice Winslow have also managed to deprive the ending of all subtlety, all suspense, and most of the "spring of felicity." In the desire to embrace a relativistic approach to marriage, Anne as narrator approves of the marriage between Mr. Elton and Mrs. Clay, saying, "There are many kinds of love. For some the right partnership can be a lucrative endeavor." Anne continues this speech as we get a high-angle view of Lady Russell considering a singles' tour of Europe that provides romantic escorts: "It's ok to find love on your terms, however unorthodox. Don't let anyone tell you how to live or who to love. I learned that the hard way." *Persuasion*, directed by Carrie Cracknell (Los Gatos, CA: Netflix / Mad Chance Productions, 2022).
58. P, 255.
59. "[The sound] was nothing more than that his pen had fallen down" (P, 254).

CONCLUSION

Coauthoring Happiness

1. Dr. Gregory writes: "without an unusual share of natural sensibility, and very peculiar good fortune, a woman in this country has very little probability of marrying for love . . . . [S]upposing a woman to have sense and taste, she will not find many men to whom she can possibly be supposed to bear any considerable share of esteem. Among these few it is a very great chance if any of them distinguish her particularly . . . . But supposing one of them should become particularly attached to her, it is still extremely improbable that he should be the man in the world her heart most approved of." John Gregory, *A Father's Legacy to His Daughters* (London: T. Cadell and W. Davies, 1808), 90–91.
2. "The eighteenth century witnessed an explosion of interest in happiness, as both a subject of inquiry and as a personal life goal. Lester Crocker once

observed a 'universal, omnipresent preoccupation' with the subject which more than one historian has described in terms of an 'obsession.'" Brian Michael Norton, *Fiction and the Philosophy of Happiness* (Lewisburg, PA: Bucknell University Press, 2012), 1.

3. In the *Essay Concerning Human Understanding*, Locke is eager to separate our perceived, momentary ideas of what might satisfy transitory desires from "our real happiness" or "true and solid happiness":

> *The necessity of pursuing happiness* [is] *the foundation of liberty*. As therefore the highest perfection of intellectual nature lies in a careful and constant *pursuit of true and solid happiness*; so the care of ourselves, that we mistake not imaginary for real happiness, is the necessary foundation of our liberty. The stronger ties we have to an unalterable *pursuit of happiness* in general, which is our greatest good, and which, as such, our desires always follow, the more are we free from any necessary determination of our will to any particular action, and from a necessary compliance with our desire, set upon any particular, and then appearing preferable good, till we have duly examined whether it has a tendency to, or be inconsistent with, our real happiness: and therefore, till we are as much informed upon this inquiry as the weight of the matter, and the nature of the case demands, we are, by the necessity of preferring and pursuing true happiness as our greatest good, obliged to suspend the satisfaction of our desires in particular cases.

Here "our greatest good" is not synonymous with our "real happiness," but rather with "the pursuit of happiness." John Locke, *Essay Concerning Human Understanding* (Rivington, 1689).

4. The phrase "pursuit of happiness" has become a cornerstone of American culture to an extent that Thomas Jefferson could never have expected. In making this substitution for Locke's well known "life, liberty, and property," Jefferson seems to be making a much broader claim for one's own ability to interpret what will bring happiness. Insofar as the phrase takes the place of Locke's "property," people have associated it with everything from the accumulation of earthly riches to sexual orientation. The tug-of-war over happy endings versus the pursuit of happiness is characteristic of all times perhaps, but it

has particular resonance in the time in which these works were written—the Age of Revolution in America and France, where expectations of rights and privileges were being actively debated. Whether in Locke, Jefferson, or Lafayette, the phrase does not promise "happiness," but rather its pursuit. Some might say that this *pursuit* of happiness *is* the core happiness—an activity rather than a state—and that the acquisition of perceived happiness quickly turns sour once one views the pursuit as completed.

5. MP, 478.

6. Elisa Galgut, "Reading Minds: Mentalization, Irony and Literary Engagement," *International Journal of Psychoanalysis* 91.4 (2010): 1–21.

7. As Wolfgang Iser describes such works, "The referential world contained in the text . . . automatically invokes a convention-governed contract between author and reader indicating that the textual world is to be viewed, not as reality, but as if it were reality." *The Act of Reading: A Theory of Aesthetic Response* (London and Henley: Routledge and Kegan Paul, 1978), 327.

8. Iser, *Act of Reading*, 327.

9. Galgut, "Reading Minds," 7–8.

10. Galgut, "Reading Minds," 9.

11. In *A Midsummer Night's Dream*, Bottom is concerned that the audience of his theatricals might be afraid of the actors' swords, taking the fight and death as *real*: "Write me a prologue; and let the prologue seem to say, we will do no harm with our swords, and that Pyramus is not killed indeed; and for the more better assurance, tell them that I, Pyramus, am not Pyramus, but Bottom the weaver: this will put them out of fear" (III, 1l. 835–41).

Index